Foreign Direct Investment and International Law

This book examines the regulatory framework for foreign direct investments, most notably the bilateral investment treaties which provide several guarantees that minimise the exposure of risks to foreign investors in a host State.

Most States have recognised that one of the ways they can improve their economic growth is by providing effective mechanisms for the attraction of foreign investments. In this regard, foreign direct investments have become a key element in the strategic vision for advancing any national economy. The book examines guarantees which have the capacity to impinge on the economic sovereignty of a State, raising questions such as: are host States obliged to comply with the rights of foreign investors to free capital repatriation in the face of economic difficulties? What power does a host State have to regulate and impose capital controls that are deleterious to the rights of a foreign investor? This book argues that policies aimed at increasing foreign direct investment need to extend beyond investment liberalisation to strike a balance between the regulatory rights of a State and the legitimate expectations of foreign investors.

Advancing the discussion on the necessity of balancing the needs of foreign investors with those of the host community and exploring the power asymmetry present in treaty negotiations, this book will be of interest to students, academics, and practitioners with an interest in international investment law.

Adaeze Agatha Aniodoh is a Lecturer in Law at the University of Leicester. She holds a PhD in Law from the University of Manchester, an LLM from the University of Sussex, and an LLB from the University of Benin, Nigeria. She also obtained a Postgraduate Certificate in Higher Education from the University of Manchester. Adaeze is called to the Nigerian Bar and has consulted for numerous organisations. She has also taught at various institutions, including the University of Manchester, Aston University in the UK, and the University of Bedfordshire.

Routledge Research in Finance and Banking Law

Crypto-Finance, Law and Regulation
Governing an Emerging Ecosystem
Joseph Lee

Regulation and Governance of Mutual Funds
United Kingdom and United States of America Perspectives on Investor Protection
Mohammed Khair Alshaleel

Regulation of Debt Collection in Europe
Understanding Informal Debt Collection Practices
Cătălin-Gabriel Stănescu

The Regulation of Megabanks
Global Systemically Important Banks and their Legal Frameworks
Katarzyna M. Parchimowicz

Regulating Open Banking
Comparative Analysis of the EU, the UK and Taiwan
Chang-Hsien Tsai and Kuan-Jung Peng

The Law of ESG Derivatives
Risk, Uncertainty and Sustainable Finance
Ligia Catherine Arias-Barrera

Financial Technology Regulation in Africa
Iwa Salami

Foreign Direct Investment and International Law
Liberalization and Economic Sovereignty
Adaeze Agatha Aniodoh

For more information about this series, please visit: www.routledge.com/Routledge-Research-in-Finance-and-Banking-Law/book-series/FINANCIALLAW

Foreign Direct Investment and International Law

Liberalization and Economic Sovereignty

Adaeze Agatha Aniodoh

Routledge
Taylor & Francis Group
LONDON AND NEW YORK

First published 2026
by Routledge
4 Park Square, Milton Park, Abingdon, Oxon OX14 4RN

and by Routledge
605 Third Avenue, New York, NY 10158

Routledge is an imprint of the Taylor & Francis Group, an informa business

British Library Cataloguing-in-Publication Data
A catalogue record for this book is available from the British Library

ISBN: 978-1-032-61452-6 (hbk)
ISBN: 978-1-041-00797-5 (pbk)
ISBN: 978-1-003-61171-4 (ebk)

DOI: 10.4324/9781003611714

Typeset in Times New Roman
by Deanta Global Publishing Services, Chennai, India

Contents

Table of Statutes

Table of Cases

Aguas del Tunari v. Republic of Bolivia, ICSID Case No. ARB/02/3
Archer Daniels Midland Company and Tate & Lyle Ingredients Americas, Inc. v. United Mexican States, ICSID Case No. ARB(AF)/04/5
Asian Agricultural Products Limited v. The Republic of Sri Lanka, ICSID Case No. ARB/87/3
Biwater Gauff (Tanzania) Ltd. v. United Republic of Tanzania, ICSID Case No. ARB/05/22
Cargill, Incorporated v. United Mexican States, ICSID Case No. ARB(AF)/05/2
CMS v. Argentine Republic, ICSID Case No. ARB/01/8
Continental Casualty Company v. Argentine Republic, ICSID Case No. ARB/03/9
Corn Products International, Inc. v. The United Mexican States (Decision on Responsibility), ICSID Case No. ARB (AF)/04/01.
Enron v. Argentine Republic, ICSID Case No. ARB/01/3
Island of Palman Case, United States v. Netherlands (1928) II RIAA 829
LG & E v. Argentine Republic, ICSID Case No. ARB/02/1
Methanex Corporation v. United States of America, UNCITRAL
National Grid v. Argentina, Case 1:09-cv-00248-RBW, IIC 361 (2008),
Richardson v. Mellish, (1824) 2 Bing. 229 at 252
Salini v. Morocco, ICSID Case No. ARB/00/4
Saluka v. Czech Republic, PCA Case No. 2001-04.
Sempra Energy International v. Argentine Republic, ICSID Case No. ARB/02/16
The White Industries Australia (WIAL) v. Coal India Limited, ICC Case No. 10558/OLG/ESR/MS
Vincent v. Lake Erie Transportation Co (1910), 124 NW 2

Acknowledgements

I would like to extend my heartfelt gratitude to my PhD supervisors at the University of Manchester, Prof Yenkong Ngangjoh Hodu and Dr Jasem Tarawneh, for their invaluable contributions and guidance throughout the course of my doctoral research. Their insightful advice, constructive feedback, and unwavering encouragement were the essential ingredients in transforming my doctoral research into what you see before you today—a monograph rather than just a thesis gathering dust. Without their dedication, this work would have remained an ambitious idea, not the fully formed project it has become.

List of Abbreviations

BIT	Bilateral Investment Treaty
BOP	Balance of Payment
CAFTA	Central American Free Trade Agreement
ECT	Energy Charter Treaty
FET	Fair and Equitable Treatment
FDI	Foreign Direct Investment
GATT	General Agreement on Trade and Tariff
GDP	Gross Domestic Product
HFCS	High Fructose Corn Syrup
ICSID	International Centre for Settlement of Dispute Resolution
ILC	International Law Commission
IMF	International Monetary Fund
ISDS	Investor States Dispute Settlement
MNC	Multinational Corporations
NAFTA	North American Free Trade Agreement
NIPC	Nigerian Investment Promotion Commission
NPM	Non Precluded Measure
NT	National Treatment
OECD	Organisation for Economic Corporation and Development
UNCITRAL	United Nations Commission on International Trade Law
UNCTAD	United Nations Conference on Trade and Development
VCLT	Vienna Convention on the Law of Treaties
WTO	World Trade Organization

1 Introduction

1.1 Introduction

Foreign direct investments (FDIs) have become an element of the strategic vision for the advancement of some national economies. This is because FDIs are largely considered to have positive impact on the economic growth of a State.[1] Most States[2] have recognised that one of the ways they can improve their economic growth is by providing effective mechanisms for the attraction of foreign investments.[3] In this regard, most developing States rely heavily on Bilateral Investment Treaties (BITs) which they believe will lead to more inflow of FDI into their region in order to: provide the financing that is otherwise unavailable,[4] stimulate their economies, trigger a reduction in poverty,[5] and lead to an all-round technological growth and advancement.[6] These States believe that signing BITs will show a form of credible commitment to foreign investors on their willingness to protect their assets, capital, and nationals, thus leading to an increased inflow of foreign investments.[7] Whether

1 Mebratu Seyoum, Renshui Wu & Jihong Lin, 'Foreign Direct Investment and Economic Growth: The Case of Developing African Economies' (2015) 122(1) *Social Indicator Research*, 48.

2 States refer to countries as political entities. Host States refers to the States where a foreign investment is made, while home States refer to foreign investors' nationality or principal place of business. Developed countries mean States with highly developed economies such as members of OECD, while developing States are those considered to be low income by the World Bank; Glen Kelley, 'Multilateral Investment Treaties: A Balanced Approach to Multinational Corporations' (2001) 39(2) *Columbia Journal of Transnational Law*, 485.

3 Andrew Newcombe, 'Sustainable Development and Investment Treaty Law' (2007) 8(1) *Journal of World Investment and Trade*, 358.

4 Alec R. Johnson, 'Rethinking Bilateral Investment Treaties in Sub-Saharan Africa' (2010) 59(4) *Emory Law Journals*, 919.

5 Issouf Sourmare & Gaston Gohou, 'Does Foreign Direct Investment Reduce Poverty in Africa and Are There Regional Differences?' (2012) 40(1) *World Development*, 75.

6 Ahmad Ali Ghouri, *Interaction and Conflict of Treaties in Investment Arbitration* (Kluwer, Kluwer Law International 2015) 14.

7 Daniel J. Blake, 'Thinking Ahead: Government Time Horizons and the Legislation of International Investment Agreement and the Legalization of International Investment Agreements' (2013) 67(4) *International Organisation*, 798.

DOI: 10.4324/9781003611714-1

these treaties attract more FDIs to States that submit to the obligations of BITs has become a matter of debate amongst legal scholars.[8]

BITs are however known to provide foreign investors with several guarantees that minimise their exposure to risks in a host State. One such guarantee is the right to repatriation of capital and transfer of profit, otherwise known as the "right to transfer of funds related to foreign investments".[9] This right is at the core of international investment law because it reinforces one of the objectives of foreign investments, which is to make and repatriate profits to a home State.[10] Amongst other driving factors, one of the main reasons investors invest is to gain returns, that is, to make profits. In addition to concerns about returns, investors are also concerned about how risks could affect the returns. Potential investments are measured alongside projected levels of risks; a greater risk would require a higher rate of return to justify an investment.[11] Risks are distinguished between commercial risks and political risks to project marginal returns. Ultimately, the end goal of the foreign investor is the expected returns from investments. Legal devices may then be viewed as primary utilities to reduce risks. In this regard, BITs play important roles in assuring the investor of minimised risks.[12] Stakeholders in the investment regime seem to agree that a free transfer clause constrains policy choices and delimits States' ability to make decisions for her sovereigns. Much of the debates on this issue centre around whether these constraints are helpful by nudging States in more predictable and productive directions or if they preclude the use of helpful policy tools.[13] Unlike other BIT provisions that focus on discriminatory actions towards a foreign investor, the clause on transfer of funds relates to broad government policy. Thus, when a dispute is based on the clause, fiscal and monetary policies of host States are reviewed by arbitral tribunals.[14]

Some BITs, especially those signed by developing countries, lack interpretative guidelines regarding the provision on fund transfers. This omission creates a challenge in balancing the rights of foreign investors to transfer funds related to their investments with the State's right to impose regulations for public interest during economic crises. The absence of permissible derogations and interpretative

8 David Collins, 'National Treatment in Emerging Market Investment Treaties' in Anselm Kamperman Sanders (ed), *The Principle of National Treatment in International Economic Law: Trade Investment and Intellectual Property* (Edward Elgar Publishing Limited 2014) 161.

9 Abba Kolo & Thomas Walde, 'Economic Crises, Capital Transfer Restrictions, and Investor Protection under Modern Investment Treaties' (2008) 3(2) *Capital Markets Law Journal*, 161.

10 Piero Bernardini, 'Investment Protection under Bilateral Investment Treaties and Investment Contracts' (2001) 2(2) *Journal of World Investment & Trade*, 243.

11 Jeswald W. Salacuse, *The Three Laws of International Investment: National, Contractual and International Frameworks for Foreign Capital* (Oxford University Press 2013) 12–13.

12 *ibid* 13.

13 Multilateral Liberalization through Bilateral Treaties? A Workshop on Global Investment Governance. Available on https://www.bsg.ox.ac.uk/sites/default/files/documents/Multilateral%20Liberalization%20through%20Bilateral%20Treaties_Final%20Memos%2028%20June.pdf [Accessed on 4 November 2024].

14 *ibid* 3.

guidance on the free transfer of funds can lead to complications for States facing balance of payments issues.[15] This is because balance of payment problems which are occasioned by reversal of capital due to lack of confidence by foreign investors and the consequent depreciation of foreign reserves in a host State can lead to a State being unable to fulfil its international obligations.[16] A free transfer of funds clause will mean that a State may find it difficult to place temporary restrictions on funds that can be repatriated in economic crisis. This inability can increase socio-economic problems such as unemployment and widespread poverty,[17] thus creating some sort of policy dilemma for policymakers and governments. Consequent attempt by States to address macroeconomic difficulties can encroach on a foreign investor's right to access his capital.

International Investment law is not well developed and unified in terms of how State response to economic crisis should be approached. Argentina has dealt with cases arising from breach of legal commitments to foreign investors on right to transfer of funds during its economic crisis. Different conclusions have been reached by arbitral tribunals in cases which bear the same or closely similar facts,[18] and, up to this moment, there is no definitive guideline nor authoritative decision to propose a clear solution to issues bordering on the adjudication of transfer of funds issues.[19] Emergency situations such as economic crisis which require treaty violations are justified under the doctrine of necessity.[20] The doctrine of necessity permits States to take measures which ordinarily would have been a breach of investment protection treaties, in so far as those measures are taken for the purpose of preserving an essential interest in times of necessity. Although this doctrine is universally acknowledged, its scope and applicability are in dispute[21] Exceptions in BITs (often encapsulated in the non-precluded measures [NPM]) and the Customary International Law on necessity which can be found in Article 25 of the International Law Commission (ILC) Draft Articles on States Responsibility both contemplate the doctrine of necessity. A major issue in crisis moments is to establish in what circumstances the doctrine can be considered. This invariably

15 *ibid* 4.

16 Marc Lavoice, 'The Eurozone Crisis: A Balance of Payment Problems or a Crisis Due to a Flawed Monetary Design? A Reply to Sergio Cesaratto' (2015) 44(2) *International Journal of Political Economy*, 158.

17 Ibironke T. Odumosu-Aganu, 'South-South Investment Treaties, Transnational Capital and African People' (2013) 21(2) *African Journal of International and Comparative Law*, 199.

18 Elizabeth Martinez, 'Understanding the Debate over Necessity: Unanswered Questions and Future Implications of Annulments in the Argentine Gas Cases' (2012) 23(1) *Duke Journal of Comparative and International Law*, 149–150

19 Youngjin Jung & Sangwook Daniel Han, 'What to Do with the Dilemma Facing the State of Necessity Defence Under the Investment Treaties and How to Interpret the NPM Clause' (2011) 12(3) *Journal of World Investment and Trade*, 397.

20 Suha Ballan, 'Economic Crises and Foreign Investors: Between Necessity and Reparations' (2018) 2(1) *International Comparative Policy and Ethics Law Review*, 4.

21 Dillon Fowler, 'Is this Really Necessary? The Scope of the Doctrine of Necessity in 21st Century Investment Treaties' (2017) 9(1) *Creighton International and Comparative Law Journal*, 2.

implies looking at the legal grounding of such derogations; in this case, the general principles of law which exempts States from liabilities in matters of necessity.[22]

Treaty provisions and obligations are often rebalanced through exceptions. This means that desirable obligations can be overridden by highly undesirable derogations because they are permitted by treaty exceptions. These exceptions could be general or specific. General exceptions are applicable to all BIT obligations while specific exceptions only apply to a limited number of BIT obligations.[23] Beyond derogations, these exceptions can enforce positive BIT duties. First, a State may be more inclined to accept BIT obligations, it would otherwise not accept. For example, a State with limited foreign reserves may be willing to conclude a BIT if it contains exceptions to allow exchange controls in emergency. Secondly, a well-crafted exception, while providing a State with freedom, will give notice to foreign investors of the possibility of derogation from general BIT norms.[24] With regards to treaty exceptions for the right to transfer funds, there is no clear definition of emergency typologies for treaty derogations, although they are evident in security and economic emergencies. The definitional gap adds to the interpretative confusion for necessity clauses. Law adjudicators have to rely on factual and legal indicators to determine the existence or otherwise of emergency situations as contemplated by a treaty's necessity clause. Law adjudicators have made recourse to institutional and expert opinions in making valuation arguments. However, the identification and application of such indicators have not been consistent.[25]

Balancing the foreign investor's interests with a State's right to regulate within these complex frameworks presents a significant challenge in international investment law.[26] The Argentinian experience imparts weighty lessons for the investment regime generally. At a time when financial markets are threatened in many States, understanding the scope of essential measures and its depth in international law is very important.[27] A significant reason for the differing interpretations and consequent conclusions reached in the Argentine cases could be that different analytical frameworks were employed by arbitrators which gave them a wide scope of subjective value choice between the need for compliance with the BIT and the seriousness

22 Antoine Martin, 'Investment Disputes after Argentina's Economic Crises: Interpreting BIT Non-Precluded Measures and the Doctrine of Necessity under Customary International Law' (2012) 29(1) *Journal of International Arbitration*, 51.

23 Kenneth Vandevelde, 'Rebalancing Exceptions through Exceptions' (2013) 17(2) *Lewis & Clark Law Review*, 452.

24 *ibid* 455.

25 Diane A. Desierto, *A Necessity and National Emergency Clauses: Sovereignty in Modern Treaty Interpretation* (Leiden, The Netherlands: Martinus Nijhoff Publishers 2012) 145.

26 Robert Brew, 'Exception Clauses in International Investment Agreements as a Tool for Appropriately Balancing the Right to Regulate with Investment Agreement' (2019) 25 *Canterbury Law Review*, 205.

27 Kathleen Cluaseen, 'The Casualty of Investor Protection in Times of Economic Crisis' (2009) 118 (7) *Yale Law Journal*, 1546–1555.

of the crisis in question.[28] Due to the inconsistencies in arbitral awards,[29] sovereigns are conflicted on whether they have ceded too many rights and the actual costs and benefits of signing investment treaties. This is because the procedural framework for resolving investment treaty disputes has created certain ambiguities about the meaning and scope of substantive guarantees and exceptions;[30] and pending the arrival of a consistent and predictable legal framework on the application of investment rights, States will be inhibited from making informed appraisals of the utility of these investment treaties. In addition to sovereignty tensions generated by BITs, it is also believed that the investor-State arbitration often activated to scrutinise State's economic decisions has become a platform which is used to attack legitimate government regulation. In essence, it appears that arbitrators are imbued with the authority to make what could otherwise be governmental decisions.[31] The high damages that result from arbitration constitute a financial limit on a State's ability to exercise its regulatory powers. The allegations of the system being pro-investor lead to questions about whether the tribunals have a chilling effect on a State's ability to exercise its regulatory powers.[32] When States invest time and resources to negotiate, sign, and ratify BITs; a consequence in part is that they are surrendering their sovereignty with the hope to receive capital by means of foreign investment. These treaties now represent a significant interference with a host State's sovereignty as they provide protections to foreign investors that are enforceable through investor-State dispute resolution.[33]The treaties give arbitrators power to determine whether foreign investors should be compensated for sovereign acts by States.

The constraint on sovereignty, the expensive investment claims arising from investment arbitration, and the prominent degree of authority given to private lawyers to determine the scope of a State's power, which leaves developing States with the short end of the stick, begs the question as to why they signed up to the treaties in the first place.[34] Since the arbitrators chosen to adjudicate investment disputes are private professionals, one of the many unanswered questions is whether private individuals should be granted wide powers over public regulations made by sovereign States.[35] It is thus acknowledged that, while foreign investments have the potential of accelerating economic development, unregulated foreign investment can cause harm to a host State. This harm provides the basis for an alternative

28 Jung & Han (n 19) 409.

29 Martinez (n 18).

30 Martin (n 22), 51.

31 Alessandra Arcuri & Francesco Montanaro, 'Justice for All: Protecting the Public Interest in Investment Treaties' (2018) 59(8) *Boston College Law Review*, 2804.

32 Julia Hueckel, 'Rebalancing Legitimacy and Sovereignty in International Investment Agreements' (2012) 61(3) *Emory Law Journal*, 613.

33 Eric Neumayer & Laura Spess, 'Do Bilateral Investment Treaties Increase Foreign Direct Investment to Developing Countries' (2005) 33(10) *World Development*, 1567.

34 Luage N. Skovguard Poulsen, *Bounded Nationality and Economic Diplomacy. The Politics of Investment Treaties in Developing Countries* (Cambridge University Press 2015) 5, 9.

35 *ibid* 3.

argument on why the international investment law should not provide absolute guarantees for foreign investments.[36]

Thus, States may need to employ appropriate techniques in order to promote consistency and coherence in arbitral decision-making process; with these, a State can assess on a more systematic basis the sovereignty it cedes and the reciprocal rights it gains for its citizens when negotiating an investment treaty.[37] This is necessary because, when economic and political stakes are high, responsibility falls on national governments to provide reasonable explanations regarding the basis for its policy choices to taxpayers. This book presents propositions intended to serve as a panacea to the investment concerns discussed above. These should aid future tribunals on how issues on transfer of funds should be considered.

1.2 Recent Trends in International Investment Law

1.2.1 Economic Crises and Investment Challenges

Globalisation is rapidly diminishing the barriers that separate the world economically and socially. This integration has led to fluctuations in investments, the growth of international trade, and the rise of transnational corporations. These shifts directly impact sovereign States' ability to manage their own affairs, with both positive and negative implications.[38] For instance, the recent global health crisis thrust the global community into a significant health and economic crisis, where critical policy decisions affecting businesses could potentially trigger investment arbitration claims under agreements across the globe.[39]

In the current landscape of financial liquidity and capital movement, States face reduced capacity for interference in their markets, making them more vulnerable to economic crises driven by external factors.[40] States in the history of financial and economic crises have deliberately intervened to advance social protection objectives that are jeopardised by market failures, and such interventions have not always gone unchallenged. The uncertainty and remit of governmental interventions during economic emergencies can conceivably result in host State breaches of investment treaty standards of protection.[41] A revision of contract to minimise the extent of economic loss and costs may contradict international obligations

36 Muthucumaraswamy Sonarajah, 'Mutations of Neo-Liberalism in International Investment Law' (2011) 3(1) *Trade Law and Development*, 205.

37 *ibid.*

38 Henri Bezuidenhout & Ewert Kleynhans, 'Implications of Foreign Direct Investment for National Sovereignty: The Wal-Mart/Massmart Merger as an Illustration' (2015) 22(1) *Nigerian Journal of International Affairs*, 95–96.

39 Sorin Dolea, 'COVID-19 and State of Necessity in Investment Arbitration' (2020) 14(4) *Romanian Arbitration Journal*, 45.

40 Ballan (n 20) 4

41 Diane A. Desierto, 'Calibrating Human Rights and Investment in Economic Emergencies: Prospects of Treaty and Valuation Defenses' (2012) 9(2) *Manchester Journal of International Economic Law*, 164.

arising from international agreements, thereby raising the cost of those immediate measures. Foreign investors can bring claims for emergency measures taken in this regard because States have investment agreements that provide obligations that must be met.[42]

During periods of economic crisis—defined as times when the real economy, which encompasses the production, consumption, and distribution of goods and services, experiences often severe and unconventional contractions[43]—conditions can create strong demand for stabilizing macroeconomic policies. Stakes are high for governments who may wish re-election, thus there is a strong incentive for the adoption of somewhat radical and immediate policy responses to the crisis.[44] Rational host States take the costs of breaching investment treaties into consideration, but those costs are uncertain. In contrast to the benefits from addressing the crisis, most costs will occur later, and most likely, investment treaties will be breached.[45] It is argued in subsequent chapters that policy decisions by most host States do not often internalise the costs and liabilities from breaching investment agreements.

States can regulate for sovereigns but not without deference to international obligations and the dictates of the real world; as the world evolves, so also should laws evolve to match the dictates of the times. BITs should be flexible to accommodate exigencies and be watertight to prevent arbitrary conduct which risks running contrary and counterproductive to the efficient functioning of the international investment regime. A relative proportion of BITs' provisions may not be consistent with the development objectives or policies of contracting States at different life span of the agreements. For example, most of them have broad and open-ended definition of investments;[46] if such treaties, in addition, provide no exception to the guarantee to transfer funds during economic crises and balance of payment difficulties, it could further compound sovereignty concerns. This is because there is scholarship that suggests that unstable capital flows may be seen as negative externalities on recipient States and that regulating cross-border flow can help mitigate economic crises,[47] thus leading to the International Monetary Funds'

42 Dolea n (39).

43 Christian Bellak & Markus Leibrecht, 'Do Economic Crises Trigger Treaty-Based Investor Disputes? (2021) 24 *Journal of International Economic Law*, 130.

44 *ibid.*

45 Moshe Hirsch, 'Compliance with Investment Treaties: When are States More Likely to Breach or Comply with Investment Treaties?' in Christina Binder et al (eds), *International Investment Law for the 21st Century: Essays in Honor of Christopher Schreuer* (Oxford University Press 2009) 869.

46 Biplove Choudhary & Parashar Kulkarni, 'Re-Crafting Bilateral Investment Treaties in a Development Framework: A Comparative Regional Perspective' in Ashwini Deshpande (ed), *Capital Without Borders* (Anthem Press 2010) 213; Nigeria-Finland BIT. Available on https://investmentpolicy.unctad.org/international-investment-agreements/treaty-files/1206/download [Accessed on 4 November 2024].

47 Kevin P. Gallagher, Sarah Sklar & Rachel Thrasher, Quantifying the Policy Space for Regulating Capital Flows in Trade and Investment Treaties, 3. Available on https://www.bu.edu/gdp/files/2019/04/Gallagher_Capital-Flows-and-Treaties.pdf [Accessed on 30 October 2024].

recommendation of a capital flow management mechanism as imperative in managing the economy alongside a sequential opening of capital accounts.[48]

Capital flow management mechanisms can be found in exceptions that permit capital flow management when there is balance of payment crises or for other prudential reasons. Thus, although most treaties advocate for open capital account and deregulation in some sectors of the economy in order to encourage foreign investors,[49] exceptions have now developed to counter what may be the impact from such policies.[50] As will be discussed later, most States are beginning to rethink the idea of an open and deregulated economy following economic crises and, therefore, opting for ways to balance the treaty objective of encouraging and facilitating foreign investments and the State's sovereign rights to regulate through exceptions and safeguards. Thus the exact scope of monetary clauses differs: while some permit free flow of capital without undue delay, modern treaties are becoming stringent with respect to regulating capital flows by having broader exceptions to the treaty obligations.[51]

A BIT that does not afford a host State the right to regulate capital through the provision of exceptions or the legitimisation of measures such as capital controls will be counterproductive to the aims of such a treaty, which are to spur and aid economic development. International capital flows in the form of FDI exacerbates economic crises. In developing States with an open capital account, often characterised by notable currency mismatches in their financial portfolio, adjustment mechanisms fail if there are any sharp changes in external resources.[52] Heavy capital inflows can fuel asset value bubbles and exchange rate appreciation, overwhelm regulatory capacity, and make an economy vulnerable to capital flow reversals.[53] The herd behaviour of moving large sums of capital out of a host State's economy by foreign investors during this period can create balance of payment problems,[54] thus making it increasingly difficult for the host State in question to adjust policies to correct the root problem. A balance of payment problem in this context is when a decrease in demand for a State's currency is so steep that it creates downward pressure on the value of its currency. This destabilises market transactions and renders

48 *ibid* 4.

49 Ross P. Buckley, 'International Capital Flows, Economic Sovereignty and Developing Countries' (1999) 4 *Yearbook of International Financial and Economic Law*, 31.

50 Camille Martini, 'Avoiding the Planned Obsolescence of Modern International Investment Agreements: Can General Exception Mechanisms Be Improved, and How?' (2018) 59(8) *Boston College Law Review* 2880–2881

51 Gallagher, Sklar & Thrasher (n 47) 5.

52 Jose Antonio Ocampo & Jose Gabriel Palma, 'The Role of Preventative Capital Account Regulation', in Jose Antonio Ocampo & Joseph E Stiglitz (eds), *Capital Market Liberalization and Development* (Oxford University Press 2008), 171.

53 Adam Feibelman, 'The IMF and Regulation of Cross-Border Capital Flows' (2015) 15(2) *Chicago Journal of International Law*, 411.

54 Pierre-Richard Agenor, 'Benefits and Costs of International Financial Integration: Theory and Facts' (2003) 26(8) *The World Economy*, 1090–1091.

citizens unable to pay for everyday necessities.[55] Balance of payment crises, which are often characterised by high current account deficit, high dollarisation, and influx of foreign currency flow, are more likely to occur in developing States.[56]

The economic crisis in Argentina in the late 1990s and early 2000s, and in Iceland and the US State of California, are a pointer to the fact that economic emergencies can happen anywhere, even in the most established financial systems and seemingly well-situated States.[57] In 1997, Thailand, a State believed to have pursued sound economic policies and gained strong economic growth was embroiled in a financial crisis which demonstrated the volatility of investment flows and the contagion effects of crises in a world that has integrated capital markets.[58] This crisis has shown that even well-situated States can experience irreparable economic damage and human welfare losses due to balance of payment difficulties.[59] Thus the question of whether capital controls can serve as effective measures to revive an economy remains a conundrum, further complicated by the lack of precedents in international arbitration regarding their regulation. The inclusion of emergency clauses in response to economic crises may help to clarify these ambiguities. To mitigate liabilities and costs, States should negotiate the applicability of both the emergency clause and the customary defence of necessity. Such provisions can be couched either as exceptions (acts capable of justifying a breach) or safeguards (measures which are excluded from the scope of treaty making).[60] This is, however, operational but in a limited context because a large percentage of BITs contain no exception nor safeguards.[61] Even when a treaty contains a safeguard or exception, a host State risks running afoul of other treaty obligations as foreign investors may bring claims in arbitration through the Most Favoured Nation Clause, the favourable treatment of another BIT which does not have provision for such safeguards or exception.

Thus the impact of BITs on the ability of developing States to control capital flows, outside of the presence of a safeguard or exception clause, remains an important topic that needs to be considered. This is because, if investment treaties

55 Chantal Thomas, 'Balance of Payment Crises in the Developing World: Balancing Trade, Finance and Development in the New Economic Order' (2000) 15(6) *American University International Law Review*, 125.

56 Oleksandr Chernyak, Vasyl Khomicik & Yevgen Chernyak, 'The Main Triggers of the Balance of Payment Crisis in the Eastern Europe' (2013) 8 *Procedia Technology*, 47–50.

57 Christina Binder & August Reinisch, 'Economic Emergency Powers: A Comparative Law Perspective' in Stephen Schill (ed), *International Investment Law and Comparative Public Law* (Oxford University Press 2010) 503.

58 Kenneth J. Vendevelde, 'Model BIT. The Way Forward' (2011) 18(1) *Southwestern Journal of International Law*, 308.

59 Peter Chowla, 'Comparing Naughty BITs: Assessing the Developmental Impact of Variation in Bilateral Investment Treaties' (2005) *Working Paper Series*, 25.

60 Jorge E. Vinuales, 'Sovereignty in Foreign Investment Law' in Zachary Douglas, Joost Pauwelyn & Jorge E. Vinuales (eds), *The Foundations of International Investment Law* (Oxford University Press 2014) 348–349.

61 *ibid.*

can be activated to prevent developing States from imposing capital controls, then a vital policy consideration is lost, and it is a loss with potentially catastrophic consequences.[62] Thus this book analyses general international law to find ways to bridge the chasm between foreign investors' interests and a State's ability to use capital control mechanisms to regulate its economy.

1.3 Aims and Objectives

To provide clarity and context to the discussions above, the book explores the following issues:

1. BIT commitments and other international agreements on the repatriation of capital and profits.
2. Useful mechanisms in bridging the chasm between State's right to regulate during economic crisis and foreign investors' right to repatriate capital.

1.4 Book Structure

This book will be divided into different chapters to facilitate discussion in small units, identify key issues, integrate ideas, and develop compelling arguments in a readable form.

Chapter 1 of this book examines the structural deficiencies in developing States' investment architecture, particularly the right to transfer funds. The objectives of the book as well as the methodologies used are also discussed. Drawing from the key issues identified therein, Chapter 2 examines the underlying basis for a BIT. Economic liberalisation, one of the aims of a BIT, is identified. Thus the chapter is based on the premise that liberal economics inform and shape the efficient development of global economics and the functioning of international investment law without insulating it from competing policy concerns.[63] It contextualises BITs within the precepts of economic liberalisation as one of the tools of liberalism in a global economy. A BIT in this regard touts itself as an instrument of economic liberalisation, that is, an instrument for the facilitation and protection of investment flows. It postulates that increased economic growth and prosperity are the natural result of a liberal regime and that, by concluding such an agreement, a developing State is seeking to attract FDI that will promote its economic growth. Chapter 3 explores the origins of the normative framework for fund transfers, tracing it back to the quest for economic liberalisation, where States had to ensure the protection of capital to instil confidence in foreign investors willing to invest in unfamiliar territories. It examines the IMF's role as a key source of international monetary law and highlights the absence of explicit investment protections within the IMF

62 Chowla (n 59) 27.

63 Kenneth J. Vandevelde, 'Investment Liberalization and Economic Development: The Role of Bilateral Investment Treaties' (1998) 36(3) *Columbia Journal of Transnational Law*, 501.

Articles of Agreement, despite its significant contribution to the expansion and growth of international trade and investment. The fact that States are willing to go above and beyond their obligations in the IMF Agreement is a precursor and illustration of the presence of strong economic incentives towards the liberalisation of international capital flows.[64]

Having explored the fundamental aim of a BIT and the possible policy collusion, Chapter 4 examines arguments that the BIT commitment on transfer of funds could possibly impact a State's sovereignty and questions the rhetoric behind such arguments. The chapter examines the concept of sovereignty as a principal cornerstone of economic relations, one which aims to protect the independence of all States, especially the less developed, in the context of their economic inequality.[65] It examines how economic integration has rendered the traditional concept of sovereignty inoperative. The traditional concept of State sovereignty is construed in relation to independence. It rebuts claims that the curtailment of State sovereignty is a recent phenomenon, but that globalisation has only brought much awareness to it as, historically, each State has always been limited by the existence of the other State and has always taken into consideration possible counteraction from the other State. Even from a philosophical point of view, independence is only permitted as much as is necessary.[66] It recognises that the world economy in the past three decades has witnessed a huge transformation, from relatively independent national economies separated by legal and geographical barriers to a more integrated and interdependent economy whereby private economic actors now enjoy new-found opportunities. As economic interactions between States expand and become multifarious, so also do capital flows and international payments become more of a frequent feature.[67] The geographic de-concentration of FDI, the changing pattern of international trade and liberalisation of financial services are testaments to this.[68] While globalisation is of great benefit to a national economy, the risk that is associated with spontaneous capital flow is the basis for the argument on the need for a new international legal order. Investment treaties reflect the increasing legalisation of international relations and consequent need to impose international legal constraints on governments.[69]

Further discussions on sovereignty are contextualised within the precincts of the BITs signed by developing States in Chapter 5. These treaties are analysed to

64 Claus D. Zimmermann, 'The Promotion of Transfer-of-Funds Liberalisation across International Economic Law' (2011) 12(5) *Journal of World Investment and Trade*, 732.

65 Nataliya Tyurina, 'Regional Economic Integration and State Sovereignty' (2014) 1(1) *Journal of International and European Law, Economics and Market*, 44

66 *ibid* 45.

67 Mahmood Bagheri & Mohammad Jafar Ghanbari Jahromi, 'Globalization and Extraterritorial Application of Economic Regulation: Crisis in International Law and Balancing Interests' (2016) 41(2) *European Journal of Law and Economics*, 394.

68 *ibid*.

69 Todd Allee and Clint Peinhardt, 'Delegating Differences: Bilateral Investment Treaties and Bargaining Over Dispute Resolution Provisions' (2010) 54(1) *International Studies Quarterly*, 3.

show the that some of them require a rebalancing between the contracting States and foreign investors' commitments as uneven regulatory protection will be counterproductive to the desired aim of the treaty. The chapter critically assesses BITs that provide for both qualified and unqualified right to transfer of funds and further discusses how developing States have responded to the issues of sovereignty diminution. Chapter 6 proposes that the proper delineation of treaty obligations can eliminate the likelihood of successful challenges to non-discriminatory public welfare measures. In this instance, precision fetters the discretion for subjective value choices and concerns about adjudicators' incompetence[70] and, furthermore, the necessity of bridging the chasm between the competing interests of the host and the foreign investor on the right to transfer funds through exceptions and treaty interpretation guidelines. Chapter 7 summarises already stated arguments and succinctly identifies the recommendations that may be necessary to bridge the chasm between the foreign investor's rights and the host State's right to regulate for her sovereignty.

1.5 Research Methodology

The methodology used in this book is the doctrinal methodology. This methodology is a distinct legal approach to research. An important element of the doctrinal methodology is that it involves a critical conceptual analysis and synthesis of relevant legislation and case laws to reveal a statement of the law relevant to the matter under investigation.[71] It is used in this research because it identifies and analyses the current law on investment with a view to proposing reforms. It transcends the discussions and critiques of the current investment regime to suggest ways in which the underlying law can be amended, and this is a hallmark of a good doctrinal study.

Doctrinal methodology draws comprehensively from different sources, journal articles, books, legislation, case laws, and websites to develop a problem-solving strategy.[72] It further involves the making of connections between seemingly disparate doctrinal strands and the challenge of extracting general principles from an inchoate mass of primary materials. It involves a unique blending of deductive and inductive reasoning and analogy; these common law tools enable lawyers to make sense of complex legal questions.[73] Questions on the efficacy of bilateral investment treaty provisions on transfer of funds within the contemporary investment regime are explored by reference to a wide range of primary and secondary sources. BITs between different States are examined while recourse is also made

70 Caroline Henckels, 'Protecting Regulatory Autonomy Through Greater Precision in Investment Treaties' The TPP, CETA, and TTP' (2016) 19 *Journal of International Economics Law*, 27.

71 Terry Hutchinson, 'The Doctrinal Method: Incorporating Interdisciplinary Methods in Reforming the Law' (2015) 3 *Erasmus Law Review*, 131.

72 Terry Hutchinson, 'Doctrinal Research' in Watson Dawn & Mary Burton (ed), *Research Methods in Law* (2nd edn, Abingdon Oxon: Routledge 2017) 16.

73 *ibid* 19.

to other substantive rules such as the IMF Articles of Agreement and the General Agreement on Trade and Tariffs amongst others.

Also, by raising normative questions, having looked at the institutional and jurisdictional framework of law, the comparative law methodology is activated, albeit to a reasonable extent. Comparative law operates on the basis that rules are referenced to organisational settings, the procedural context, and the conceptual structure within which legal problems emerge and the rules are operated.[74] In this book, jurisdictional practices between different States are compared. This is because the goal of law in different rules and institutions or social context can create normative questions. Discussions borrow from partial legal solutions in other legal systems and contextualises them within the current social and economic climate without emphatically relying on rules and legislation. For example, the Indian and American model BITs are referenced in subsequent chapters. Also, the Argentine financial crisis and its legal implications are concurrently evaluated alongside other incidents of economic crisis to understand the likely effects of BIT provisions during an economic crisis and what legal solutions work best for developing States. For a full understanding of the discourse, resources beyond BITs and legal texts are used. As the investment regime derives from public international law, recourse is made to customary international law, the Vienna Convention on the Law of Treaties (VCLT), the IMF Articles of Agreement, and the United Nations Conference on Trade and Development to reflect the interdisciplinary nature of discussions.

1.6 Conclusion

This book contributes to the discourse on the challenges faced by investment regimes in developing States, emphasizing the need to balance the interests of foreign investors with those of local communities, particularly concerning the right to transfer funds related to investments. It outlines potential safety measures for tribunals, States, and other stakeholders involved in drafting,negotiating and interpreting treaty clauses on fund transfers. The aim is to provide developing States with similar economic characteristics a framework for future negotiations. It aspires to be relevant to international law students and all stakeholders in international investment law. Contemporary and provocative, the book addresses critical subjects such as the erosion of sovereignty and the implications of recent global crises on foreign investment regulation.

74 John Bell, 'Legal Research and the Distinctiveness of Comparative Law' in Van Hoecke Mark (ed), *Methodologies of Legal Research: Which Kind of Method for What Kind of Discipline?* (1st edn, London: Bloomsbury Publishing Plc 2011) 170.

2 Economic Liberalisation through the Channels of a BIT Framework

2.1 Introduction

The nexus between States and BITs points to FDI: the quest to protect foreign investments as a signal of credible commitment. In this sense, a BIT becomes a device for achieving democratic consolidation, market stability, and increased investments.[1] This relationship between States and BITs has to a reasonable extent been characterised by a dichotomy between sovereignty and investment protection: State sovereignty over natural resources versus State responsibility for injuries to aliens; domestic laws clashing with international minimum standards of treatment; and the State's public policies running counter to legitimate expectations of foreign investors.[2] At the root of this clash is the complexity of the foreign investment phenomenon with its distinctive characteristics: capital flows out of the home State into the host State and the conflicting interest in the foreign investment continuum, which is foreign investors seeking to maximise profit and undertake strategic alliances and the State seeing the investment as an opportunity to promote economic growth. While a foreign investor rallies on the protection shield in the form of right of property, the State seeks to reinforce its sovereignty to control its internal matters and the economy.[3]

Many States have adopted policies of economic liberalisation in order to encourage capital flows and speed up economic growth regardless of the economic disruptions that high volumes and volatility of capital inflows and outflows can create.[4] A common policy frequently prescribed along this line is the need for the "liberalisation of the capital account".[5] This would entail the allowance of a free flow of funds in and out of a country's economy—inherently alluded to as an essential

1 Seok-ju Cho, Yong Kyun Kim & Cheol-Sung Lee, 'Credibility, Preferences and Bilateral Investment Treaties' (2016) 11(1) *The Review of International Organization*, 26.

2 Omar E. Garcia-Bolivar, 'Sovereignty vs. Investment Protection: Back to Calvo' (2009) 24(2) *ICSID Review*, 465.

3 *ibid.*

4 Wassem Mina, 'Political Risks Guarantees and Capital Flows: The Role of Bilateral Investment Treaties' (2015) 9(1) *Economics: The Open Assess, Open-Assessment E-Journal*, 5.

5 Uan Noy & Tan B. Vu, 'Capital Account Liberalization and Foreign Direct Investment' (2007) 18 *North American Journal of Economic and Finance*, 176.

DOI: 10.4324/9781003611714-2

step in the process of economic development.[6] The degree of liberalisation of the capital account depends on the capital controls. Lesser controls on capital flows will lead to greater capital account liberalisation.[7]

The international investment law system has deep roots in capitalism and capital accumulation. The shortcomings in the economic growth of States lacking modern economic structures adopt the logic and simplicity of the Marshall Plan Concept.[8] This ideation rests on the injection of massive capital into poor States to facilitate development. Capital is deemed to maintain its quantity while transferring its form. They are first seen in the form of "monetary advances", usually symbolising financial wealth or income-generating funds but having a definite monetary magnitude. [9] This could possibly explain the link between the concepts of foreign investments and massive capital flows. The second view of capital is related to mechanised production which encompasses capital goods or stocks of physical instruments that possess sets of qualities that are valuable to productivity. Political economists argue that both the qualitative and quantitative function of capital should be subsumed and treated as funds necessary to assist the original factors of production in the form of land and labour.[10]

The quantitative and qualitative facets of capital and capital goods have greatly influenced legal thought. In this sense, capital is often referred to as the contribution, which could be money, property, and services, that owners of a business invest in equity. In general, they are attributed to various economic interests which includes any form of value, monetary worth or physical property and, in capitalist enterprise, elements of privatisation and profit orientation. These economic interests are invariably connected with the concept of growth and development and undoubtedly amongst the rights that are protected by international investment law.[11] The distributional effects of capital mobility amongst States have effects on different actors in the system: owners of capital, workers in different sectors, producers in non-traded goods and international investors.[12] These lead to political re-alignments amongst different actors. Increased capital mobility is known to benefit owners of financial services and the foreign investors who hope to gain returns. The adoption of policies liberalising capital flow concur with the growing advocacy for capital mobility by financial institutions and foreign investors. These identified sources offer explanations for the demand of liberalisation policies.[13]

6 Eswar S. Prasad & Raghuram G. Rajan, 'A Pragmatic Approach to Capital Account Liberalization' (2008) 22(3) *Journal of Economic Perspective*, 149.

7 Mahendra Pal Singh, Wolfram Cremer & Niraj Kumar, *Open Markets, Free Trade and Sustainable Development* (Springer Nature Singapore Pte Ltd 2019) 264.

8 Priscilla Schwartz, 'Capitalism, International Investment Law and the Development Conundrum' (2013) 6(2) *Law and Development Review*, 223.

9 *ibid.*

10 *ibid.*

11 *ibid* 224.

12 *ibid.*

13 Quan Li & Dale L. Smith, 'The Dilemma of Financial Liberalization: State Autonomy and Societal Demands' (2002) 64(3) *The Journal of Politics*, 766.

Many States in recent times are responding to the increased global demand and competition of FDIs (a form of capital) by implementing investment-related policies. As a result of this, a range of measures have grown exponentially both locally and internationally. Amongst the leading instruments of investment protection, are investment agreements which provide protection to foreign investments from risks such as expropriation and remittance control which are perceived to be prevalent in developing States. In general, international investment agreements have proliferated at the bilateral, regional, and interregional levels over the last past decade, and developing States have been active actors in signing investment treaties.[14]

Capital-exporting States seek guarantees of protection that are both precise and comprehensive with the primary aim of protecting existing and future investments.[15] This means that they anticipate investment agreements that guarantee investors the right to transfer revenue and capital from an investment in all cases, outside of the host State, while capital-importing States seek to negotiate for exceptions in appropriate cases, so that a compulsory transfer obligation will be extinguished to preserve policy space if need be. In most cases, negotiations that successfully result in an agreement are those that do not materially depart from the capital-exporting State's model.[16] Many developing States who are capital importing have liberalised their capital and, consequently, their ability to control domestic monetary policy.[17] And it is not unexpected that more States would sign investment agreements if the grand bargain of increased foreign investments following investment protection is anything to go by. Some States are taking proactive steps to modernise investment frameworks and adopting treaties that reflect their own preferences, which is a paradigm departure from models that seem unfavourable to them. For example, African States are now negotiating BITs that provide innovative features that are primarily aimed at sustainable development and safeguarding the right of a host State to regulate.[18] The Morocco-Nigeria BIT, considered in detail in Chapter 5, exemplifies the new-generation BIT that enables a State to retain the capacity to implement beneficial national policies .

In summary, BITs advertise themselves as important components of economic liberalisation—in this regard, as instruments for facilitating and protecting international investment flows. They also treat increased prosperity for both

14 Biplove Choudhary & Parashar Kulkarni, 'Recrafting Bilateral Investment Treaties in a Development Framework: A Comparative Regional Perspective' in Ashwini Deshpande (ed), *Capital Without Borders* (Anthem Press 2010) 209–210.

15 Jeswald Salacuse, 'BIT by BIT: The Growth of Bilateral Investment Treaties and Their Impact on Foreign Investment in Developing Countries' (1990) 24(3) *The International Lawye*r, 663–664

16 *ibid.*

17 Jonathan Crystal, 'Sovereignty, Bargaining and the International Regulation of Foreign Direct Investment' (2009) 23(3) *Global Society*, 226.

18 Hamed El-Kady & Mustaqeem De Gama, 'The Reform of the International Investment Regime: An African Perspective' (2019) 34(2) *ICSID Review*, 483.

parties as the consequential result of a liberal investment regime.[19] The benefits of FDIs are unrivalled in terms of their ability to generate economic growth and advance technological development; however, they have influenced the ability of the State to act as sovereign in its territory, thus rendering the traditional concepts of sovereignty obsolete as foreign investors gain special status of private actors in international law. This assertion can best be understood if the relationship between the foreign investor and the State is viewed alongside the concepts of FDI and BIT, with its enclosed system that imbues the foreign investors with rights and States with duties and no rights.[20] To provide context, this chapter discusses BITs within the parameters of FDIs. Subsequent sections establish the nexus between these treaties and FDIs and further examine the dichotomy between States and foreign investors.

2.2 FDI Regulation and Bilateral Investment Treaties

FDI is traditionally defined as forms of international inter-firm competition that involves a significant equity stake or effective management control of foreign enterprises.[21] It is basically an investment by foreign nationals that is large enough to grant the investor a significant amount of capital control. It has long term horizons and is generally not done for speculative purposes, but, rather, to exploit natural resources, serve the domestic market, and provide platforms to serve the world market through exports.[22] In the operational features of a multinational corporation, FDI is considered to be the end result of broad corporate strategies and investment decisions of profit-maximising organisations that face worldwide competition where significant differences in cost structures, due to factor productivity and remuneration differentials across States support cross-border investment and production relocation.[23] In contrast to FDI, there is portfolio investment, which is sometimes protected by BITs. A portfolio investment is a passive investment in the securities of another State such as stocks and bonds.[24] Discussions on FDI remain the primary focus of this book; however, the risks inherent in the protection of portfolio investments will be considered, albeit briefly to show good cause why some BITs need revisiting.

19 Kenneth J. Vandevelde, 'Investment Liberalization and Economic Development: The Role of Bilateral Investment Treaties' (1998) 36(3) *Columbia Journal of Transnational Law*, 503.

20 James Thuo Gathli & Harrison Otieno Mbori, 'Reform and Retrenchment in International Investment Law: Introduction to a Special Issue' (2023) 24 *Journal of World Investment & Trade*, 538.

21 Luiz R. De Mello Jr, 'Foreign Direct Investment in Developing Countries: A Selective Survey' (1997) 34(1) *The Journal of Development Studies*, 4.

22 Andrew Kerner, 'Why Should I Believe You? The Costs and Consequences of Bilateral Investment Treaties' (2009) 53(1) *International Studies Quarterly*, 53.

23 *ibid* 56.

24 Adeleke Kunle M., Olowe, S.O. & Fasesin Oladipo Oluwafolake, 'Impact of FDI in Nigeria Economic Growth' (2014) 4(8) *International Journal of Academic Research in Business and Social Sciences*, 234.

FDIs often involve a very complex process; aside from the capital they bring, they also include a very complex process of modern technology, managerial skills, and knowledge transfers.[25] FDIs are known to have led to the expansion of a State's industrial base; the growth of industrial opportunities; and the improvement of balance of payments.[26] In addition, they aid a State's industrialisation growth and development strategies through technical and managerial skills and are considered to be a source of employment opportunities for a State, transforming an economy from a primary agrarian enclave to an industrial one by facilitating the importation of a technology that has led to the greater utilisation of the State's natural resources.[27] The centrality of FDI attraction is the sanctity of property rights of foreign investors. While FDI is considered essential to economic development, BITs are regarded as the main extraterritorial legal devices through which States can strengthen the legal environment for multinational companies.[28] Thus the global network of BITs signed by States over the years has been built on the premise of promoting FDIs and are often reflective in a BIT's preamble.[29] They have become the most popular international legal mechanism for the promotion and governance of FDI amongst policymakers in developing States.[30]Investment treaties are now viewed as admission tickets to investment markets.[31] Whether they boost FDI flows remains a matter of debate.[32] There are, however, mixed and conflicting results on whether BITs encourage FDI and reduce the likelihood of State interference in the activities of multinational corporations.[33] Scholars who subscribe to the law and development orthodoxy have examined the correlation between FDI and BITs; however, the results are inconsistent and contradictory.[34]

25 Petrovic-Randelovic Marija, Ksenija Dencic-Mihajlor & Others, 'An Analysis of the Location Determinants of Foreign Direct Investment: The Case of Serbia' (2013) 81(1) *Social and Behavioural Science*, 182.

26 Chi-Chi Onuorah Anastasia, 'Relationship between Foreign Direct Investment Inflow, Sub-Saharan Africa and Nigeria Economic Development' (2012) 1(11) *Kuwait Chapter of the Arabian Journal of Business and Management Review*, 30.

27 *ibid.*

28 Sarah Bauerle Danzman, 'Contracting with Whom? The Differential Effects of Investment Treaties on FDI' (2016) 42(3) *International Interaction*, 452.

29 Jeswald Salacuse, 'BIT by BIT: The Growth of Bilateral Investment Treaties and Their Impact on Foreign Investment in Developing Countries' (1990) 24(3) *The International Lawyer*, 661.

30 Eric Neumayer & Laura Spess, 'Do Bilateral Investment Treaties Increase FDI to Developing Countries?' (2005) 33(10) *World Development*, 1567.

31 Rudolph Dolzer & Christopher Schreuer, *The Principles of International Investment Law* (2nd edn, Oxford University Press 2012) 14.

32 David Collins, 'National Treatment in Emerging Market Investment Treaties' in Anselm Kamperman Sanders (ed), *The Principle of National Treatment in International Economic Law: Trade Investment and Intellectual Property* (Edward Elgar Publishing Limited 2014) 161.

33 Williams C., Luoianova T. & Marinez C., 'The Moderating Effect of Bilateral Investment Treaties Stringency between Political Instability and Subsidiary Ownership Choice' (2017) 26(1) *International Business Review*, 1.

34 Jason Webb Yackee, 'BIT, Credible Commitment, and the Rule of (International) Law: Do BITs Promote Foreign Direct Investment?' (2008) 42(4) *Law and Society Review*, 806.

There are potential rewards for investing in developing States, although this also comes with its own risks: the risks associated with unstable political and regulatory frameworks.[35] There are two kinds of risk here: first, a systematic domestic risk typical to all investors and related to the quality of domestic institutions and, secondly, an idiosyncratic risk specific to each pair of home and host States resulting from interpersonal relations.[36] The relations between political interactions of a host State with regards to foreign investment can either lead to positive or negative outcomes. A retaliatory effect of deteriorating relations between the home State and host State could lead to expropriations. In this regard, BITs function most by offsetting political tensions between States and, secondly, as a costly signal that a host government will not diminish the protection of property rights granted by domestic institutions.[37] In essence, they reduce policy uncertainty and guarantee the presence and adoption of rules for foreign investment by establishing clear rules on expropriation and the circumstances under which expropriation can take place.[38] A State that exhibits strong institutional regulations inspires confidence to invest in the State, since economic activities that occur within its boundary are likely to flourish due to less interference. In this context, contracts can be enforced, and defaulters can be pursued in a functioning court of law. In such politically stable States, government officials have a limited ability to make discriminatory and erratic policy changes that may adversely affect multinational corporations. Thus environmental uncertainty exogenous to the firm is diminished.[39]

The impact of politics in encouraging foreign investors to negotiate for more stringent BITs becomes more evident when contracting with unstable States. Instability in a political environment increases the likelihood of political turmoil.[40] Governments may attempt to alter property rights by means of nationalisation, money supply regulations, and taxation. Therefore, bargaining for rights becomes quite ambivalent in driving economic reforms because politicians can sometimes be inconsistent. Political uncertainty will reinforce the notion and possibility that regulations will be hard to predict and invested assets harder to protect. Since multinational corporations are vulnerable in this circumstance, they may choose minority ownership in investment while limiting commitments or press for stringent conditions.[41] Thus the disparity in the capacity of developing States to attract foreign investors rests on the credible promise to uphold property rights and policy commitments. And there is evidence to suggest that BITs that include access to

35 Robert Ginsburg, 'Political Risk Insurance and Bilateral Investment Treaties: Making the Connection' (2013) 14(1) *The Journal of World Investment and Trade*, 943.

36 *ibid.*

37 Rudolph Desbordes & Vincent Vicard, 'Foreign Direct Investment and Bilateral Investment Treaties. An International Political Perspective' (2009) 37(3) *Journal of Comparative Economics*, 373.

38 Mina Wassem, 'Political Risk Guarantees and Capital Inflow: The Role of Bilateral Investment Treaties' (2015) 9(26) *Peer Review Journal*, 1.

39 Williams, Luoianova & Marinez (n 33) 2.

40 *ibid.*

41 *ibid.*

investor-State' arbitration mechanisms are consistently associated with increased investments in infrastructural projects.[42]

Other non-political factors that may affect investments are the possibility of the imposition of exchange controls, restrictions on repatriation of profits, disruptions in production caused by strikes, and abrupt changes in economic policies. These variables affect the present and expected future profits of a given firm and, as such, investors incorporate these variables into the firm's value maximisation framework.[43] Thus, economic policies of a host State are also of great concern to a foreign investor. Unsound monetary and fiscal policies (usually captured by high inflation and large fiscal deficits), external imbalances, and rapid credit creation may shift investors' confidence towards investing or leaving a State:[44] for example, foreign exchange control laws that place restrictions on currency convertibility are likely to deter FDI.[45]

Some scholars are of the opinion that a BIT stabilises a host State's existing investment environment and provides substitutes for weak domestic laws that are not developed enough to protect FDI, thereby emitting signals to potential investors of a credible commitment to the protection of foreign investments by developing States.[46] However, some scholars have termed the equation of BITs to a correlative effect on FDI as "naïve legal formulism"—a belief that the rules of contract law are central and germane for economic transactions in a modern capital economy, whereas the realities of a modern commercial practice prove otherwise.[47] Investment agreements do not in their entirety attract investment, rather, they complement the main determinants of FDI flows. .[48] It appears that business executives who make investment decisions in business have little or no accurate knowledge of governing legal rules. BITs remain an overlooked tool in the legal arsenal of multinational corporations. Even when this specialised legal knowledge is within the purview of lawyers that are in the general counsel's office, the knowledge may not flow to the non-lawyer managers who make the investment decisions. If the investor's knowledge of BITs is weak, then the obsolescing bargain risk reduction that BITs envisage is redundant. There is little reason to believe that the presence or absence of a treaty will

42 Danzman B. S., 'Contracting with Whom? The Differential Effects of Investment Treaties on FDI' (2016) 42(3) *International Interaction*, 453–454.

43 Romita Biswas, 'Determinants of Foreign Direct Investment' (2002) 6(3) *Review of Development Economics*, 494.

44 Cesar Calderon & Megumi Kubota, 'Sudden Stops: Are Global and Local Investors Alike?' (2013) 89(1) *Journal of International Economics*, 124.

45 Elizabeth Asiedu, 'On the Determinants of FDI to Developing Countries: Is Africa Different?' (2002) 30(1) *World Development*, 111.

46 Alec R. Johnson, 'Rethinking Bilateral Investment Treaties in Sub-Saharan Africa' (2010) 59(4) *Emory Law Journal*, 925.

47 Yackee (n 34) 810.

48 Carlos G. Garciia, 'All the Other Dirty Little Secrets: Investment Treaties, Latin America and the Necessary Evil of Investor-States Arbitration' (2004) 16(2) *Florida Journal of International Law*, 315.

have a significant effect on particular investment decisions, thus prompting suggestions that the formal trappings of the law only have modest effect in private decisions.[49]

Although there is no conclusive theoretical literature on whether BITs constitute major determinants of FDI, there are scholars who suggest that, due to some differences in national rules, a BIT may be the cause of higher transaction costs and uncertainty from a firm's perspective.[50] Although this point would support an argument for a multilateral investment treaty, these scholars acknowledge that differences in economic, political, cultural, and general business climate characteristics are more important determinants of the transaction costs associated with FDI.[51] Though investment treaties have been quite significant in the establishment decisions of some investors (in terms of acknowledging the legal structure they provide for their investment), in overall terms the impact of treaties on investment flows to the developing world has been small.[52] However, negotiation of BITs continue unabated even though it has been found that they are highly ambiguous regarding whether host States gain more attractiveness by offering better protections and more rights to foreign investors.[53] In other words, there appears to be no clear-cut clarity on whether the protections offered by BITs are the main source for the attraction of FDI to States that sign up to them.

2.3 The Liberalising Effect of Bilateral Investment Treaties

BITs rest on three principles: facts, causation, and rectitude. The first principle stems from a belief that FDI flows will increase prosperity.[54] The second, from the belief that the protection of FDI will promote investment flows.[55] While the

49 Yackee (n 34) 810–811.

50 Peter Egger & Michael Pfaffermayr, 'The Impact of Bilateral Investment Treaties on Foreign Direct Investment' (2004) 32 *Journal of Comparative Economics*, 789.

51 Karl P. Sauvant & Lisa E. Sachs, *The Effect of Treaties on Foreign Direct Investment: Bilateral Investment Treaties, Double Taxation Treaties, and Investment Flows* (Oxford University Press 2009) 254.

52 Muthucumaraswamy Sornarajah, *Bilateral Investment Treaties in the International Law on Foreign Investment* (16th edn, Cambridge University Press 2010) 172–235.

53 Axel Berger, Mathias Busse, Peter Nunnenkamp & Martin Roy, 'More Stringent BITs, Less Ambiguous Effects on FDI? Not a Bit!' (2011) 112(3) *Economic Letters*, 270.

54 Depending on the sector, FDI may have huge or little impact on the economy of a State. Foreign investments in the primary sector have generally few linkages to the local economy and contribute little to economic growth and employment generation. Investments in the manufacturing sector are known to lead to much technological growth and employment of labour. Even though it is not in all cases that FDI stimulates growth and technological growth, discussions in this book proceed from the premise that FDI is fundamental to the economic growth of a State, since this represents a larger percentage of the effect of FDI in a State; Liesbeth Colen, Damiaan Persyn & Andrea Guariso, 'Bilateral Investment Treaties: Does the Sector Matter?' (2016) 83 *World Development*, 194.

55 This is because, *post ante*, actors will suffer if they do not follow through with BIT commitments; and, *ex ante*, because the cost-sinking nature of BITs potentially separates sincere and insincere actors; Kerner (n 22) 76.

third one emanates from the belief that BITs, after the end of the Cold War, was imperative for promoting a liberal international order.[56] The first and second principles have already been discussed above, thus the last principle forms the basis for further discussion. The presence of legal frameworks and the removal of policies which were once roadblocks to free movement of goods and capital have led to, at least, positive outcomes for most States. There is now, more than ever, a willingness to open up national economies to global market forces. Economists surmise the gains to developing States from a liberalised investment regime to be in the billions of dollars of added GDP growth.[57] They also acknowledge human insecurity and instability to have left in the wake of economic liberalisation.[58] Thus, economic liberalisation is one of the approaches that developing States have used in attracting FDI.[59]

The right to repatriation of capital and profit (otherwise known as "the right to transfer of funds") evidence economic liberalisation. Its rationale is to aid mobility of capital and thereby promote foreign investment. It signals to foreign investors that they can, at any point, bring in capital to a host State and repatriate it either as capital or profit to their home State. However, the freedom to transfer funds related to foreign investments in and out of a State will affect a State's capital account. This is because the capital account is an integral part of the balance of payment of any State, as it reflects the net ownership of assets.[60] Thus the degree of liberalisation of the capital account of a State depends on the capital controls that are imposed at any given time. The less the controls on capital flows, the greater the capital account liberalisation. If capital controls are eliminated, then there is full capital account convertibility.[61] Whether free mobility of capital should be encouraged has become a moot point amongst academic scholars.[62]

Some BITs between developed States are carefully crafted, often incorporating nuanced exceptions that reflect a depth of legal insight that is typically beyond the reach of many developing States. This advantage is largely due to the stronger negotiating position held by the developed States.[63] Some BITs signed by developing States are however not thorough, in the sense that they do not create room for exceptions to tackle unanticipated economic problems, nor do they differentiate between different kinds of capital or under what circumstances capital movement

56 Jonathan Bonnitch, Lauge N. Skovgaard Poulsen & Micheal Weibel, *The Political Economy of the Investment Treaty Regime* (Oxford University Press 2017) 8.

57 Beth A. Simmons & Zachary Elkins, 'The Globalisation of Liberalisation: Policy Diffusion in the International Political Economy' (2004) 98(1) *American Political Science Review*, 171.

58 *ibid.*

59 Saeed Rasekhi & Zeinab Seyedi, 'An Examination of Economic Liberalisation Impact on Foreign Direct Investment in Selected Developing Countries' (2010) 14(25) *Iranian Economic Review*, 2.

60 Prabhash Ranjan, 'Capital Flows into India-Role of Monetary Transfer Provisions in India's International Agreements' in Mahendra Pal Singh, Wolfram Cremer & Niraj Kumar (eds), *Open Markets, Free Trade and Sustainable Developments: Perspectives from EU and India* (Springer 2019) 264.

61 *ibid.*

62 *ibid.*

63 *ibid.*

should be curtailed.[64] Broad and vague terms of the BIT provision on capital movement lead to misunderstandings as to the correct application and interpretation of the relevant law. In like cases that border on capital movement, different decisions have been reached by investment arbitral tribunals primarily due to the incoherence of such BIT texts and lack of precedence in arbitral decisions.[65] Also, the risks associated with large and volatile capital flows put in question the quest for full capital account liberalisation, which has been fervently pursued by international economic policymakers.[66] There is now a major rethink on the issue of capital account liberalisation. In December 2012, the IMF endorsed the regulation of cross-border finances in some circumstances; it further pointed that many trade and investment treaties do not provide the appropriate policy to regulate cross-border finance when needed. This policy departure from full capital account liberalisation is owing to the effects of capital flow mechanisms during economic crisis,[67] thus prompting the need to review capital flow mechanisms, the IMF's "new position", and investment agreements to ensure interpretative coherence.

2.4 Economic Theory of Capital (Account) Liberalisation

International monetary and financial liberalisation revolve around three foreign economic policy areas. The first is the liberalisation of the current account, which involves the payment of goods and services, foreign debt repayment, and invisibles.[68] The second is capital account liberalisation: this entails the removal of rules that discourage the free movement of investment funds in and out of a State. The third policy is the unification of exchange rates and multi-layered systems that can serve as discrimination to trading partners or kinds of transactions.[69] Whichever policy a State chooses to pursue could be due to direct economic competition or prevailing global norms.[70]

The basis of a liberal economic theory is that free markets will provide the most efficient use of resources and the greatest productivity. To have free markets, there must exist a unique relationship between the market and the State. The State must ensure that all actors in the marketplace have secure rights that they can offer to

64 Luke Eric Peterson, Bilateral Investment Treaties and Development Policy-Making. Available on https://pravo.hse.ru/data/2012/10/05/1244483607/READER_Bilateral%20Investment%20Treaties%202004.pdf [Accessed on 4 November 2024].

65 Cynthia C. Galvez, 'Necessity, Investor Rights, and State Sovereignty for NAFTA Investment Arbitration' (2013) 46(1) *Cornell International Law Journal*, 151–152.

66 Menno Broos & Sebastian Grund, 'The IMF's Jurisdiction Over the Capital Account—Reviewing the Role of Surveillance in Managing Cross-Border Capital Flows' (2018) 21 *Journal of International Economic Law*, 491.

67 Kevin P. Gallagher, Sarah Anderson & Annamaria Viterbo, 'Capital Flow Management and the Trans-Pacific Partnership Agreement' (2013) G-24 *Policy Brief No.* 79, 1.

68 Beth A. Simmons & Zachary Elkins, 'The Globalization of Liberalization: Policy Diffusion in the International Political Economy' (2004) 98(1) *American Political Science Review*, 171.

69 *ibid* 172.

70 *ibid.*

exchange for FDI, and the State must enforce those exchanges to which the parties agree.[71] Principles of a liberal economic theory entail that the State intercedes with the relevant civil societies to establish and protect the rights of parties to a treaty.[72] This requires the creation of the legal framework that enables investment stakeholders to bargain effectively and establish rights that offer secure exchange of values. The legal system must offer both substantive and procedural rights that are independent, which should not be unduly interefered with. Secondly, the State must defer to the market's allocation of resources, in the sense that it must allow any existing contract or treaty to prevail, by allowing the market to guide the allocation of resources within the State.[73] Thirdly, the State may interfere with the market to correct anomalies or market failures where necessary, for example, to counteract inefficiencies that are caused by externalities.[74] A liberal international investment regime is one in which all of the three principles work hand in hand and complement each other.[75] According to liberal economic theory, States with limited distortions will tend to perform better than States with heavy regulations that impede the market. Some economists, supported by empirical studies in the last few decades, conclude that freer trade in goods and services results in faster economic growth.[76] Investment liberalisation however involves some fundamental issues in contemporary governance and legal questions of considerable interest.

Although liberalisation has required deregulation through the dismantling of structural barriers to market access and border control, it has also introduced the re-regulation of investment through the introduction of formalised rules for business conduct and prudential requirements for intermediaries. While costs and benefits incentives drive developing States to sign BITs, not much attention has been paid to potential risks that come with the signing and ratification of the treaties. Capital movement between States has thus become highly debated following the economic benefits, costs, and consequences for States.[77]

71 Kenneth J. Vandevelde, 'Investment Liberalization and Economic Development: The Role of Bilateral Investment Treaties' (1998) 36(3) *Columbia Journal of Transnational Law*, 504.

72 *ibid* 505.

73 *ibid.*

74 *ibid* 506.

75 *ibid.*

76 Sebastian Edwards, 'Capital Mobility, Capital Controls and Globalization in the Twenty-First Century' (2002) 579(1) *The Annals of the American Academy*, 263.

77 Amr Abbas Mohammed Adel Abbas Aly Hussein, Bilateral Investment Treaties Treatment of International Capital Movement: Time for Reform, p. 26. Available on https://qmro.qmul.ac.uk/xmlui/bitstream/handle/123456789/2514/HUSSEINBilateralInvestment2012.pdf?sequence=1 [Accessed on 4 November 2024].

2.4.1 The Drive Towards Economic Liberalisation

Economic liberalisation stimulates FDI through the reduction of obstacles to FDI flows.[78] The drive towards economic liberalisation has largely been motivated by some mutually reinforcing developments, for example, the growing importance of international private capital flows to developing States, a global shift towards neoliberal economic policy and the influence of interest groups and the IMF.[79] The end of the socialist model of development through central planning at the end of the 1980s, along with the surprising economic growth achieved by several Asian economies between 1970 and 1980, has influenced the postulation that economic growth is directly linked to, and can be achieved through, the liberalisation of the economy.[80] In addition, the imposition of structural adjustment policies on developing countries as a condition for receiving loans have arm-twisted developing States into adopting liberal policies to some extent even when they are sceptical about such policies.[81] Capital flows are largely deemed important means for the allocation of savings, promotion of economic growth, and the facilitation of balance of payments adjustments.[82]

Perspectives on the efficacy of capital flows vary. First, capital flows are viewed as an engine of economic growth, in the sense that that catalyse institutional change and relax constraints on resource mobilisation. The idea generally is to enact policies that encourage funds to flow from capital-exporting States to capital-importing States.[83] Secondly, capital mobility can be seen as a source of instability because they operate in a place where there are information asymmetries following the distance between the lenders and borrowers of capital.[84] Flows can turn on a dime and, when they do, they can bring the entire financial infrastructure crashing down. Here, the idea is to enact policies that insulate economies from this risk by limiting volatile forms of foreign lending.[85] Those who propose or argue from these two perspectives are quick to enlist history to support their claims. In the nineteenth century, there is evidence that suggests that foreign investments contributed massively to the formation and growth of economies in emerging markets. In the late 19th and early 20th centuries, Argentina experienced a significant resurgence in foreign trade and capital flows, particularly from European countries. This influx of investment played a pivotal role in the country's economic transformation dur-

78 Saeed Rasekhi & Zeinab Seyedi, 'An Examination of Economic Liberalisation Impact on Foreign Direct Investment in Selected Developing Countries' (2010) 14 (25) *Iranian Economic Review*, 10.

79 Joon Chang & Ilene Grabel, *Reclaiming Development. An Alternative Economic Policy Manual* (Zed Books Limited 2004) 153.

80 Vandevelde (n 71) 502.

81 *ibid.*

82 Deborah E. Siegel, 'Using Free Trade Agreements to Control Capital Accounts Restrictions: Summary of Remarks on the Relationship to the Mandate of the IMF' (2004) 10 *ILSA Journal of International and Comparative Law*, 300.

83 Barr Eichengreen, *Capital Flow and Crises* (Massachusetts Institute of Technologies 2003) 13.

84 *ibid.*

85 *ibid.*

ing this period. The funds received were primarily channelled into key infrastructure projects, including the construction of railways, ports, and other public works. These developments were crucial for integrating Argentina's vast interior with its coastal cities, facilitating the export of agricultural products to global markets, particularly Europe.[86]

One of the most notable outcomes of this foreign capital infusion was the rapid modernisation of Buenos Aires, which became the focal point of Argentina's economic and cultural growth. The modernisation of Buenos Aires not only bolstered Argentina's export economy but also laid the foundations for its emergence as a significant player in global trade.[87] On the other side, the risk associated with capital flows is evident in the crises that engulfed emerging markets in the 1880–1913 period.[88] The capital flows, while helping to develop key infrastructure, also exposed Argentina to the volatility of international markets and foreign creditors, a factor that would later contribute to economic instability in the country during the 20th century,[89] thereby making it hard to think of another issue where the stake for policy is higher.

Prior to the era of economic liberalisation, Mercantilism reigned supreme. The emergence of modern States in Europe in the sixteenth and seventeenth century was accompanied by the development of the theory of Mercantilism.[90] It advocated extensive State regulation of economic activity for national interest.[91] Those who propagated this theory equated national wealth with the quantity of gold held by the State and sought to restrict imports while increasing exports to increase the gold supply. Mercantilism perpetuated colonialism because resources were acquired from colonial subjects following the absence of readily available resources in the colonial master's territory. In essence, Mercantilism and colonialism were mutually reinforcing.[92] Mercantilism was premised on the quality of money having a direct correlation to a nation's economic and imperial health and therefore involved a systematic blueprint for constructing and maintaining imperial economic hegemony. It influenced State actions throughout the seventeenth and eighteenth century.[93]

The theory of Mercantilism was challenged in the eighteenth century by liberal economic theorists Adam Smith and David Ricardo.[94] These liberals argued that

86 Mitchener K. J. Weidenmier, 'The Barring Crisis and the Great Latin American Meltdown of the 1980's' (2008) 68(2) *The Journal of Economic History*, 462–464.

87 *ibid.*

88 Eichengreen (n 83) 14.

89 Weidenmier (n 86).

90 Kenneth J. Vandevelde, 'Sustainable Liberalism and the International Investment Regime' (1988) 19(2) *Michigan Journal of International Law*, 375.

91 *ibid.*

92 *ibid.*

93 Jonathan Barth, 'Reconstructing Mercantilism: Consensus and Conflict in British Imperial Economy in the Seventeenth and Eighteenth Centuries' (2016) 73(2) *The William and Mary Quarterly*, 262.

94 Kenneth J. Vandevelde, 'Bilateral Investment Treaties: History, Policy, and Interpretation (Oxford University Press 2010) 24–25.

productivity was best achieved by an unregulated market and not by the amount of gold in the treasury. The theory of Mercantilism thus conflicted with the theory of liberal economy. Britain, the dominant economic power in the nineteenth century, embraced the liberal economy, leading to a big drive towards freer trade in Europe and beyond.[95] In the nineteenth century, liberalism faced opposition from the rise of economic nationalism, which emerged as a successor to mercantile theory. Economic nationalism emphasised the importance of State interests (raison d'état) and supported government regulation of the economy, including international trade, to protect the national interest. This approach aligned with the surge of nationalist sentiment that spread across Europe in the second half of the nineteenth century. As a result, European trade policies became increasingly protectionist after the 1870s. A consequence of these policies led to the reduction of world trade supply and in turn to reduced demand in goods, high unemployment, decreased populations, the Great Depression of the 1930s,[96] and ultimately the Second World War.[97] [98]

Thus the liberal economic theory was quickly reverted to following the consensus that half of the havoc emanating from the Second World War was caused by economic nationalism. The allies who had won the war resolved to create a liberal economic order. A prominent feature of the agenda for future cooperation was the creation of international institutions to govern international trade, investment, finance, and development.[99] This saw the creation of the General Agreement on Tariffs and Trade (GATT), pivotal to building a liberal regime for international trade; foreign investment regulation however proved to be controversial:[100] the Havana Treaty, which was intended for both trade and investment, failed to materialise because the United States withdrew its support. However, GATT set in motion the beginning of a liberal international economic order, even though it did not specifically address investment issues.[101] Nonetheless, capital movement peaked, to the extent that a legal regime to regulate it emerged. Since the underlying assumption for a liberal economy is that property protection through an independent legal system is paramount, it was only necessary that a body of international investment law was needed, thus the emergence of BITs.[102] From the late 1980s, many developing States that had formerly built their economies on State planning and enterprises, tight regulation of the private sector, and restricted

95 Kenneth J. Vandevelde, 'Sustainable Liberalism and the International Investment Regime' (1988) 19(2) *Michigan Journal of International Law*, 375.

96 *ibid*, 378.

97 Jonathan Michie, 'The Coming Financial Crisis' (2022) 36(3) *International Review of Applied Economics*, 291–292.

98 *ibid.*

99 Nicolas M. Perrone, 'The Governance of Foreign Investment at a Crossroad: Is an Overlapping Consensus the Way Forward?' (2015) 15(1) *Global Jurist*, 10.

100 *ibid.*

101 *ibid.*

102 Vandevelde (n 95) 382.

economic interactions with other States began to jettison these policies in favour of a neoliberal economic model otherwise known as the "Washington Consensus".[103] This approach looks to markets rather than the State's plans in resource distribution. It highlights deregulation of economies and openness to international economic transactions such as FDI.[104] Although, the goal of market liberalisation is not explicitly mentioned in BITs, they have formed one of the frameworks for the negotiation of these treaties, and scholarship largely suggests that the success of BITs points to the contemporary emergence of neoliberal market fundamentalism which relies on the State playing a limited role in the economy.[105]

2.4.2 Capital Account Liberalisation

Capital account liberalisation is evidenced in BITs through the obligations imposed on a State to permit all transfers made freely in and out of its territory. These transfer provisions are enforced more rigidly in some agreements than others.[106] South-South treaties tend to have more policy space for capital flow management measures whereas North-South and North-North treaties have more restrictive terms.[107] This suggests that the policy preferences of developing States in the global south, who apparently prefer treaty flexibility, succumb to the preferences of the developed States, thereby highlighting the likelihood of negotiating power imbalances.[108] The IMF has recommended that treaties should have policy space for capital regulation within parameters set by the IMF Agreement. Even if such recommendations were to be strictly enforced, the world economy still has a myriad of treaties that do not permit capital flow; and there is no global order to harmonise or address inconsistencies across global treaty regimes.[109]

However, the use of capital controls is perhaps a great indicator of an increased autonomy that most policymakers in developing States are willing to find advantageous. Now more than ever, States are willing to consider capital control mechanisms to manage their economies. This "new normal" which began slowly but unevenly after the East Asian crisis shows the new openness and policy practice in the context of a long process of legitimation of capital controls. Ideational change is evident: the thinking and practice on capital controls, although incoherent,

103 Ziyad Motola, 'Free Trade, the Washington Consensus, and Bilateral Investment Treaties the South African Journey: A Rethink on the Rules on Foreign Investment by Developing Countries' (2017) 61(1) *American University Business Law Review*, 35.

104 Jeswald Salacuse, 'The Emerging Global Regime for Investment' (2010) 51(2) *Harvard International Law Journal*, 440.

105 Dini Sejko, 'Sovereign Investors as ICSID Claimants: Lessons from the Drafting Documents and the Case Law' (2023) 56 *Vanderbilt Journal of Transnational Law*, 857.

106 Kevin P. Gallagher, Sarah Anderson & Annamaria Viterbo, 'Capital Flow Management and the Trans-Pacific Partnership Agreement' (2013) G-24 *Policy Brief No*. 79, 1.

107 Rachel D. Thrasher, Sarah Sklar & Kevin P. Gallagher, 'Policy Space for Capital Flow Management: An Empirical Investigation' (2021) Journal of International Economic Law, 792.

108 *ibid* 780, 781.

109 *ibid*.

are evolving.[110] The after-effects of capital liberalisation validate other protective national policy responses, one of which is the self-insurance provided by the over-accumulation of currency reserves.[111] These resources help States to consolidate their increasing policy autonomy as they can deploy capital controls without worrying about the negative reactions by the IMF or investors. This policy space proves useful during an emergency or intensity of a turbulence.[112] While BITs have been concluded to achieve remarkable milestones such as investment protection and liberalisation, not much thought has been given to the policy space of contracting States, particularly those that are self-insufficient or struggle with currency reserves and may not have the requisite policy autonomy.[113] Such States are at the risk of arbitral decisions that undermine the host State's policy measures, as protectionist acts could be interpreted a treaty breach.[114]

This should prompt caution as the basic bargain of BITs (the promise to protect the investment of a foreign investor by a host State in return for the protection of its own national investment in the foreign investor's country), evident in the broad and vague substantive rights in BITs, is unlikely to materialise for one contracting party. In real terms, nationals from developing States are unlikely to invest abroad.[115] Thus the proliferation of BIT negotiations is quite astonishing and remarkable since these agreements limit the ability of States to make policies for the public interest[116] and are based on principles which developing States had previously rejected.[117] For instance, BITs constitute the Hull Rule, which provides for "prompt, adequate and effective payment" in the event of a taking;[118] effective compensation in cases of expropriation;[119] and the right of foreign nationals to institute claims against a host State in international arbitration, which developing States had previously loathed.[120] This astonishing turn of events is linked to the change in economic and political events in the 1980s which left developing

110 Ilene Grabel, 'Capital Controls in a Time of Crisis' in Philip Arestis & Malcolm Sawyer (eds), *Financial Liberalisation: Past, Present and Future* (Palgrave Macmillan 2016) 179.

111 *ibid* 182.

112 *ibid* 183.

113 Julie Kim, 'Balancing Regulatory Interests through an Exceptions Framework Under the Right to Regulate Provisions in International Investment Agreements' (2018) 50(2) *George Washington International Law Review*, 289.

114 *ibid* 291.

115 Jeswald Salacuse, 'The Emerging Global Regime for Investment' (2010) 51(2) *Harvard International Law Journal*, 440.

116 Dominic Dagbanja, 'Changing Pattern and Future of Foreign Investment Law and Policy in Ghana: The Role of International Investment Treaties' (2011–2012) 19 *African Yearbook of International Law*, 85.

117 Cai Congyan, 'International Treaties and the Formation, Application and Transformation of Customary International Law Rules, (2008) 7(3) *Chinese Journal of International Law*, 664.

118 Todd Alle & Clint Peinhardt, 'Evaluating Three Explanations for the Designs of Bilateral Treaties' (2014) 66(1) *World Politics*, 49.

119 Kenneth J. Vandevelde, 'The Economics of Bilateral Investment Treaties' (2000) 41(2) *Harvard International Law Journa*l, 470.

120 *ibid.*

States with no other option but to liberalise their investment regimes to attract foreign investment. Thus developing States have been pushed towards economic liberalisation because of the need to attract capital in the form of FDI, due to low availability of commercial loans because of the third world crisis and the absence of domestic savings.[121]

Capital account liberalisation amplifies the disjointed relationship between economic theory and actual events in the real world. Neoclassical theory suggests that the free movement of capital should help smoothen State's consumption and be equilibrating. However, there are indications from the Asian and Latin American financial crises in the 1990s that short term capital account liberalisation can contribute to economic crises.[122] It has been canvassed that developing States need to do a short-to medium-term liberalisation of capital flows such as FDI while still controlling short term flows.[123] And it is on this basis that further discussions underscore the need for the control and monitoring of capital as they may contribute to financial fragility, especially in developing States, and may not always serve the purpose of economic development.

2.5 Myths and Realities of Economic Liberalisation

It is not always the case that economic liberalisation is associated with positive development. Developing States that open their economies to the full force of global competition are not immune from the risks that are associated with this process. A downside of economic liberalisation is that, contrary to the neoliberal view, the financial innovation and consequential increase in capital that accompany economic liberalisation impart greater risk and instability in the economy of the host State. Indeed, there are alternative arguments on the efficacy of FDIs. Marxist theorists argue that FDI impacts negatively in developing States because it leads to a pattern of underdevelopment and dependency.[124] In addition to this, some academic scholars have argued that the movement of private capital in the 1990s was the cause of the financial and currency crises that occurred in developing States during that time. [125]They opine that increased capital movement results in rising costs and is therefore of no benefit to developing States. And since developing States lack modern financial institutions, the impact of a global financial market is

121 Kenneth J. Vandevelde, 'Investment liberalization and Economic Development: The Role of BITs' (1998) 36(3) *Columbia Journal of Transnational Law*, 502.

122 Anwar Shaikh, *Globalization and the Myths of Free Trade: History, Theory and Empirical Evidence* (Routledge 2007) 259.

123 *ibid* 260.

124 Kenneth J. Vandevelde, 'Sustainable Liberalism and the International Investment Regime' (1988) 19(2) *Michigan Journal of International Law*, 378.

125 Sebastian Edwards 'Capital Mobility, 'Capital Controls and Globalization in the Twenty-First Century' (2002) 579 (1) *The Annals of the American Academy*, 263.

higher. Developing States do not have the required institutions to effectively manage large movement of capital.[126]

The promotion of capital markets increases the problem of financial fragility. These risks often culminate in national economic crises, the burdens of which fall disproportionately on economically vulnerable and political weak groups within the society. Some economists believe that the cause of the financial crises that erupted in Asia was the vulnerability of the financial sector, which stemmed from the under-regulated expansion of capital and financial markets. Many years before the crises, most Asian States opened their financial markets, which steered the undermining of their monetary and financial regulation. South Korea, for instance, adopted a liberal stance towards foreign capital and finance following the IMF's strong recommendation that foreign capital should be liberalised in the early 1990s.[127] It has been suggested by observers that the moral hazard in this instance was over-guaranteed but under-regulated financial intermediaries.[128] Economic crisis is likely to occur where the liberalisation of capital occurs before the development of domestic financial regulations and regulators to handle financial volatility, especially where States are eager to attract foreign capital before domestic financial regulations and regulators are prepared to handle volatility.[129]

Unregulated capital flow can instigate economic instability and financial crisis when inflows and outflows are too rapid, with the poor disproportionately affected.[130] The ideology promoted by international financial institutions such as the IMF, which championed favourable financial expectation of a liberalised economy, was said to have contributed to the tremendous flow of foreign capital into Argentina in the 1980s; its subsequent flight is however, amongst others, one of the biggest contributing factors to the crisis.[131] Argentina's crisis was against the backdrop of IMF's recommendation for economic stabilisation and development which required reducing trade barriers and regulation of capital flows in and out of a State.[132] After many years of championing the liberalisation of capital across national frontiers, the IMF has indeed come to the realisation of the limits of capital account liberalisation and the merits of capital control, and thus has begun

126 *ibid* 265.

127 Catherine Lee, 'To Thine Self be True: IMF Conditionality and the Erosion of Economic Sovereignty in the Asian Financial Crisis' (2003) 24(4) *University of Pennsylvania Journal of International Economic Law*, 887.

128 *ibid.*

129 *ibid* 891.

130 Kenneth J. Vandevelde, 'Investment liberalization and Economic Development: The Role of BITs' (1998) 36(3) *Columbia Journal of Transnational Law*, 502.

131 Sarah F. Hill, 'The Necessity Defense and the Emerging Arbitral Conflict in Its Application to the US-Argentina Bilateral Investment Treaty' (2007) 13(3) *Law and Business Review of the Americas*, 548.

132 John V. Paddock, 'IMF Policy and the Argentine Financial Crisis' (2002) 34(1) *The University of Miami Inter-American Law Review*, 158.

endorsing the use of capital control under certain circumstances.[133] Yet a plethora of BITs in force around the globe significantly circumscribe the ability of States to put in place capital account regulations to guard against the risk of capital fluctuation.[134] However, any attempt to introduce capital control will run contrary to the ideals of economic liberalisation.

During economic crises, foreign investors are known to move capital invested in a range of emerging markets into safe heavens. In economies where this takes place, they are known to face rapid capital outflows. For those with open capital account and freely floating exchange rates, the result is a weakening of the exchange rate.[135] The global economic crises of 2008 illustrate the dangers associated with increased financial liberalisation, free capital movement, and weak regulations; apart from capital flight and currency instability, economic crises also lead to the erosion of policy sovereignty. In the case of policy sovereignty, there is a stranglehold of government, thereby preventing them from exercising independent control over economic policy.[136] In fact, foreign investors have been shown to be willing to initiate investor-State arbitration where States have regulated in a *discriminatory fashion* while addressing the adverse effects of past economic crises.[137] Remedies in this instance are usually monetary compensation, leaving States with little possibility to retaliate through a cross-claim or invoking the International Centre for Settlement of Dispute Resolution (ICSID) system.[138] If the promises offered by FDI are to materialise or translate to real economic development, States need to apply post-establishment restrictions to regulate the impact of the investment on the local economy. Host States must have the capability to reduce any adverse effects on foreign investment or prevent capital flight by imposing exchange controls to prevent investors from transferring the returns on the investment out of the host States, albeit in a reasonable manner.[139]This could be done through a review of the BIT provision on transfer of funds, which is the operative tool for capital movement.

133 Kevin P. Gallagher, 'The IMF, Capital Controls and Developing Countries' (2011) 46(19) *Economic and Political Weekly*, 13.

134 Terra Lawson-Remer, Economic Instability, Capital Controls and Bilateral Investment Treaties. Available on https://www.cfr.org/blog/economic-instability-capital-controls-and-bilateral-investment-treaties [Accessed on 4 November 2024].

135 Andrew Yianni & Carlos de Vera, 'The Return of Capital Control' (2010) 73(4) *Law and Contemporary Problems*, 357–358.

136 Kalim Siddiqui & Phil Armstrong, 'Capital Control Reconsidered: Financialization and Economic Policy' (2018) 32(6) *International Review of Applied Economics*, 715.

137 Anne Van Aaken & Jurgen Kurtz, 'Prudence or Discrimination? Emergency Measures, The Global Financial Crises and International Economic Law' (2009) 12(4) *Journal of International Economic Law*, 861.

138 *ibid.*

139 Kenneth J. Vandevelde, 'The Economics of Bilateral Investment Treaties' (2000) 41(2) *Harvard International Law Journal*, 484–485.

2.6 Conclusion

The validity of the free-market orthodoxy that has dominated for the past 30 years is now being challenged, signalling a shift towards a more regulated economy. This transition includes not only calls for increased regulation but also a demand for reform of both the global financial system and the international monetary system to reduce instability. Globalisation has rendered State isolation in the international community nearly impossible, further entrenching economic liberalisation. Given that BITs embody a liberalised investment regime, it is essential to reevaluate overly rigid commitments that lack flexibility, as these may undermine the protections offered by BITs and provide inadequate safeguarding of FDI in the long run. In the following chapters, it is proposed that BITs should include specific "carveout" provisions that delineate areas of protection for host States. Financial sectors, in particular, should be exempted from the general scope of treaties to allow for preferential treatment during potential economic crises. This approach would enable States to maintain their regulatory rights while fostering a sustainable framework for economic development and ensuring a steady inflow of foreign investments. Achieving this balance necessitates a comprehensive understanding of the theoretical concepts and normative values associated with capital controls, which may challenge economic liberalisation. This discussion will be elaborated in the next chapter.

3 Theoretical Underpinnings of Capital Control and the Right to Transfer Funds

3.1 The Theory of Capital Control

During economic crises, firmly held ideas are tested by a rival set of ideas about their functionality, how economies work, and how crises should be managed. Under the uncertainty that pervades in such periods, key actors can be open to alternative ideas that help manage such uncertainty.[1] In most cases, they have recourse to economic measures. Though it is not easy to surmise and, in some cases, quantify these economic measures, they can however be seen in the form of interventions in the foreign exchange market, adoption of capital controls, lender of last resort or bail outs, and prudential regulations.[2] The restriction of capital flow has proven to be one of the most controversial of them because of policy effects and is therefore the subject of analysis.

The main rationale for capital control is that global governance will have an adverse negative effect on domestic economy. Over the last 20 years, various States have imposed capital control to protect their domestic economies from the effects of a liberalised financial market. The IMF simply refers to it as a "capital flow management mechanism".[3] Capital control is, therefore, any instrument that limits the free movement of capital between a State and the rest of the world to a certain extent. It may be given effect through administrative measures that exert a direct rule upon capital flows or through incentive mediums implemented via the market. It can be created upon the inflow and outflow of a capital; it could either be a permanent or temporary measure.[4] When permanent, it implies that the costs of financial integration are considered to exceed the benefits. When temporary, economic liberalisation is seen as crucial, and controls should exist only until the establishment of the necessary conditions that will allow the State to fully

1 Federcio Lupo-Pasini, 'Monetary Measures in Investment Law: The Uneasy Relationship between Monetary Stability and Investment Protection' in Thomas Cottier, Rosa M. Lastra, Christian Tietje & Lucia Satragno (eds), *The Rule of Monetary Affairs* (Cambridge University Press 2014) 573.

2 *ibid* 586.

3 Kalim Siddiqui & Phil Armstrong, 'Capital Control Reconsidered: Financial Liberalisation and Economic Policy' (1997) 11(1) *International Review of Applied Economics*, 3.

4 André De Melo Modenesi & Rui Lyrio Modensi, 'Capital Controls and Financial Liberalization: Removing the Ideological Bias' (2008) 30(4) *Journal of Post Keynesian Economics*, 567.

DOI: 10.4324/9781003611714-3

maximise the benefit of the liberalisation of its capital account. And, as soon as the economy is mature and ready to benefit from financial integration, controls must be removed.[5] It is used mainly during economic crises to manage exchange-rate volatility, provide independent monetary policy, and limit speculative activity in the economy.[6]

Also, capital control can either be price or quantity based.[7] The former involves the alteration of foreign capital such that there is taxation on inflows and outflows of capital while the latter involves capping certain types of capital outflows. Some measures combine both the price- and quantity-based measures; in such case, a cap on capital flows must be placed in the central bank to hold some investments back in the State in the case of capital flights.[8] There is however no globalised position on when and whether, or not, to use this mechanism. Even the IMF, which regulates financial matters amongst States, has been found to approve and disapprove at the same time.[9] Most western States view capital controls as obstacles to economic globalisation, while some developing States have argued that they are important tools for managing economies. Each side has been found to pitch its tent where it suits it the most.[10]

Fighting financial instability is a very big policy challenge. Recent economic crises have been triggered, partly, by large policy reversals in international capital flows, even in seemingly well-situated States with good monetary and sound fiscal policies.[11] Policymakers have struggled with whether to protect their economies from such instability by using macroprudential regulation on domestic financial transactions or imposing heterodox policy measures such as capital control.[12] Capital controls have, however, been found to stabilise short-term volatile capital flows during economic crises;[13] they provide policymakers additional policy instruments that allow them more efficient and less costly macroeconomic stabilisation

5 *ibid.*

6 *ibid.*

7 Joseph E. Stiglitz & Jose Antonio Ocampo, *Capital Market Liberalization and Development* (Oxford University Press 2008) 30.

8 Kevin P. Gallagher, 'The IMF, Capital Controls and Developing Countries' (2011) 46(19) *Economic and Political Weekly*, 12.

9 Kevin P. Gallagher, 'Contesting the Governance of Capital Flows at the IMF' (2015) 28(2) *An International Journal of Policy, Administration, and Institutions,* 187

10 David Pabian, 'Capital Controls in International Law: Clarity through a Central Regulatory System' (2014) 24 *Journal of International Law*, 8.

11 Anton Korinek & Damiano Sandri, 'Capital Controls or Macro Prudential Regulation' (2016) 99(1) *Journal of International Economics*, 527.

12 *ibid.*

13 In the 1990s, Malaysia was known to have imposed capital controls aimed at the offshore national currency: ringgit. The capital control involved bringing the ringgit on shore (since it was believed that the offshore markets prevented Malaysia's ability to bring interest rates down) and hold on the repatriation of portfolio capital flows. The control was placed in February 1999 and relaxed in September 1999; Catherine Lee, 'To Thine Self Be True: IMF Conditionality and the Erosion of Economic Sovereignty in the Asian Financial Crisis' (2003) 24(4) *University of Pennsylvania Journal of International Economic Law*, 887.

measures.[14] They can increase economic efficiency and promote growth by reducing finance volatility, and, consequently, discourage long term capital outflows.[15] Thus, in crisis moments, the use of capital controls may be advantageous as it may not be practical to allow for unregulated capital movement.

To maintain equilibrium in a monetary union, which is the endeavour of independent States, and the core of economic policy formulation, economists believe there is need for economic interventions to correct anomalies. Things change from what was envisaged and the market may not always function as anticipated so there should be interventions. To achieve this equilibrium, a fixed exchange rate, free capital movement, and an independent monetary policy is said to be impossible to co-exist.[16] The level of autonomy a government possesses at a given time derives from a complex interaction of international and domestic forces that is best known through the Mundell-Fleming approach to payment balances.[17] Although there are other theoretical approaches or models that define open economies, the Mundell-Fleming model is considered here because it is thought to be a fundamental theoretical framework for the analysis of the effects of economic policy in developing economies, and it is also the preferred model for both analysis and pedagogy.[18]

The Mundell-Fleming framework posits that a State can, at most, have only two of the following conditions: (i) fixed exchange rate, (ii) monetary policy autonomy, and (iii) capital movement.[19] National monetary policy autonomy refers to the ability of domestic policymakers to implement monetary policies that differ from those of the countries with which their economies are closely linked.[20] In an economy with high capital mobility and fixed exchange rates, any attempt by the government to set interest rates independent from the rates of the nations with which they are financially linked is likely to be offset by counteracting speculative flows. Under full capital mobility, a change in monetary policies will lead domestic investors to send their money abroad in search of better economic prospects.[21] This is explained as the *impossible trinity* or *trilemma*.[22]

14 Barry Eichengreen & Andrew Rose, 'Capital Controls in the 21st Century' (2014) 48 *Journal of International Money and Finance*, 3

15 Kevin P. Gallagher & Yuan Tian, 'Regulating Capital Flows in Emerging Markets: The IMF and the Global Financial Crisis' (2017) 7(2) *Review of Development Finance*. 96.

16 Hanno Beck & Aloys Prinz, 'The Trilemma of a Monetary Union: Another Impossible Trinity' (2012) 47 *Intereconomics*, 39.

17 *ibid.*

18 Tomislav Coric, Hrvoje Simovic & Milan Deskar-Skrbic, 'Monetary and Fiscal Policy Mix in a Small Open Economy: The Case of Croatia' (2015) 28(1) *Economic Research-Ekonomska Istraživanja*, 458.

19 William Roberts Clark, Usha Nair Reichart, Sandra Lynn Lomas & Kevin L. Parker, 'International and Domestic Constraints on Political Business Cycles in OECD Economies' (1998) 52(1) *International Organization*, 92.

20 *ibid.*

21 *ibid* 93.

22 M. R. Venkatesh, *Mamohan Sigh- A Decade of Decay* (1st edn, Rare Publication 2013) 350.

It is difficult to maintain a stable exchange rate where there is high surge of forex outflows, when this happens the domestic currency depreciates, and the government must intervene either by devaluating the local currency or adopting capital control mechanisms. It is on this basis that it is often said that governments cannot effectively meet all the demands of the three conditions but only two at the same time.[23] An economist puts it succinctly:

> The point is you can't have it all: A State must pick two out of three. It can fix its exchange rate without emasculating its central bank, but only by maintaining controls on capital flows; it can leave capital movement free but retain monetary autonomy, but only by letting the exchange rate fluctuate; or it can choose to leave capital free and stabilise the currency, but only by abandoning any ability to adjust interest rate to fight inflation.[24]

This simply means that a State that attempts to peg its exchange rate cannot have both effective monetary policy and open capital markets;[25] the "impossible trinity" creates a policy dilemma of some sort, most likely in a rapidly globalising world. At critical financial stages, the defining role of the sovereign monetary authority either expands or contrasts depending on whose ox is gored. Whether as a result of a desire to prevent or respond to a crisis, the imposition of capital controls raises issues that have wide implications under international agreements such as the IMF Articles of Agreement and Bilateral Investment Treaties (BITs). A governmental intervention in the form of capital control upholds the monetary autonomy of a State while upsetting the assurances upon which foreign investment thrives on.

3.2 Treaty Provision on Transfer of Funds: The Operative Tool of Capital Movement and Control

Foreign investments involve the transfer of funds or capital which can be in the form of tangible or intangible assets from one State to another to generate wealth for use, under the total or partial control of those assets.[26] Recent BITs now define foreign investment in general terms as pre-establishment rights, for example, expenditures of an investment prior to the enablement to invest in a State and any benefits which accrue from the use of capital.[27] Thus capital and benefits thereon are usually protected by investment treaties. A foreign investor has a right to the income generated from his investment and the return on his investment (profit). This right is enshrined in most BITs as the right to repatriation of capital and

23 *ibid.*

24 Clause D. Zimmerman, *A Contemporary Concept of Monetary Sovereignty* (Oxford University Press 2013) 4.

25 Micheal B. Devreux & James Yetman, 'Capital Controls, Global Liquidity Traps, and the International Policy Trilemma' (2014) 116(1) *The Scandinavian Journal of Economics*, 159.

26 Getahun Seifu, 'Regulatory Space in the Treatment of Foreign Investment in Ethiopian Investment Laws' (2008) 9(5) *Journal of World Investment & Trade*, 406.

27 *ibid* 406–407.

transfer of profit, otherwise known as the "right to transfer of funds", and is usually expressed as monetary transfer provisions.[28] They are negotiated and included in BITs because foreign investors regard the ability to transfer income and capital, and to make foreign expenditures freely as essential to operating and profiting from their investment project. Thus home States, through BIT negotiations, seek for unrestricted guarantees to make transfers.[29]

The basic issues that are considered during the negotiation process are: (a) the general nature of the investors' rights to make monetary transfers, (b) the nature of payments that are covered by the right to make transfers, (c) the type of currency which should be used in making such transfers, (d) the exchange rate that should apply, and (e) the period within which the host State must allow the investors to make transfers.[30] The exercise of the right to repatriate capital can occur at any point: (a) upon the abandonment of the contract, (b) at the end of the contract once its aim has been achieved, (c) at the end of the duration the contract was stipulated to exist, or (d) if the domestic organisation of associated labour closes business or ceases to exist.[31] The freedom to transfer investment-related funds to and from the host States is at the core of international investment law. It evidences a liberalised investment regime. It recognises that foreign investors should be allowed not only to transfer funds to the host State to fund their investment but also to repatriate the connected profits and, in the case of divestment both the principal and capital gains, where applicable.[32] The provisions aimed at guaranteeing the "free transfer of funds" are contained in all BITs even though content and requirements may differ in the texts due to the need to strike a balance due to differing priorities.[33]

The logic of repatriation is built on the premise that multinational corporations penetrate underdeveloped States to maximise corporate profits[34] and to distribute the dividends thereon to its shareholders who may reside in either the host State, the home State of the foreign investors or in several other States. Repatriation of funds may also be relevant to serve other purposes such as the payment of licence fees and royalties, purchase of raw materials and machinery for production, and servicing of external loans and payment for other services: all of which are crucial for the success of an investment. It therefore makes practical sense that guaranteeing

28 Mahendra Pal Singh, Wolfram Cremer & Niraj Kumar, *Open Markets, Free Trade and Sustainable Development* (Springer Nature Singapore Pte Ltd 2019) 264.

29 Jeswald Salacuse, 'BIT by BIT: The Growth of Bilateral Investment Treaties and Their Impact on Foreign Investment in Developing Countries' (1990) 24(3) *The International Lawyer*, 663–664.

30 *ibid.*

31 M. E. Coronna, 'The Right to Repatriation of Capital and Transfer of Profits for Foreign Investors in Yugoslavia Joint-Ventures' (1986) 12 *Review of Socialist Law*, 143–144.

32 Annamaria Viterbo, *International Economic Law and Monetary Measures. Limitations to State Sovereignty and Dispute Settlement* (Elgar International Economic Law 2012) 238.

33 *ibid* 244.

34 John M. Rothgeb, Jr., 'Foreign Investment and the De-capitalization of Underdeveloped Host Countries' (1990) 27(4) *The Social Science Journal*, 458.

the right to repatriation of profit will attract foreign investors.[35] It is also imperative that foreign exchange is available for effectual exercise of the right to transfer capital. Thus the right to transfer of funds is considered breached if authorities of a host State restrict the availability or use of foreign exchange necessary to make the transfer in question.

The right to repatriation of profits and capital, and monetary transfers related to investments, are of practical significance to the operational condition of FDI.[36] For both a host State and its foreign investors, the BIT provisions on monetary transfers and repatriation of profits are of utmost importance in a treaty and often the hardest to conclude due to conflicting interests. Foreign investors consider the ability to transfer capital and income and make foreign expenditures freely very important in the operation of their investment project. BIT negotiations suppose that an unrestricted right in this regard will be essential for operational purposes.[37] States that experience chronic balance of payment difficulties considerably reduce their willingness to grant foreign investors unrestricted right to make monetary transfers so as to be able conserve foreign exchange to pay for essential goods and services when need be.[38] In such case, capital outflow control mechanisms may be used to provide a hedge for developing State to build strong monetary and financial systems, and sophisticated and well-resourced prudential regulations. Developed States can stimulate their economy during or in anticipation of a recession through deficit spending without prompting a retreat of foreign investors because they reasonably believe in the capabilities of the State's reserves in keeping a rein on the money supply and, invariably, on inflation.[39] Contrastingly, this same deficit spending approach by a developing Statet will lead to a quick withdrawal of capital by foreign investors for fear of inflation and currency depreciation.[40] Capital controls may be necessary for a developing State to revitalise and reflate the economy during or after a crisis. Thus, if a State must pursue expansionist fiscal policies, then outflow controls may well be necessary.[41] These conflicting goals between the desire of States to control capital outflows and the foreign investors to pull out of the economy in crisis moments make negotiations on monetary transfer provisions in BITs very difficult to negotiate or conclude. Thus reinforcing the need for rebalancing the competing interests of stakeholders in the investment regime.

35 Muthucumaraswamy Sornarajah, 'State Responsibility and Bilateral Investment Treaties' (1986) 20 *Journal World Trade Law*, 95.

36 Rod Farley & Neil Foster-Mc Gregor, 'Heterogeneous Effects of Bilateral Investment Treaties' (2017) 153(4) *Review of World Economics*, 632.

37 Jeswald W. Salacuse & Nicholas P. Sullivan, 'Do BITs Really Work: An Evaluation of Bilateral Investment Treaties and Their Grand Bargain' (2005) 46(1*) Harvard International Law*, 128.

38 Restrictions on Foreign Investors/Currency Exchange Controls. Available on (https://ppp.worldbank.org/public-private-partnership/legislation-regulation/framework-assessment/legal-environment/foreign-investor-currency-exchange-restrictions [Accessed on 4 November 2024].

39 Ross P. Buckley, 'International Capital Flows, Economic Sovereignty and Developing Countries' (1999) 4 *Yearbook of International Financial and Economic Law*, 31.

40 *ibid* 33.

41 *ibid.*

Poorly worded monetary transfer provisions contribute to interpretative and applicability problems. Some States define the transfer obligations in more general terms, while some are more thorough, going into considerable detail by stating the type of transfers that are covered and proffering definitive convertibility obligations.[42] However, key applicability and interpretative problems likely to emanate from a BIT's monetary transfer provisions in balance of payment problems, economic crises or common contract issues are: what types of transfers have been covered; what the scope is of monetary transfer convertibility; and the nature of exceptions and limitations that are likely to apply to the treaty's obligation. Most BITs generally prescribe that the currency to be transferred must be "freely convertible" at the market rate of foreign exchange prevailing on the date of transfer.[43] "Freely Convertible" is a vague term with no clear-cut definition. Potential issues in this situation include identifying which currencies qualify as freely usable. According to the IMF Fund Agreement, freely convertible currencies are defined as the United States dollar, the Japanese yen, the British pound, and the euro, and these are the ones that should be available to foreign investors. [44] For those not referencing the IMF Fund Agreement, it is important to determine which currency qualifies as "freely usable" and to understand the nature of transactions relevant to this assessment.

It is not uncommon to find that BITs fail to address the prevailing market exchange rate, particularly on the date of transfer, given that there is the possibility that there might not be any market rate at all.[45] This consideration is important because, for example, a shortage of foreign exchange, essential for facilitating profit transfers, led to dissatisfaction and criticism amongst foreign investors in Yugoslavia. This prompted legislative changes to the country's foreign exchange laws to streamline and support fund transfers. The government further stipulated that, in cases of foreign exchange scarcity due to balance of payments issues, available foreign currency should be prioritised for specific payments related to investments.[46] These legislative measures reflect Yugoslavia's recognition of the vital role foreign investments play in the economy and the need to reassure investors about their right to repatriate capital and profits.[47] Consequently, Yugoslavia took steps to inspire confidence in this regard.[48]

42 *ibid* 30.

43 Bilateral Investment Treaties 1995–2006: Trends in Investment Rule Making, p. 56. Available on https://unctad.org/system/files/official-document/iteiia20065_en.pdf [Accessed on 2 December 2024].

44 IMF Fund 1976 Articles XXX(f).

45 Michael Waibel, 'BIT by BIT – The Silent Liberalization' in Christina Binder, Ursula Kriebaum, August Reinisch & Stephan (eds), *International Investment Law for the 21st Century: Essays in Honour of Christopher Schreur* (Oxford University Press 2009) 513.

46 M. E. Coronna, 'The Right to Repatriation of Capital and Transfer of Profits for Foreign Investors in Yugoslavia Joint-Ventures' (1986) 12(1) *Review of Socialist Law*, 141.

47 *ibid.*

48 *ibid* 143.

The right to transfer of funds is a right that is sui generis and must be distinguished from the general treatment obligation that applies to foreign investments. It therefore requires a careful approach. Unlike national treatment that requires that foreign investors are treated no less favourably than a host State's own nationals,[49] the right to transfer funds provides foreign investors with preferential treatment and, if circumscribed when guaranteed, it could be argued that expropriation has taken place. State regulation that significantly impairs the operation of an investment may be considered indirect expropriation regardless of whether the State has acted for legitimate economic or social reasons.[50] Regimes of constant regulatory takings which weaken the economic value of an investment may well qualify as regulatory takings and could therefore give rise to a duty to pay compensation under international investment law.[51]

3.3 Conflict of Obligations: The Monetary Regulatory Dilemma

Where a monetary transfer provision in a BIT protects the rights of a foreign investor to convert investments into foreign currency for repatriation, any exchange control regulation can be illegal from an international investment law perspective. Exchange control policies are one of the most vital policies most governments often rely on to influence trade, industry, and financial sectors. Foreign investors wishing to repatriate their investment and convert it into another currency or wishing to rely on a stable exchange rate to manage their business might suffer considerable loss in the event of a restriction or devaluation. A frequently cited example in this regard is the Argentinian monetary crisis of 2000.[52] Thus there is a dilemma when it comes to obliging the right to repatriation of capital and profit in times of economic crisis, especially when they encroach on the traditional limits of State sovereignty. Often questioned is a State's right to breach a monetary treaty provision when there are legitimate reasons for its non enforcement, for example in balance of payment problems. The shortage of foreign currency reserves that makes FDI attractive for host States also makes it difficult for them to allow for the loss or depletion of foreign exchange in the form of capital flights during economic crises.

49 Nicolas F. Dieibold, 'Standards of Non-Discrimination in International Economic Law' (2011) 60(4) *The International Law and Comparative Law Quarterly*, 831.

50 Lucien J. Dhooge, 'The Revenge of the Trailer Smelter: Environmental Regulation as Expropriation Pursuant to the North American Free Trade Agreement' (2001) 38(3) *American Business Law Journal*, 526.

51 Peter T. Muchlinski, 'Regulating Multinationals: Foreign Investment, Development, and the Balance of Corporate and Home State Rights and Responsibilities in a Globalized World' in Jose E. Alvarez & Karl P. Sauvant (eds), *The Evolving International Investment Regime: Expectations, Realities, Options* (Oxford University Press 2011) 36.

52 Federico Lupo-Pasini, 'Monetary Policy Measures in Investment Law: The Uneasy Relationship Between Monetary Stability and Investment Protection' in Thomas Cottier, Lastra Rosa & Christian Tietje (eds), *The Rule of Law in Monetary Affairs: World Trade Forum* (Cambridge University Press 2014) 576.

The range of measures necessary to address economic crises is wide and far reaching and may include regulatory measures, controlling the economy, and ensuring that other measures to protect the banking and financial institutions are put in place.[53] Usually States that are wary of the economic disruptions that accompany capital flows may be tempted to impose capital controls on international capital movement.[54] When faced with balance of payment difficulties,[55] developing States must maintain a fixed exchange rate in order to preserve the purchasing power of their citizens and to prevent a "consumption crisis" in which sharply depreciated currency prevents people from purchasing basic necessities.[56] The preservation of such an exchange rate to prevent a consumption crisis however creates a crisis of another sort—those that arise from recurrent demands to maintain the currency value.[57] Herein lies the problem with capital controls. The inconsistency in the desire to control capital movement and the desire to attract FDI has not been adequately addressed despite its relevance to policymakers, who are keen on attracting these investments, and, on the other hand, multinational corporations, who are anxious to recoup the dividends and profits of their investments. Foreign capital by its character challenges the role of the State in promoting domestic development. In response to these challenges, States must devise policies to balance the costs and benefits of this foreign resource.[58]

Arguably, there is a conflict between the necessity of maintaining a host State's monetary stability through the adoption of monetary measures that are beneficial to its citizens and the competing interest of a foreign investor to be protected at all reasonable costs in their legitimate expectations on investment protection. In other words, monetary sovereignty and investment liberalisation are two reinforcing terms, which, though reasonable, are mutually incompatible when applied together. Thus the rights of foreign investors within a liberalised international regime are a concern. There is apprehension about the restrictions that investment treaties and investment treaty arbitration impose on the regulatory power of a State. This is because there are BITs that do not define classes of exceptions to the protection granted to foreign investors during economic crises nor expressly list the conditions under which the host State can restrict investors' rights, unlike other international

53 Christina Binder & August Reinisch, 'Economic Emergency Powers: A Comparative Law Perspective' in Stephen Schill (ed), *International Investment Law and Comparative Public Law* (Oxford University Press 2010) 503.

54 Mihir A. Desai, C. Fritz Foley & James R. Hines Jr, 'Capital Controls, Liberalization and Foreign Direct Investment' (2006) 19(4) *The Review of Financial Studies*, 1433.

55 Chantal Thomas, 'Balance of Payment Crises in the Developing World: Balancing Trade, Finance and Development in the New Economic Order' (2000) 15(6) *American University International Law Review*, 1252–1253.

56 *ibid.*

57 *ibid* 1253.

58 Chu Huang, 'The State and Foreign Investment: The Cases of Taiwan & Singapore' (1989) 22(1) *Comparative Political Studies*, 94.

treaties.[59] Possibly, due to the open-ended language of investors' rights, tribunals may abridge the role of States as regulators without giving due consideration to the rationality of public interest protection for either economic, environmental, health, human rights, or emergency purposes.[60] Evident in most investment arbitration is that the time of legislation may not always meet public demands, and this creates a consequent need for a State to exercise its sovereignty to promote policies that protect economic growth and are favourable to its own populace.[61]

The general stance amongst sovereigns especially in democratic settings is that it should be the exclusive right of each government to adjust to economic realities without incurring liabilities for any resulting change in the value of assets.[62] Attempts by States to extend FDI regulation beyond that allowed by BITs are a growing concern in the international arena given that arbitrators are empowered through BITs to review sovereign control of money, which is often regarded as one of the most guarded national prerogatives.[63] Guidance on resolving this dilemma remains limited in scope, and the sensitive issue of sovereignty costs preclude dense hard law when compared to other areas of international economic relations, such as in goods and services.[64]

Under customary international law, State sovereignty is prioritised, and it presupposes that a State can control its currency and exchange transactions, and possibly impose exchange control restrictions without incurring international responsibility.[65] This hegemonic status can culminate in protectionism: as shown in the previous chapter, it contributed significantly to the Second World War, in turn leading to the development of the IMF Articles of Agreement (Fund Agreement) to create orderly international monetary relations.[66]

Despite States' prerogative to regulate for sovereignty, a long-standing approach of the IMF is that State interference is only permitted as is necessary to address economic anomalies. Member States are constrained on the exercise of once unfettered access to exchange controls.[67] The IMF prescribes two important obligations to member States in the conduct of their external monetary policies, which can be

59 Benedict Kingsbury & Stephen Schill, 'Public Law Concepts to Balance Investors' Rights with State Regulatory Actions in the Public Interest – The Concept of Proportionality' in Schill S. (ed), *International Investment and Comparative Law* (Oxford University Press 2010) 76.

60 *ibid.*

61 Leila Choukroune, *Judging the State in International Trade and Investment Law. Sovereignty Modern, the Law and Economics* (Springer Nature Singapore 2010) 2.

62 Joseph E. Stiglitz, 'Proceedings of the Annual Meetings' (2007) 101 *American Society of International Law*, 5.

63 Beth A. Simmons, 'The Legalization of International Monetary Affairs' (2000) 54(3) International Organization, 573.

64 *ibid.*

65 Abba Kolo, 'Transfer of Funds: The Interaction between the IMF Articles of Agreement and Modern Investment: A Comparative Law Perspective' in Stephen Schill (ed), *International Investment Law and Comparative Public Law* (Oxford University Press 2010) 345.

66 *ibid* 348.

67 *ibid* 349.

found in Article VIII of the Fund Agreement. The article proscribes exchange-rate systems that favour certain trade partners or transactions.[68] It also prohibits restrictions in payments and transfers for current accounts. It also provides for governments to make foreign exchange available for goods, services, and invisibles, and obliges them to refrain from delaying, limiting or imposing changes or currency transfers if they have the effect of inhibiting or increasing the costs of making payments.[69] This obligation does not extend to international capital transfers that do not qualify as payments for current transactions. Article VI (3) of the Fund Agreement permits member States to make such controls that are necessary to regulate international capital movement but not on payments that pertain to current transactions, or which will unduly delay transfer of funds in settlements of commitments.[70] Thus the right to restrict transfer of capital outflows is subject to some exceptions. These varying provisions in Articles VI and VIII draw an important distinction between a "capital" transaction and a "current" transaction'. It has been widely accepted that:

> a capital transfer is one that has as its counterpart a claim to future return, while the counterpart to a payment for a current transaction is the receipt of goods or services .... In other words, if a payment made by a resident to a non-resident results in goods or services being brought to, or performed in, the territorial jurisdiction of the member in which the payer is resident, the payment is a payment for current transaction. If, on the other hand, the payment does not result in such an immediate return of goods or services, it would be treated as capital transfer[71]

The IMF has no mandatory procedures to address currency issues and has been reluctant to enforce its rules through legal sanctions.[72] IMF members can choose to declare themselves bound by the IMF rules. New members can choose to make use of transitional provisions under Article XIV of the Fund Agreement. The effect of Article XIV is to oversee the practices a member State engaged with before their commitment to the Fund Agreement. Such members are, however, expected to have regards to the purposes of the Fund and lift capitals controls as soon as balance of payment problems are resolved.[73] Though compliance to these rules is voluntary, most States are willing to commit to avoid reputational costs. The IMF does not provide any negative or positive incentive for adherence to the provision

68 Simmons (n 63) 574.

69 *ibid* 580.

70 Abba Kolo, 'Transfer of Funds: The Interaction between the IMF Articles of Agreement and Modern Investment: A Comparative Law Perspective' in Stephen Schill (ed), *International Investment Law and Comparative Public Law* (Oxford University Press 2010) 350.

71 *ibid.*

72 Philip J. MacFarlance, 'The IMF's Reassessment of Capital Controls after the 2008 Financial Crisis: Heresy or Orthodoxy?' (2015) 19 *UCLA Journal of International Law and Foreign Affairs*, 194.

73 Article XIV (s 1–2) of the International Monetary Fund Articles of Agreement. Available on https://www.imf.org/external/pubs/ft/aa/pdf/aa.pdf [Accessed on 4 December 2024].

of its articles.[74] However, the executive board can declare a member non-eligible to use its resources where there has been failure to fulfil its rules by a member State and sometimes non-compliance interrupts drawings from a standby or extended arrangement even though these remedies are used sparingly.[75]

From an investor's perspective, the Fund Agreement does provide an important but incomplete protection as it does not prohibit a host State from restriction on capital transfers, including transfers of the proceeds from the liquidation or sale of an investment. Also, the Fund Agreement does not adequately deal with multiple currency practices which are prevalent in most States, and it is not unusual to find that multiple currency practices are either discriminatory or non-discriminatory.[76]

Capital controls have become contentious as to whether they are the best available options to States that face an economic crisis given the policy dilemma they present.[77] Capital control has its merit and demerits; it is recognised that capital control policies have the capacity to protect a State facing a turbulent external situation. This is surmised from the premise that capital controls can reduce exposure to economic chaos in the interim.[78] The United Nations Conference on Trade and Development (UNCTAD) further identifies four reasons why the imposition of capital controls are necessary: (a) for the prevention of exchange-rate appreciations that may reduce the State's competitiveness with regards to its trading partners because high value of a State's currency will make exports from a State more costly than imports, as such industries may not be able to export more goods and services; (b) to prevent capital flight on the slightest sign of difficulties. Speculators (usually portfolio investors) who have no long term interest in a host economy are likely to flee at the sign of economic crisis; if they are not restrained, a massive exit of capital will not only lead to the depletion of a host State's reserves but also to economic turmoil; (c) to prevent large inflows of capital that may overheat the system and also create distortions in the financial market; and (d) capital control is an important element of fiscal sovereignty by host States which can be exercised when confronted with balance of payment difficulties.[79]

Controls on capital are expected to protect States, especially in developing regions, from speculative attacks. The use of this policy is not entirely new in international economics. Dating as far back as 1974, it has been argued that a tax on foreign exchange will reduce speculative flows in international currency markets.[80]

74 Simmons (n 63) 582.

75 *ibid.*

76 Joseph Gold, *The Fund Agreement in the Court* (Washington D.C: International Monetary Fund 1989) 128–130.

77 Abba Kolo, 'Investor Protection vs Host State Regulatory Autonomy during Economic Crisis: Treatment of Capital Transfers and Restrictions under Modern Investment Treaties' (2007) 8(4) *The Journal of World Trade Investment and Trade*, 457.

78 Using Capital Controls to deal with Financial Crisis. By Martin Khor. Available on https://StateState.globalpolicy.org/component/content/article/220/47393.html [Accessed on 5 December 2024].

79 Shikuan Chen & Min-Jen Chang, 'Capital Control and Exchange Rate Volatility' (2015) 33(1) *North American Journal of Economics and Finance*, 167–168.

80 *ibid.*

Notwithstanding the usefulness of this policy in addressing economic issues, capital controls may discourage foreign investors since they emit a wrong signal about a State's macroeconomics and its political risks, and, consequently, result in low ratings at the international capital market. These controls not only raise the costs of local borrowing but also the costs associated with complying with repatriation regulations.[81] It has been argued that capital controls limit individual liberty and work against the ideal of a free society, and are ineffective because economic agents will always find legal gaps in order to preclude their influence.[82] To address the conflicting goals from both parties to a BIT, different States have adopted different techniques to possibly obviate any legal problems.

The first technique is to provide for a free transfer that is unrestrained by domestic laws or economic circumstances of the host State. This evident in Article 6 of the 2007 Germany-Nigerian BIT: it stipulates that payments should be made without delay at the market exchange rate applicable on the day of the transfer. If there is no foreign exchange market, the cross rate derived from the rates applied by the IMF on the date of payment should be used to convert the relevant currencies into special drawing rights.[83] A second technique used by some States, as seen in the BITs of Turkey-China[84] and Canada-China,[85] is to subject the free transfer to the host State's internal laws on foreign exchange or other treaties such as the IMF Agreement.[86] While a third technique is to provide exceptions to the freedom to transfer funds by acknowledging measures taken during the periods of balance of payment difficulties provided that such measures are necessary, consistent with IMF or GATT rules, are non-discriminatory, and are on a temporary basis.[87] The fourth technique, which is somewhat similar to the first, is to subject the right to transfers to the domestic laws and regulations of the host State. Measures imposed

81 Abba Kolo, 'Investor Protection vs Host State Regulatory Autonomy during Economic Crisis: Treatment of Capital Transfers and Restrictions under Modern Investment Treaties' (2007) 8(4) *The Journal of World Trade Investment and Trade*, 4.

82 André De Melo Modenesi & Rui Lyrio Modenesi, 'Capital Controls and Financial Liberalization: Removing the Ideological Bias' (2008) 30(4) *Journal of Post Keynesian Economics*, 567.

83 Germany-Nigeria BIT. Available on http://investmentpolicyhub.unctad.org/Download/TreatyFile/1382 [Accessed on 4 December 2024].

84 Turkey-China BIT. Available on https://investmentpolicy.unctad.org/international-investment-agreements [Accessed on 4 December 2024].

85 Canada-China BIT. Available on https://investmentpolicy.unctad.org/international-investment-agreements [Accessed on 4 December 2024].

86 Abba Kolo A. & Thomas Walde, 'Capital Transfer Restrictions under Modern Investment Treaties' in August Reinisch (ed), *Standards of Investment Protection* (Oxford University Press 2019) 221.

87 For example, Article 6 of the France-Uganda BIT permits the restriction of transfers provided that there is serious case of balance of payment difficulties. The restriction is expected to not be more than six months and must be consistent with provisions of the IMF and imposed in a non-discriminatory manner; Available on https://investmentpolicy.unctad.org/international-investment-agreements [Accessed on 4 December 2024]; Abba Kolo, 'Investor Protection vs Host State Regulatory Autonomy during Economic Crisis: Treatment of Capital Transfers and Restrictions under Modern Investment Treaties' (2007) 8(4) *The Journal of World Trade Investment and Trade*, 473.

during economic difficulties should be non-discriminatory and in accordance with IMF rules. However, such measures are insulated from third-party scrutiny.[88]

Conflicts can potentially arise when contracting parties to a BIT have included explicit guarantees for the repatriation of funds while also being members of the IMF. This raises important questions, such as: how should the provisions of the BIT on the transfer of funds interact with the IMF Articles of Agreement (Fund Agreement) covering the same topic? In cases of conflicting provisions, should the treaty obligations or the IMF provisions take precedence, or should both be applied concurrently? Additionally, how should an arbitral tribunal determine consistency when a BIT explicitly requires that a host State's measures align with the IMF Fund Agreement? These questions highlight the potential for conflicting objectives when States enter into BITs that offer guarantees for capital repatriation while simultaneously adhering to other international agreements, such as the IMF Fund Agreement, that may not include such provisions. This situation underscores the complexities of harmonising international investment law with global financial regulations and the challenge of ensuring that conflicting obligations do not undermine the objectives of each agreement.

The IMF acknowledges the necessity of policy space for States to manage their economic policies effectively. Senior IMF officials have argued that BITs should include provisions allowing for at least temporary derogations to address balance of payments difficulties. The IMF has raised concerns that US Free Trade Agreements (FTAs) and BITs do not provide sufficient flexibility for host States to regulate their capital accounts as needed.[89] Academic scholar Sean Hagan has also voiced similar concerns, emphasising that when one nation (such as the US) restricts a host State from implementing short-term capital controls while allowing such measures under agreements with other countries, it creates a situation that leads to market distortions and amounts to discrimination. This lack of policy flexibility can place host States at a disadvantage, inhibiting their ability to respond to economic crises effectively.[90] In a comparable context, cases involving BITs signed by certain European Union (EU) member States have highlighted similar issues. The *effet utile* (usefulness) of treaty provisions granting rights related to capital movement restrictions became contentious when these provisions conflicted with EU law, particularly the Treaties of the European Union (TEU). The EU has expressed concern over BITs that commit member States to ensuring the unimpeded transfer of payments related to investment without including any safeguard or exception clauses that would allow for the rapid implementation of capital restrictions when necessary. This has raised questions regarding the compatibility of such BITs with

88 *ibid.*

89 Kevin P. Gallagher, 'Trading Away Financial Stability: Reconstructing Capital Account Liberalization as Trade and Investment Policy' in Kevin P. Gallagher (ed), *Ruling Capital: Emerging Markets and the Reregulation of Cross-Border Finance* (Cornell University Press 2015) 182.

90 *ibid* 169–195.

EU law and the ability of member States to exercise their sovereign right to regulate their financial systems in response to economic challenges.[91]

It is also problematic that many BITs, particularly those of older design, grant exclusive rights to investors while placing nearly all obligations on the host States.[92] These treaties establish a comprehensive framework that dictates the conduct of host States in their treatment of foreign investors, without balancing these obligations with expectations or duties for investors regarding their business practices and operational procedures. Consequently, this one-sided structure leads to a situation where foreign investors are frequently in a position to challenge the actions of host States. The primary issue lies in the fact that investment treaties predominantly impose obligations on host States, leaving them with little room for policy discretion, while simultaneously bestowing substantial and procedural rights upon investors. This imbalance not only limits the regulatory autonomy of host States but also reinforces a system where the interests of investors are prioritised without equivalent responsibilities or safeguards in their business conduct.[93]

Where a State guarantees free transfer of funds, they may lack the necessary policy space to adopt capital controls. There is a propensity for capital control measures that diminish the value of an investment to be classified as "takings" associated with expropriation within the regulatory framework for foreign investment. Whether they would be regarded as non-compensable taking or as takings which should be compensated according to the rules of international law will be subject to debate.[94] A foreign investor may invoke the expropriation provisions of an investment treaty or customary international law to challenge a host State's exchange restrictions, which they claim have significantly impacted the value of their investment. This could include situations where the investor is unable to repatriate funds to purchase essential inputs, equipment, or machinery, or to service external loans—actions that increase the business's debt and significantly reduce the value of the investment. The burden of proof lies with the foreign investor to demonstrate that the exchange restrictions substantially affected or undermined the value of the investment, thus constituting expropriation.[95]

Expropriation is one extreme on a continuum of acts of regulation/interference with foreign investment, and it has historically been the focus of international law due to its significance. As a result, there is a substantial body of State practice,

91 Marise Cremon, 'Who Can Make Treaties? The European Union' in Duncan B. Hollis (ed), *The Oxford Guide to Treaties* (Oxford University Press 2012) 117.

92 José Alvarez, 'Book Review: Investment Treaty Arbitration and Public Law by Gus Van Harten' (2008) 102 *American Journal of International Law*, 912.

93 Jan Kleinheisterkamp, 'Investment Treaty Law and the Fear for Sovereignty: Transnational Challenges and Solutions' (2015) 78(5) *The Modern Law Review Limited*, 795.

94 Muthucumaraswamy Sornarajah, 'Protection and Guarantees of Investment' (2000) 26(2) *Commonwealth Bulletin*, 1293.

95 Kolo & Walde (n 86) 228.

treaty law, and expressed opinions surrounding this particular issue.[96] Although the focus of recent discussions has shifted to other regulatory concerns, expropriation remains central in shaping the broader debate over the treatment of foreign investment, with the capital-exporting perspectives shaped by this issue continuing to influence wider discussions.[97] While there is no clarity as to what constitutes indirect expropriation, it could be argued in future that changes in policies which have the effect of diminishing the profitability of foreign investments would be classified as "taking".[98] In the case that an investment tribunal considers such "takings" to constitute expropriation (a treaty breach), then the host State would be required to pay compensation to the foreign investors who have suffered a substantial loss or diminution of investment.[99] In this regard, circumscription of the right to repatriation of profits when assured will be considered as takings as a denial of this right would amount to a deprivation of something of value to the foreign investors' rights.

3.4 Conclusion

The free market is increasingly yielding to demands for a more regulated economy, alongside a growing clamour for reform of both the global financial system and the international monetary system to address their inherent instability. In an era of globalisation that has rendered State isolation in the international community virtually impossible, economic liberalisation has become a permanent fixture. Within this liberalised investment regime, bolstered by the legal framework of BITs, the constraints on contractual provisions present a modern dilemma and a significant concern for host States. Overly stringent commitments, lacking sufficient flexibility, may compel States to take actions that undermine the protections afforded by BITs, ultimately providing less security for FDI over time. To pre-empt potential economic crises, a reassessment of the protection scope provided by BITs is essential. This review should enable States to maintain their regulatory rights while fostering a sustainable framework for economic development. By striking this balance, host States can protect the ongoing inflow of foreign investments while addressing the complexities of an evolving global economic landscape.

96 Fiona Beveridge, *The Treatment and Taxation of Foreign Investment under International Law* (Manchester University Press 2000) 6.
97 *ibid.*
98 Sornarajah (n 94).
99 Emma Aisbett, Larry Karp & Carol McAusland, 'Compensation for Indirect Expropriation in International Investment Agreements: Implications of National Treatment and Rights to Invest' (2010) 1(2) *Journal of Globalization and Development*, 1.

4 The Right to Repatriation of Capital

A Trammel of State Sovereignty?

4.1 Introduction

Globalisation signifies the reality that we live in an era where the boundaries of sovereignty no longer serve as barriers to the movement of capital, labour, information, and ideas, nor can they effectively shield against harm or damage. This view, expressed by former President of the International Court of Justice, Judge Rosalyn Higgins, reflects the prevailing perspective on the future of global governance,[1] the realisation that globalisation presents a reality of possible erosion or elimination of nation-States.[2] Indeed, globalisation, evident in the rise of international trade and capital markets, does affect sovereignty. The "new" international law generated in part by organisations that States have derogated their authority to has placed limitations on the independent control of domestic policies.[3]

The international system of nation-States offers numerous opportunities that national policies can leverage, such as increased capital flows and economic security. However, as international space continues to shrink, these capital flows will require large-scale human efforts that extend beyond the capacity of individual nation-States. This shift is leading to growing interdependence amongst States, presenting new and complex challenges. Multinational corporations serve as a compelling example of how modern technology enables the creation of integrated organisations that connect different economies to achieve specific corporate goals,[4] thereby fostering a certain level of dependency amongst States. This interdependence of advanced countries disconcerts those invested in the sphere. What happens in one national economy becomes a problem for others. There are concerns that the operations of these corporations are extensions of a State's hegemony: States worry about the extent to which the global interests of foreign investors could conflict with national interests, thereby creating a latent tension with their presence.[5]

1 Julian Ku & John Yoo, 'Globalization and Sovereignty' (2013) 31(1) *Berkley Journal of International Law*, 210.
2 *ibid.*
3 *ibid.*
4 Raymond Vernon, 'Economic Sovereignty at Bay' (1986) 47(1) *Foreign Affairs*, 114.
5 *ibid* 117.

DOI: 10.4324/9781003611714-4

The liberalisation of capital movement has certainly led to the ending of direct State intervention, whether by structural controls, ownership, informal support of cartels, and entry restrictions.[6] There is now a growth of regulation, most of it originating from international or supranational bodies. This has been followed by the transformation of laws and norms to conform to international standards; in fact, the law in turn, is metamorphosing internal sovereignty.[7] In this regard, it could be argued that BITs provide guarantees that rob States of their sovereign immunity. States sovereignty is called into question through legal claims brought by foreign investors alleging breach of promised commitments when the investor's return goes awry due to the sovereign's role in the regulation of economic affairs.[8] In claims against protectionist regulations, the prioritisation of the interpretation of investments wholly from an investment perspective ruins BIT ideals. This is because it leaves out the concerns of the sovereign by solely focusing on profits and returns on investments; when this happens, the investors' values dominate.[9] It is for this reason that there are claims that the prevailing investment regime is "pro-investors".[10]

The controversies surrounding BITs have kept most governments' eyes peeled on the associated risks and costs relative to sovereignty. The influence and power of States have been so reduced in recent times, that this has led to greater fiduciary risks; take for instance, legal actions by foreign investors against States in arbitral tribunals, such that concerned and alert citizens are weary and resenting the shifts in the bargaining power caused by these treaties.[11]The growing trend of foreign investors challenging sensitive legislative acts that ordinarily fall within the purview of States has legitimised the concerns of these States.[12] While foreign investors are likely to focus on discordant and incoherent arbitral decisions, States for their part are worried about whether they have relinquished too much power; and whether the threat of investor-State arbitration is disregarding their domestic measures.[13] This is because, following the protection offered by the International

6 Sol Picciotto, 'Linkages in International Investment Regulation: The Antinomies of the Draft Multilateral Agreement on Investment' (1988) 19(3) *University of Pennsylvania Journal of International Economic Law*, 735.

7 *ibid.*

8 Joseph Thaliath, 'Bilateral Investment Treaties and Sovereignty: An Analysis with Respect to International Investment Law' (2016) 5(2) *Christ University Law Journal*, 3.

9 *ibid.*

10 Horatia Muir Watt & Diego P. Fernandez Arroyo, *Private International Law and Global Governance* (Oxford University Press 2014) 346.

11 Klaus Meyer & Daniel Rottig, 'International Trade and Investment Agreements: Sovereignty at Bay in the 21st Century?' (2016) 16(1) *AIB Insights*, 3.

12 Dickson Moses Oruaze, 'Rebalancing International Investment Agreements in Favour of Host States' (2018) 60(2) *International Journal of Law and Management*, 453; Lone Pine Resources Inc. v. The Government of Canada, ICSID Case No. UNCT/15/2; Occidental Petroleum Corporation and Occidental Exploration and Production Company v. The Republic of Ecuador, ICSID Case No. ARB/06/11.

13 George K. Foster, 'Investors, State and Stakeholders: Power Asymmetries in International Investment and the Stabilizing Potential of Investment Treaties' (2013) 17(2) *Lewis & Clark Law Review*, 366.

Centre for Settlement of Dispute Resolution (ICSID), foreign investors are able to shield themselves from new policies and laws which require compliance from both States and non-States actors or even seek compensation from the government for the costs of compliance. Also, the choosing of arbitrators from different fields of work who interpret treaty provisions expansively while examining politically sensitive actions against sovereigns has exacerbated this issue.[14] Vague treaty texts have resulted in expansive legal interpretation and, consequently, led to monetary claims by foreign investors while unduly circumscribing regulatory spaces in the form of regulatory chill.[15] These legal claims brought by foreign investors against host States elevate them to a pedestal in international law that do not avail non-States actors and distinguish BITs from most international agreements where access to dispute settlement is restricted to sovereign States.[16]

The ability of foreign investors to sue for alleged treaty breaches and the increasing numbers of investors' claims challenging sovereign States have evoked concerns about BITs' inherent costs. This prompts questions regarding what can be done to shield sovereign States from the diminutive erosion of their rights to legislate when need be; whether broad concessionary rights from BITs encroach on the traditional limits of State sovereignty; and what scope of authority a nation should cede over their economic policies to achieve global efficiency in an increasingly interdependent world. These questions are explored because they probe the level of international economic relations on global efficiency and their effect on national sovereignty. The rights that BITs bestow on non-State actors to seek legal recourse against a State is novel in character. Foreign investors need not follow the traditional means of obtaining redress against a foreign State in international law, which requires seeking diplomatic protection and espousal of its claim by the home State:[17] foreign investors now sue States directly. It is however important that a State's perceived loss of political, cultural, and economic autonomy linked with the greater foreign ownership of the host economy must be weighed in the balance with any expected benefits from FDI.[18] Thus it is considered in subsequent sections if a State's right to regulate in economic crisis and monetary sovereignty is truly eroded bearing in mind that treaties require voluntary commitment.

14 Suzanne A. Spears, 'The Quest for Policy Space in a New Generation of International Investment Agreements' (2010) 13(4) *Journal of International Economic Law*, 1038–1039.

15 Kavaljit Singh & Burghard Ilge, *Rethinking Bilateral Investment Treaties: Critical Issues and Policy Choices* (Both Ends, Madhyam, Somo 2016) 4.

16 Kyla Tienhaara, 'Once BITten, Twice Shy? The Uncertain Future of 'Shared Sovereignty' in Investment Treaty Arbitration' (2011) 30 *Policy and Society*, 185.

17 Paolo Di Rosa, 'The Recent Wave of Arbitrations against Argentina under Bilateral Investment Treaties and Principle Legal Issues' (2004) 36(1) *The University of Miami Inter-American Law Review*, 42.

18 John Crystal, 'Sovereignty, Bargaining and the International Regulation of FDI' (2009) 22(3) *Global Society*, 228.

4.2 The Sovereignty Conundrum

The new pattern of global economic integration is virtually the cause of the controversies surrounding BITs being regulatory chill. In observing the circumstances around us, the world is increasingly becoming intertwined and interdependent following economic activities amongst States. If we look at BITs, the North American Free Trade Agreement (NAFTA), and other investment agreements, we can see the manifesting of a greater globalisation and transnational integration. The deepening regulation of international economic sphere by legal constructs and the intrusion of what was once termed "sovereign prerogative" are however frustrating to many national leaders because it prevents them from effectively meeting their constituents' needs as they so wish.[19] The increasing number of international commitments and obligations which modern States are expected to fulfil has virtually rendered the State subservient to various international economic forces. In effect, this makes for a significant departure from the conventional conceptualisation of State sovereignty.[20]

Sovereignty, traditionally understood, means that States may regulate their national economies as they deem fit.[21] Thus foreign investors could be subject to a plethora of regulations relating to the different spheres of governance and management by a State, and a State determines what sectors of the economy they can allow foreign investors to operate in. On the other hand, a State following their international commitment is obliged to respect foreign investors operating within their States if they have signed any treaty in this regard. BITs are products of State sovereignty, as they were formed through voluntary agreements from contracting States. However, in another way, they fundamentally contradict traditional notions of sovereignty, as these agreements erode the political and economic autonomy of the States involved. Tension over sovereignty arises between a home State and a host State when a foreign investor challenges the host State's policies. This happens because a BIT, which governs FDI, grants authority to all parties involved. BITs underpinned into two activities: standard prescription and dispute resolution impact State sovereignty. The ante- and post-commitment costs associated with credible commitments from BITs have led to all manner of policies being challenged in BIT-related suits. The investor-State arbitration provided for under a BIT enables foreign investors to bypass domestic courts to initiate arbitration claims if there is an infringement of the domestic law or prescription of an investment treaty.[22] The replacement of the traditional medium of dispute settlement in customary

19 John Jackson, 'Reflections on International Economic Law' (1996) 17(1) *University of Pennsylvania Journal of International Economic Law*, 24–25.

20 Leila Choukroune, *Judging the State in International Trade and Investment Law: Sovereignty Modern, the Law and the Economics* (Singapore: Springer 2016) 157.

21 Claus D. Zimmermann, 'The Concept of Monetary Sovereignty Revisited' (2013) 24(3) *The European Journal of International Law*, 798–799.

22 Chang-fa Lo, 'Relations and Possible Interactions between State-State Dispute Settlement and Investor-State Arbitration under BITs' (2013) 6(1) *Contemporary Asia Arbitration Journal*, 9.

international law, which involves an exchange between the home State and the host State, with a system in which investors can seek relief for losses due to host State actions without the approval of the home State, is the most revolutionary aspect of international law in the past half century.[23] As one legal scholar puts it, this is "one of the most dynamic and controversial areas of international law today".[24] A government's reluctance to introduce policies to pre-emptively avoid investor's claims echoes the criticism of the investment regime on creating sovereignty cost for host States.[25]

The case of *Philip Morris Asia Limited v the Commonwealth of Australia*[26] is indicative of how far-reaching foreign investors rights go.[27] Philip Morris Asia initiated claims against Australia for the enactment of the Australian Tobacco Plain Packaging Act of 21 November 2011 which imposed restrictions on the appearance and retail packaging for tobacco products, and use of trademarks thereon. The claimant contended, amongst others, that Australia had breached Article 10 and 2 of the 1993 Agreement between Australia and Hong Kong (the latter being the home State of the claimant) because of the substantial deprivation of the value of its intellectual property and goodwill in Australia; treatment of claimant's investments unfairly; impairment of their full use and enjoyment; and failure to provide full protection. Although the tribunal ruled that they had jurisdiction on the case, it nonetheless dismissed the claim because the act complained of took place before protected investment as defined in the treaty became operative.[28] Consequently, the Australian government has withdrawn from the investment-dispute resolution mechanism in future agreements, which is a detour from the preferred strategy of other developed countries in recalibrating their exposure to investment law and moved to tightening substantive provisions in investment agreements.[29] It is believed that the questioning of the domestic legality of the Australian measures in protecting their citizens from the harmful effects of tobacco may have contributed to this.[30]

However, a tribunal is known to have ruled in favour of a Spanish company in claims challenging the Mexican government after its hazardous waste confinement

23 Beth A. Simmons, 'Bargaining over BITs, Arbitrating Awards: The Regime for Protection and Promotion of International Investment' (2014) 66(1) *World Politics*, 17.
24 *ibid* 13.
25 Julia Calvert, Charlotte Rommerskirchen & Arjen van der Heide, 'Does Ownership Matter? Claimant Characteristics and Cases Outcomes in Investor-State Arbitration' (2022) 27(5) *New Political Economy*, 791.
26 UNCITRAL PCA Case No. 2012–12.
27 Ulf Linderfalk, 'Philip Morris Asia Ltd. v. Australia-Abuse of Rights in Investor-State Arbitration' (2017) 86 *Nordic Journal of International Law*, 403–406.
28 *ibid* 408.
29 Jurgen Kurtz, 'Australia's Rejection of Investor-State Arbitration: Causation, Omission and Implication' (2012) 27(1) ICSID Review, 67, 68.
30 *ibid* 71.

plant had its permit revoked for environmental concerns.[31] These suits/limitations portend serious political costs to those who pursue these BITs. A mere threat of litigation is also quite unsettling and can affect national policies, for example, the Canadian government may not be able to expand into health care services provided by foreign investors due to its BIT commitment to foreign investors.[32] While the international investment regime presents itself not as an exception to national sovereignty, but rather as extensions of contemporary international law, investment treaties are regarded as exceptions to national sovereignty.[33]

4.2.1 What Is Sovereignty?

Sovereignty has been recognised as a legal principle and a cornerstone of international relations aimed at protecting the independency of all States, especially the less developed ones in the context of their economic non-equality.[34] Sovereignty and independence are not entirely synonymous as there is no fixed distinction between independence and loss of independence.[35] It is a matter of fact which is dependent on opinions. Thus the concept of sovereignty is fluid with varied interpretations in public international law. A State may construe sovereignty to justify a conduct, while, in some other cases, it will refer to it to denounce the same act.[36] The indeterminacy of what constitutes the precise scope of sovereignty creates a weakness in legal arguments in the sense that, when law is minimised, international lawyers argue that States' conduct is not regulated and States are conferred with unrestrained powers but, when the same law is prioritised, international lawyers could rely on norms that provide for idealised behaviours which may not be apropos.[37] This is why theories of sovereignty are nuanced and complex, and constantly evolving to the dictates of international relations. Therefore, what really constitutes State sovereignty under international law is quite ambiguous. Due to the indeterminate nature of the concept of State sovereignty, its tenets will however be contextualised and restricted to how it relates to international economic law. Sovereignty will be addressed in the context of globalisation and economic relations.

31 Andrew Kerner, 'Why Should I Believe You? The Costs and Consequences of Bilateral Investment Treaties' (2009) 53(1) *International Studies Quarterly*, 76, 79.

32 Bilateral Investment Treaties and Development Policy-Making, 30. By Luke Eric Peterson. Available on https://www.iisd.org/system/files/publications/trade_bits.pdf [Accessed on 4 December 2024].

33 Georgia Dimotropoulus, 'National Sovereignty and International Investment Law: Sovereignty Reassertion and Prospects of Reforms' (2020) (21)1 *Journal of World Investment Trade* 74.

34 Natatliya Tyurina, 'Regional Economic Integration and State Sovereignty' (2014) 1(1) *Journal for International and European Law, Economics and Market Integrations*, 44.

35 *ibid.*

36 Edward Guntrip, 'Self Determination and Foreign Direct Investment: Reimaging Sovereignty in International Investment Law' (2016) 65(4) *International and Comparative Law Quarterly*, 830.

37 *ibid* 832.

Jean Bodin, a French philosopher, once defined sovereignty as the "supreme power over citizens and subjects, unrestrained by law".[38] Its notion is referred to as the triple capacity of the State which comprises: the absolute supremacy on domestic affairs within its territory; the absolute right to govern its people; and the freedom from any interference in the State's affairs.[39] While the notion of sovereignty can be distilled into different subprinciples, it is still at the same time meaning the authority to exercise power within a certain territory.[40] In essence, sovereignty is the supreme and independent power or authority in government as possessed or claimed by a State or community in a defined territory.[41] A State's right to enact laws and develop public policy is a right that is established by State sovereignty; it dates back to the Treaty of Westphalia in 1684[42] and is still observed today, albeit in a more qualified order. The year 1684 is often noted as the birth year of the sovereign States, for it was on 30 January 1684 that the Peace of Westphalia, otherwise known as the Treaty of Munster, was concluded between the Kingdom of Spain and United Netherlands. This treaty marked the end of an 80-year war and the formal recognition of United Netherlands. In Article 1 of the treaty, the King of Spain recognises the United Netherlands as "free and sovereign" with untrammelled powers over their territory.[43] This Peace of Westphalia ushered in a new era of sovereignty and independent States in Europe which no longer had to defer to a higher authority.[44]

Different adjectives have been used to qualify sovereignty, some of the most popular ones are territorial,[45] absolute,[46] relative,[47] internal and external authority, and functional;[48] each of these epithets indicate qualifications which can differ depending on the subject matter and historical moment.[49] Thus sovereignty is fluid.

38 Wm A. Dunning, 'Jean Bodin on Sovereignty' (1896) 11(1) *Political Science Quarterly*, 92.

39 LEKA Dukagjin, 'Challenges of State Sovereignty in the Age of Globalisation' (2017) 13(2) *Acta Universitatis Danubius Journal*, 63.

40 Dimotropoulus (n 33) 73.

41 Dukagjin (n 39) 64.

42 The treaty made the territorial State the cornerstone of the modern-day system, and it spelt out the terms of diplomatic relations; Andreas Osiander, 'Sovereignty, International Relations, and the Westphalian Myth' (2001) 55(2) *International Organization*, 261.

43 Nico Schrijver, 'The Changing Nature of State Sovereignty' (2000) 70(1) *The British Year of International Law*, 66–67.

44 *ibid.*

45 Merje Kuus & John Agnew, 'Theorizing the State Geographically: Sovereignty, Subjectivity, Territoriality' in Kevin R. Cox, Murray Low & Jennifer Robinson (eds), *The SAGE Handbook of Political Geography* (SAGE 2007) 102.

46 D. Engster, 'Jean Bodin, Scepticism and Absolute Sovereignty' (1996) 17(4) *History of Political Thought*, 495.

47 Eiki Berg & Ene Kuusk, 'What Makes Sovereignty a Relative Concept? Empirical Approaches to International Society' (2010) 29 *Political Geography*, 41.

48 Nico Schrijver, 'The Changing Nature of State Sovereignty' (2000) 70(1) *The British Year of International Law*, 70; Ronald A. Brand, 'External Sovereignty and International Law' (1994) 18(5) *Fordham International Law Journal*, 1689.

49 Schrijver (n 48) 70.

In the case of Island of Palman (1928) between Netherlands and the United States, it was succinctly put that:

> Sovereignty in the relations between States signifies independence. Independence in regard to a portion of the globe is the right to exercise therein, to the exclusion of any other State, the functions of a State .... Territorial sovereignty involves the exclusive right to display the activities of a State.[50]

What is clear in today's modern world is that sovereignty is not absolute; the State is limited by the demands of the rule of law.[51] The quest to address modern challenges by States has led to a more interconnected and interdependent world, and this has contributed to the change and reduction of State sovereign powers.[52] Today, all the States in the world are largely involved in or are members of international organisations bound and regulated by treaties they have all mutually consented to. Foreign investors, typically multinational corporations (MNCs) have a major impact in the development of this global economic interdependence. Many States have had to adapt their governmental, monetary, and fiscal policies with efforts to attract foreign investment.[53] Though there is no quantifiable data to describe the extent to which activities by MNCs have brought changes to the State-based international legal order, what is plausible, however, is that sovereign governments have lost the historical monopoly to formulate and administer economic policies to conduct State-to-State relations essentially as they deem fit. This sacrifice is premised on the likelihood that mutual corporation with other States will be instrumental in achieving a larger policy objective in the national economy and other spheres of government.[54]

States are the very essence of international law; they make international law and make themselves bound to their obligations. States are sovereign in nature: in the simplest terms, this connotes that they have the obligation not to interfere with each other's affairs. In a broader sense, States cannot seek to influence the internal policies of other States. The interdependence of States amongst themselves has made it imperative for the existence of special rules to govern inter-State relation. These rules cannot be overarchingly made by one State, or else there would be a global breakdown of law and order. And if there were to be a blatant disregard of the rules

50 *ibid.*

51 Alan O. Sykes, 'Regulatory Protectionism and the Law of International Trade' (1999) 6(1) *The University of Chicago Law Review*, 6.

52 Kal Raustiala, 'Rethinking the Sovereignty Debate in International Economic Law' (2003) 6(4) *Journal of International Economic Law*, 842.

53 Dukagjin (n 39) 65.

54 Stephen D. Cohen, 'Multi-national Corporations versus the Nation-State' in Stephen D. Cohen (ed), *Multinational Corporations and Foreign Direct Investment: Avoiding Simplicity, Embracing Complexity* (Oxford University Press 2007) 234.

of international law there would be no basis for State-State relations required by the existential interdependence of the several sovereign States.[55]

When States contract themselves to treaties, sovereignty in this instance must be qualified, or else one would assume the total loss of sovereignty.[56] The acknowledgement of this can lead to the acceptance of the notion of relative sovereignty instead of absolute sovereignty. Even with the normative difference between absolute and relative sovereignty, with respect to the latter, a State cannot be forced into new obligations without its consent. States are now recognised to be sovereign if they are subject only to the rules of international law and not any other law. The claim to absolute sovereignty by States based on the supposition that pure rules of market economy governed international economic relations has been dispelled as rhetoric.[57] If we claim that States have absolute sovereignty going by the traditional definition of sovereignty—States must pursue whatever policies they deem fit and decree whatever laws they deem necessary without interference—then we fail to recognise obligations flowing from the reciprocity of the sovereignty concept. If we put the absolute sovereignty claims on paper and juxtapose them with the realities of the modern world, we find that this claim is otiose; no State, either internally or externally, has so-called unqualified rights because of the establishment of legal limitations in the form of constitutional law and international law respectively and the growing cross-border economic relations and interdependence amongst States following globalisation. BITs and the imperatives of customary international law have put a lid on the claims of sovereign absolutism.[58]

4.2.2 Economic Sovereignty and International Economic Relations

International economic relation presupposes international exchange of goods; parties to such relations rely on the fulfilment of the bargains of reciprocity and mutuality of State relations. This interdependence has been loathed by States as a limitation on their being the director of their own affairs. In considering this, one must recognise the surrendering of partial authority to supranational bodies. French scholars postulate that a preference for the interdependence of States should override State sovereignty in any interpretation of international economic law matters.[59] This position may underplay the fact that deference to international organisations and laws only become possible if a State chooses to be a member of such organisation and the laws, only with its consent, are adopted unanimously or ratified by the State. However, interdependence in international relations vis-à-vis States is

55 Ignaz Seidl-Hohenveldern, *International Economic Law* (3rd edn, Kluwer Law International 1992) 3.

56 Eric A. Posner & Alan O. Sykes, *Economic Foundations of International Law* (Harvard University Press 2013) 39.

57 Seidl-Hohenveldern (n 55).

58 Simona Tutuianu, *Towards Global Justice: Sovereignty in an Interdependent World* (Springer 2013) 1.

59 Seidl-Hohenveldern (n 55) 20.

usually in tandem with binding obligations which are mutually consented to, that is, ratification by a government.[60] When consented to, it begs a question of how much is too big or too little sovereignty to cede as a State.

International law is built on the principle of State sovereignty, which is shaped by evolving norms and perspectives within the international community. Thus it is flexible, adapting to the changing views of the global order. While international law is distinct from international relations, it both reflects and influences these shifting dynamics. Over the past fifty years, developments in international economic relations have reshaped the traditional notion of sovereignty.[61] A key issue is whether contemporary international law reflects this transformation. In the context of foreign investment, tensions have arisen between developed (capital-exporting) States and developing (capital-importing) States in the way that international law applies. Historically, sovereignty in economic relations was viewed as political equality amongst States, regardless of their relative economic or social power. States had the formal right to make and honour binding commitments, and the principle of *pacta sunt servanda*-the obligation to respect agreements freely made-played a key role in foreign investment discourse.[62]

Two key principles emerged in this context: first, newly independent States were expected to honour agreements made by former colonial powers, even if these agreements (such as resource extraction concessions) were often seen as unjust or overly restrictive on the State's regulatory authority. Second, agreements between newly independent States and foreign investors were also upheld by international law, despite the fact that private entities were not traditionally considered subjects of international law.[63] These liberal principles of State sovereignty and commitment to agreements were challenged by the emerging claims of newly independent States, which sought to assert control over their national economies. The idea of political independence without economic autonomy became increasingly untenable, leading to widespread economic reforms in these States. Thus the notion of economic sovereignty gained prominence, reshaping the global debate on sovereignty and foreign investment.[64] This trend was not limited to developing States. In post-war Europe, there was also a significant increase in State control, particularly in heavy industry and utilities. However, the ways in which governments sought to regulate the economy for the broader public interest varied widely. During this period, it became widely accepted that one of the key functions of government was to regulate private interests for the public good and to play a central role in directly providing public services or facilitating their provision.[65]

60 Jeffrey S. Lantos, *The Life and Death of International Treaties, Double Edged Diplomacy and the Politics of Ratification in Comparative Perspective* (Oxford University Press 2009) 3.

61 Fiona Beveridge, *The Treatment and Taxation of Foreign Investment under International Law* (Manchester University Press 2000) 6–7.

62 *ibid.*

63 *ibid.*

64 *ibid* 8.

65 *ibid.*

To achieve full economic independence, many developing States at the time tried to renegotiate the existing contracts and foreign investment agreements, failing which they nationalised foreign enterprises.[66] It was argued by some Eastern European States that inherent in the sovereignty of a State is the right to control and regulate and, in worst case scenario, the right to nationalise property if need be. The so-called "Hull formula", endorsed by developed countries and calling for "prompt, adequate, and effective" compensation for expropriation, was rejected by developing countries.[67] It was argued that accepting the Hull Rule would mean that States would have no lawful right to expropriate foreign property at all. Under this rule, when a State nationalised property, it would be obligated to use the expropriated asset to generate funds for compensation, effectively returning control to the foreign investor and preventing the State from benefiting economically from the property.[68]

The end of colonialism in the 1960s fuelled the agitation for economic sovereignty, with the United Nations becoming a combat arena for the public manifestation of these grievances; the new States were able to push through their agenda via the 1962 Resolution on Permanent Sovereignty over Natural Resources.[69] This resolution contained a provision on the obligation of States to foreign investors in the case of expropriation and taking to pay "appropriate compensation" instead of "adequate compensation",[70] a partial deviation from the elements of Hull Rule.[71] To reinforce this, a resolution in the form of the Charter of Economic Rights and Duties of States, which was later adopted by the General Assembly in 1974, restated that "appropriate compensation" shall be paid in accordance with the rule in force on the taking. Of particular importance is the disappearance of "in accordance with international law", a phrase hitherto present in the 1962 Resolution.[72] However, under this "New International Economic Order", which followed the adoption of the Charter of Economic Rights and Duties of States, the requirement for "appropriate compensation" for expropriation remained in place, but any disputes (or "controversies") had to be resolved in accordance with the domestic law of the nationalising State and by its own tribunals, rather than through an international tribunal under international law.[73]

66 Subhash C. Jain, 'Permanent Sovereignty Over Natural Resources and Nationalisation in International Law' (1977) 19(3) *Journal of the Indian Law Institute*, 241.

67 Patrick Dumberry, 'Are BITs Representing the New Customary International Law in International Investment Law?', (2010) 28(4) *Penn State International Law Review*, 677.

68 Elihu Lauterpacht, 'International Law and Private Foreign Investment' (1997) 4(2) *Indiana Journal of Global Legal Studies*, 263–245.

69 Karol N. Gess, 'Permanent Sovereignty over Natural Resources: An Analytical Review of the United Nations Declaration and its Genesis' (1964) 13(2) *International and Comparative Law Quarterly*, 408.

70 *ibid.*

71 Cai Congyan, 'International Treaties and the Formation, Application and Transformation of Customary International Law Rules' (2008) 7(3) *Chinese Journal of International Law*, 669–670.

72 Jain (n 66) 247.

73 Dumberry (n 67).

Even then, these efforts did not yield a greater effect; because the dichotomy between the capital-exporting States and the capital-importing States began to wane following the awareness that private investment, a medium for economic development, will only go to the safest place. Consequently, a competitive rush for FDI led to a reinforcement of the customary international law on Hull Rule; a subject that had once been abhorred.[74]

Nonetheless, the merely decorative allure of political sovereignty does not entirely entail the presence of economic sovereignty. Although, both aspects of sovereignty are distinct they are still intertwined. Full State independence requires the legitimate pursuance of all aspects of sovereignty. There cannot therefore be political sovereignty without economic sovereignty as it is tantamount to a mockery of independence. The autonomy and power of States to enter into economic treaty obligations therefore rests on the notion of economic sovereignty. And this relates to a State's permanent resources, its economic ecosystem, and the laws of engagement in international economic relations.[75] A validity test of economic sovereignty will involve a consideration of three elements: (1) any interference with a persisting fundamental State policy, (2) the relationship between the party to the dispute and the State policy, and (3) the presence or threat of injury to the State itself.[76]

4.3 Sovereignty Qualification in International Investment Law

States exchange credibility for sovereignty to an unusual extent when they sign treaties; this implies that the legality of any subsequent State practice is referred to these standards and, consequently, subject to control through international adjudication.[77] These standards have generated widespread debate on the extent to which investment treaties delimit State sovereignty.[78] Thus one of the most sensitive issues regarding a BIT is that it involves sovereignty costs.[79]

The rules of investment touch on a diverse range of domestic regulations such as administrative principles, labour law, environmental law, and property law; and a conventional understanding of the concept of sovereignty detached from international economic relations and realities may lead to the view that the international rule on foreign investment is on a borderline of what is considered acceptable.

74 *ibid.*

75 Uba S. F. Nnabue, 'Principles of International Economic Law and the Right to Economic Development', (2011) 2 *Nnamdi Azikiwe University Journal of International Law*, 2.

76 Spencer Weber Waller & Alan M. Simon, 'Analysing Claims of Sovereignty in International Economic Disputes' (1985) 7(1) *Northwestern Journal of International Law and Business*, 8.

77 Anne Van Aeken, 'International Investment Law between Commitment and Flexibility: A Contract Theory Analysis' (2009) 12(2) *Journal of International Economic Law*, 508.

78 Edward Guntrip, 'Self Determination and Foreign Direct Investment: Reimaging Sovereignty in International Investment Law' (2016) 65(4) *International and Comparative Law Quarterly*, 830.

79 Jonathan Crystal, 'Sovereignty, Bargaining and the International Regulation of Foreign Direct Investment' (2009) 23(3) *Global Society*, 228.

It is becoming more clear that regulations on foreign investment may reach far into that which was traditionally reserved for States.[80] This development has led to the concerns not just about the preservation of national sovereignty but also about the democratic legitimacy by which the laws of foreign investment are made and applied.[81] Developing States that sign BITs will have sovereignty concerns and risk costly arbitration proceedings, notwithstanding the belief that increased inward investment will stimulate growth and prosperity. Unfortunately, it is not in all cases that FDI has contributed to development objectives.[82] Investment treaties which focus on economic liberalisation diminish the regulatory space of the host State to a large extent because a State will have a lesser degree of control over the entry and establishment of FDI.[83] Such liberalisation comes at the cost of weakening a nation's "economic sovereignty", such as the erosion of permanent and exclusive privileges over its economic activities, wealth and natural resources.[84] The 2001 Argentine financial crisis has shown that international investment agreement has the capacity to constrain a State's autonomy in mitigating adverse effects of economic crisis. State intervention through implementing national economic policies have led to grave complexities, both for the States and private actors in international economic relations.[85]

4.3.1 The Recognition of Private Actors under International Law

A treaty is power-conferring:[86] beyond the attempt to capture an agreement between parties to the treaty, it creates a framework where the views and wishes of entities other than the parties to the treaty can have an important role in the treaty operation. A consequence of this is that treaty interpretation which would ordinarily be interpreted in a manner to achieve the goals of the parties will also have to be interpreted to achieve the goals of the non-party.[87] This highlights the important need to identify the entities that have been given powers under the treaty and how they are expected to utilise them.

80 Rudolf Dolzer & Christopher Schreuer, *Principals of International Investment Law* (2nd edn, Oxford University Press 2012) 24.

81 *ibid.*

82 Gordon Sirr, John Garrey & Liam Gallagher, 'Bilateral Investment Treaties and Foreign Direct Investment: Evidence of Asymmetric Effects on Vertical and Horizontal Investment' (2017) 35(1) *Development Policy Review*, 93.

83 Muthucumaraswamy Sornarajah, 'A Law for Need or a Law for Greed? Restoring the Lost Law in the International Law of Foreign Investment' (2006) 6 *Int Environ Agreements*, 339.

84 A. E. Oji & M. V. C. Ozioko, 'Effect of Globalisation on Sovereignty of State' (2011) 2 *Nnamdi Azikiwe University Journal of International Law*, 268.

85 Akbar Adibi, 'The Challenge of the Economic Independence and the Sovereignty of State: A Review of the Problem of Legitimacy of Economic Sanctions in the Reality of International Legal Order' (2017) 5(3) *Russian Law Journal*, 114.

86 Tony Cole & Anuj Kumar Vaksha, 'Power-Conferring Treaties: The Meaning of Investment in the ICSID Convention' (2011) (24)1 *Leiden Journal of International Law*, 309.

87 *ibid.*

MNCs, otherwise known as foreign investors, now play a direct role in the expansion of foreign investment law following their rights to bring direct claims against a State, which is a rare phenomenon when compared to other areas of international law.[88] Unlike other non-State actors, like non-governmental organisations and public interest groups who do not have rights or likelihood of directly initiating claims against a State, an MNC can bring claims against a State. Although a BIT equates to a relationship between two sovereigns, it can be reconceptualised as a tripartite agreement going by the parties who end up being beneficiaries from the treaty. Thus an agreement entered into by two sovereigns, a home State and a host State, in practice, creates protections for the benefits of, and usually enforced by, an investor from one State against the other.[89] The report of the Executive Directors of the World Bank which can be found in the ICSID convention reinforces the right of both the host State and the foreign investor to have access to investment arbitration under the convention. It states that:

> While the broad objective of the Convention is to encourage a larger flow of private international investment, the provisions of the Convention maintain a careful balance between the interests of investors and those of host States. Moreover, the Convention permits the institution of proceedings by host States as well as by investors and the Executive Directors have constantly had in mind that the provisions of the Convention should be equally adapted to the requirements of both cases.[90]

Most investment treaties impose duties on host States and give substantial and procedural rights to investors; this creates a situation where the investors are entitled to argue against the host State's conduct. Unlike contractual arbitration, in a treaty-based investor-State dispute settlement (ISDS) the investors have the sole prerogative to submit a claim.[91] By accepting investor-State arbitration, States accept a process whereby they are routinely cast as respondents.[92] However, this does not preclude treaty parties from bringing claims against each other concerning the interpretation or application of the treaty.[93] Disputes like these are usually solved diplomatically and, as a last resort, referred to arbitration. Investors on their

88 Jean D'Asperemont, Micheal Reisman & Matt Noortmaan, *Participants in the International Law Investment Regime: Multiple Perspectives on a Non-State Actor in International Law* (Abingdon: Routledge 2013) 260.

89 Anthea Roberts, 'Triangular Treaties: The Extent and Limits of Investment Treaty Rights' (2015) 56(2) *Harvard International Law Journal*, 354.

90 ICSID Convention. Available on https://icsid.worldbank.org/en/Documents/resources/2006%20CRR_English-final.pdf [Accessed on 5 December 2024].

91 Margie-Lys, Jaime, 'Relying Upon Parties Interpretation in Treaty Based Investor-State Dispute Settlement: Filling the Gaps in International Investment Agreements' (2014) 46(1) *Georgetown Journal of International Law*, 272.

92 Anthea Roberts, 'Power and Persuasion in Investment Treaty Interpretations: The Dual Role of States' (2010) 104 (2) *American Journal of International Law*, 180.

93 *ibid* 183.

own part can bring a claim against a sovereign for violation of a treaty.[94] Up until recently, a little more than 1% of the cases registered at the ICSID were brought by a host State (State entity) against a foreign investor.[95] It could therefore be argued that the lack of balance in investment treaties is because treaties were primarily aimed to correct asymmetries that might exist at the place where an investment is situated, that is, where the host States can exercise their authority over foreign investors.[96]

Foreign investors enjoy different degrees of protection depending on whether the home State has actively negotiated a treaty and the negotiations reached. For example, different BITs provide distinctive sets of protective clauses and avenues for legal recourse. In some cases, some foreign investors may not even be entitled to certain protective measures that are present in other treaties because their home State has not concluded an agreement with the host State in that regard. In such cases, it raises the issue of discriminatory treatment against foreign investors and a governmental barrier to competition and a restriction on the freedom to compete.[97]

The legal relationship between the foreign investor and the State can be categorised either as direct rights, derivative rights, or intermediate/contingent rights.[98] If investment treaties were intended to create their own self-enclosed system, then the rights contained therein could be considered to be direct rights of the investors which should not be tampered with through State actions that may be considered as countermeasures, which are recognised in customary international law.[99] If, however, investment treaties are considered solely within the confinement of international law, it would therefore mean that the rights of investors are derivative rights and can be understood as intergovernmental commitments which can be compromised by countermeasures undertaken by States in so far as they are expressly desired by the States.[100] If this position is accepted, one may therefore question if the infringement of an investor's right should be accepted as a countermeasure and the investor should therefore reckon with it or if the foreign investor should be entitled to compensation if his rights were recognised as a direct infringement.

94 Susan D. Frank, 'The Nature and Enforcement of Investor Rights under Treaties: Do Investment Treaties have a Bright Future' (2005) 12(47) *U.C. Davis Journal of International Law and Policy*, 53–54.

95 Gustavo Laborde, 'The Case for Host State Claims in Investment Arbitration' (2010) 1(1) *Journal of International Dispute Settlement*, 100.

96 Jaime (n 91).

97 Erik Denters, 'Preferential Trade and Investment Treaties' in Tarcisio Gazzini & Eric De Brabendere (eds), *International Investment Law. The Sources of Rights and Obligations* (Martinus NIJHOFF Publishers 2012) 56.

98 Tillman Rudolf Braun, 'Globalisation-Driven Innovation: The Investor as a Partial Subject in Public International Law. An Inquiry into the Nature of and Limits of Investors Rights' (2014) 15(1–2) *American University International Law Review*, 77.

99 *ibid.*

100 *ibid.*

At the centre of the derivate rights is the idea that investment treaties institutionalise and reinforce the system of diplomatic protection.[101] The derivate rights approach suggests in itself that foreign investors do not have rights under investment treaties. This view is premised on the "orthodox positive doctrine", which prescribes States as the only subjects that can be recognised in public international law.[102] Consequently, investment treaties cannot vest independent rights on foreign investors. Some arbitral tribunals have echoed this argument in favour of some States. The nature of the rights of foreign investors was contested in the case of *Archer Daniel* (2007),[103] *Corn Product* (2008),[104] and *Cargill* (2009).[105] The claimants, of American origin and one of the largest cereal processors, had filed a claim against the Mexican government for introducing a high fructose corn syrup (HFCS) tax in order to combat the rise of American HFCS in Mexico after it became a threat to the domestic Mexican sugar industry.

The main issue was whether a foreign investor in his own right has a direct right to foreign investment protection (the direct theory) or his right is derived on behalf of, and subsumed under, the home State's right (the derivative theory).[106] The American government had argued that the aim of investment arbitration was to depoliticise economic relations by granting direct rights to foreign investors against a host State in contrast to diplomatic protection. In response, the Mexican government argued that the legal position of the investor is a derivative right which is dependent on the relationship between the host State and the home State. And that, in this instance, the HFCS tax introduced by the Mexican government was a countermeasure (a legitimate defence in customary international law) to the previous violation of international law on the part of the United States. The United States had previously denied the Mexican sugar industry access to the American market and rejected the appointment of an arbitral panel in accordance with Article 2008 of NAFTA and as a result breached their contractual rights under NAFTA.[107]

It was however ruled that the private claims were merely allowed for convenience to enforce what is in the origin—the rights of the party States.[108] In the award, a majority of the arbitrators admitted the justification of the tax introduced by

101 Zachary Douglas, 'The Hybrid Foundations of Investment Treaty Arbitrations' (2004) 74(1) *British Yearbook of International Law*, 163.

102 Hersch Lauterpacht, 'The Subject of the Law of Nations' (1947) 63(4) *Law Quarterly Review*, 439–440.

103 *Archer Daniels Midland Company and Tate & Lyle Ingredients Americas, Inc. Mexico*, ICSID Case No. ARB (AF)04/05.

104 *Corn Products International, Inc. v. The United Mexican States (Decision on Responsibility)*, ICSID Case No. ARB (AF)/04/01.

105 *Cargill, Incorporated v. United Mexican States*, ICSID Case No. ARB(AF)/05/2.

106 Nicolas M. Perrone, 'The International Investment Regime and Foreign Investors Right: Another View of a Popular Story' (2014) 11(3) *Manchester Journal of International Economic Law*, 65.

107 Braun (n 98) 79.

108 Duijzentkunst Bart L. Smit, 'Treaty Rights as Tradable Assets: Can Investors Waive Investment Treaty Protection?' (2010) 25(2) *ICSID Review-Foreign Investment Law Journal*, 412. The correct citation as seen on the journal article is 'ICSID Review-Foreign Investment Law Journal'

Mexico as a countermeasure under customary international law. But they did not consider the preconditions for a countermeasure to have been adequately met, the reason being that the introduction of HFCS tax was, obviously:

> To protect the domestic cane sugar industry, rather than inducing the United States to comply with the NAFTA [and was thus] not a valid countermeasure within the meaning of Article 49 of the ILC Articles on States Responsibility … a clearly disproportionate measure may well be adjudged not to have been necessary to induce the responsible State to comply with its obligations but to have a punitive aim and to fall outside the purpose of countermeasures enunciated in article 49 …. Therefore, the Tax was not necessary and reasonably connected with the aim purportedly pursued.[109]

According to *Archer Daniels*, a State could possibly take countermeasures, but in this instance, due to a lack of proportionality, they did not appear to be justifiable. However, the arbitral tribunals in the *Corn Products* and *Cargill* qualified the protection standard contained in NAFTA to be the direct rights of an investor.[110] *Corn Products* and *Cargill* generally condemned the substantiation of the countermeasure as not permissible to infringe on the individual rights of third parties such as the material rights deriving from NAFTA in favour of the investor.[111] A centrism of the direct right and derivative right will lead to a contingent right theory. The contingent right model is also known as the intermediary theory or procedural direct model. According to this model, the substantive protection standards enshrined in investment treaty remain at an intergovernmental level while the procedural right to arbitration applies to the investor as its own right after the filing of a notice of arbitration. The filing of a notice of arbitration is what qualifies it as a contingent right.[112]

Despite the nuanced interpretation of the foreign investor's right, one of the main aims of BITs has always been to erase the uncertainties that were associated with customary international law and the abolition of diplomatic espousal. The right of a foreign investor to make claims based on exclusive rights in an investment treaty, and also not under any legal obligation to notify a home State of its intention to enforce treaty standards in international law, speak volumes of the direct right of a foreign investor.[113] In other words, treaties give private actors or non-State actors, otherwise referred to as foreign investors, a right to sue States directly for compensation and damages before an international tribunal, a paradigm shift from the customary practice of State-to-State relation. This private right to sue a State for compensatory damages represents one of the most revolutionary aspects

109 Braun (n 107).
110 *ibid.*
111 *ibid* 81.
112 *ibid* 93–95.
113 *ibid.*

of international law on foreign investments.[114] This is also evident in other regional or sector-specific investment treaties such as the Energy Charter Treaty (ECT), NAFTA and the Central American Free Trade Agreement (CAFTA) following the rights and privileges conferred on MNCs.[115]

It could be argued that, even though it is the foreign investor that brings and controls investor-State arbitration under a BIT, the substantive rights guaranteed are those of the home State and not those of the foreign investor. Nonetheless, although the foreign investor is ultimately enforcing its home State's right, it has been granted the power to pursue a claim that its home State may find inconvenient to pursue due to diplomatic or political reasons. More so, it is the foreign investor and not the home State that determines the issues that will be raised and the argument that will be advanced in the treaty interpretation.[116] Thus foreign investors are entitled to trigger dispute settlement mechanisms and seek legal redress for breach of investment treaties before international investment tribunals.[117] This system is a cornerstone for the international regulation of States in order to protect the interest of foreign investors within the swathe of economic globalisation. The emergence of this system, though dependent on the ultimate authority of States for its establishment and efficacy, reflects the expansion of private authority as a method of regulation.[118]

As specific as the rights granted to foreign investors under BITs may appear, they are, in a real sense, often quite broad and vague, with low-level precision.[119] A consequence, in part, is that decision makers are left to ascertain the normative content and the precise standards that are applicable to specific circumstances. Ultimately, the definitive status of these substantive rights is determined by the body that is charged with interpreting and applying these standards, a body which usually has wide discretion and often does not put into consideration the views of the States or the treaty parties but builds its jurisprudence in tandem with tribunal awards and academic opinions.[120] It is now a practice for an investment treaty to give the investor a right to choose a desired method of dispute resolution. Often, the choice is between a national or international dispute settlement system, and, when the latter is chosen, there is a further choice of whether an ad hoc international arbitration or institutional arbitration settlement system should be a final

114 Beth A. Simmons, 'Bargaining over BITs, Arbitrating Awards: The Regime for Protection and Promotion of International Investment' (2014) 66(1) *World Politics*, 17.

115 *ibid.*

116 Tony Cole & Anuj Kumar Vaksha, 'Power-Conferring Treaties: The Meaning of Investment in the ICSID Convention' (2011) 24(1) *Leiden Journal of International Law*, 312.

117 David Schneiderman, 'Investing in Democracy-Political Process and International Investment Law' (2010) 60(1) *University of Toronto Law Journal*, 911.

118 Gus Van Harter, 'Private Authority and Transnational Governance: The Contours of the International System of Investor Protection' (2005) 12(4) *Review of International Political Economy*, 602.

119 Anthea Roberts, 'Power and Persuasion in Investment Treaty Interpretations' (2010) 107 *American Journal of International Law*, 190.

120 *ibid* 179.

choice.[121] Once a decision is made all other choices are excluded.[122] Just like every other treaty, the acceptance of investment treaty by a State and the obligations contained therein represents an exercise of a sovereign right. However, once the sovereign commits itself to a treaty, the balance of interests and aspirations become excluded to unilateral decisions. The investors upon the conclusion of an investment treaty are entitled to rely on the scheme mutually agreed on by the host States as long as the treaty remains in force.[123]

Host States exercise their sovereignty when they consent to investment protections that are contained in investment treaties; the legality of any subsequent State practice is restricted by reference to these standards. The increase in the number of claims submitted and the corresponding publication of resulting awards show that arbitral tribunals often interpret BITs inconsistently which leads to lack of clarity and transparency as to the precise nature and extent of the commitment made by the States.[124] In some cases, foreign investors who have structured their investment in a way that they benefit from the protection afforded them by BITs may suddenly discover that they will not benefit from those treaties. The States on the other hand may find themselves in a difficult position of explaining to taxpayers why they are subject to damages in one case but not in another.[125] These inconsistencies around investment arbitration affect not only foreign investment decisions and foreign relations but also economic development in the long run.[126]

The varying interests of stakeholders in an investment agreement are considered to be both paramount and have always been advocated to not be sacrificed for the other. In *Saluka* v. *Czech Republic*, the tribunal was very clear that, in interpreting a BIT, none of the interests mentioned in the preamble of the United States-Argentina BIT should be sacrificed for the other. In *Saluka*'s case it was held that:

> The protection of foreign investments is not the sole aim of the Treaty, but rather a necessary element alongside the overall aim of encouraging foreign investment and extending and intensifying the parties' economic relations. That in turn calls for a balanced approach to the interpretation of the Treaty's substantive provisions for the protection of investments, since an interpretation which exaggerates the protection to be accorded to foreign investments may serve to dissuade host States from admitting foreign investments and so

121 *ibid.*

122 *ibid.*

123 Rudolf Dolzer & Christopher Schreuer, *The Principles of International Investment Law* (Oxford University Press 2012) 20.

124 Bernard Hanotiau, 'Are Bilateral Investment Treaties and Free Trade Agreements Drafted with Sufficient Clarity to give Guidance to Tribunals?' (2016) 5(3) *American University Business Law Review*, 314.

125 *ibid* 315.

126 Susan D. Frank, 'The Nature and Enforcement of Investor Rights under Treaties: Do Investment Treaties have a Bright Future' (2005) 12(47) *U.C Davis Journal of International Law and Policy*, 57.

> undermine the overall aim of extending and intensifying the parties' mutual economic relations.[127]

Whether this notion is one which is adhered to by arbitral tribunals remains a matter of debate. Arbitral awards which prioritise international investments over State sovereign powers have raised concerns at the international investment sphere and has further led to the criticism of investor-States dispute settlement as being one of the ways in which foreign investors are permitted to undermine a host State's regulatory power.[128] Thus it could be argued that these rights conferred on foreign investors are ominous and portend great danger to a State. And just like any other treaty or legal text which does not speak for itself, but requires interpretation, discordant tunes from investment arbitration have helped compound the sovereignty conundrum.

4.4 Arguments on Diminution of States Sovereignty: Mere Rhetoric?

The consideration of sovereignty as the bedrock principle of international law has led to a straw-horse debate alleging unease between the State-centred international legal system resulting from perception and the increasing recognition of fluid and evolving international norms, those which function contrary to the conventional dogma of the State-centred system.[129] State participation in international law adds an additional dimension to the basic concept of sovereignty. If we are to assume, going by the traditional definitions of sovereignty, that States have external sovereignty—the ability to exclude relations with other States—internal sovereignty—the ability to pilot its own institution without undue interference—and territorial sovereignty—the ability to interact on its own accord with all persons and things within it territory[130]—then the imposition of certain standards of treatment by supranational bodies or international law challenges the principle of non-intervention and sovereign equality of States. There are, however, arguments that international law cannot be imposed: States have the option to opt in or opt out, thus reinforcing the doctrinal strand of sovereignty.[131]

However, there are instances where a State need not consent to international law before being bound by its dictates. The legal doctrine of jus cogens limits

127 Brigitte Stern, 'The Future of International Investment Law: A Balance between the Protection of Investors and the State Capacity to Regulate' in Jose E. Alvarez & Karl P. Sauvant (eds), *The Evolving International Investment Regime: Expectations, Realities, Options* (Oxford University Press 2011) 192.

128 Vera Korzun, 'The Right to Regulate in Investor-State Arbitration: Slicing and Dicing Regulatory Carve-outs' (2017) 50(2) *Vanderbilt Journal of Transnational Law*, 358.

129 John Hilla, 'The Literary Effect of Sovereignty in International Law' (2008) 14(1) *Widener Law Review*, 78.

130 Tania Voon, 'Multinational Enterprises and State Sovereignty under International Law' (1999) 21(2) *Adelaide Law Review*, 225–226.

131 *ibid* 227.

State sovereignty;[132] this is because there are basically inviolable rules which are of utmost importance to the international community from which no derogation is permitted.[133] They serve to curtail the excess and unbridled nature of States.[134] Economic integration has revolutionised public international law, and this has become the motivation for new legislation and constitutionalising in international law and perhaps the impetus for revising the unquestioned margin of deference accorded to States.[135]

With the law being a seamless web, there must be the recognition of the subtle relationships between different States because decisions taken in one State can have effect on another State, and a decision taken in one functional area of public policy can have an effect in other functional areas of governance.[136] These aspects of conceptual synthesis and transformation are not new at all or may be new but of a different kind. Globalisation, evident in the formulation of world capitalism and its century's transformation has occasioned the systemic changes in the State sovereignty nomenclature.[137] Several increasingly influential processes subsumed under the caption of globalisation are systematically undermining the capacity of policymakers to act independently or effectively within their national jurisdictions. If sovereignty is considered within the precincts of globalisation, then the question of whether sovereignty is being transformed or eroded emerges.[138]

An underlying theory of a BIT is that it is aimed at moderating the untrammelled exercise of sovereign power by host States. Foreign investors, who are by nature alien to the host State's political process, are vulnerable to sustain the intemperate exercise of that sovereign power.[139] An investment treaty limits the sovereign right of a State to subject foreign investors to its domestic administrative legal system.[140] The regulatory choices of a State are scrutinised by international investment arbitration when they encroach or create an impending encroachment on the substantive rights of foreign investors in a host State. This is evident in the aftermath of the Argentine financial crisis wherein the Argentine government was forced to invoke

132 Felix Lange, 'Challenging the Paris Peace Treaties, State Sovereignty, and Western-Dominated International – The Multifaceted Genesis of the Jus Cogens Doctrine' (2018) 31 *Leiden Journal of International Law*, 830.

133 Thomas Weatherall, *Jus Cogens: International Law and Social Contract* (Cambridge University Press 2015) 5.

134 *ibid* 4.

135 Joel P. Trachtman, 'The International Economic Law Revolution' (1996) 17(1) *University of Pennsylvania Journal of International Economic Law*, 36.

136 *ibid.*

137 Don Kalb, Marco Van der Land, Richard Staring, Nico Wilterdink & Bart Van Steenbergen, *The Ends of Globalization* (Rowman & Littlefield 2000) 125.

138 Mark Beeson, 'Sovereignty under the Siege: Globalisation and the State in Southeast Asia' (2003) 24(2) *Third World Quarterly*, 357.

139 Gustavo Laborde, 'The Case for Host State Claims in Investment Arbitration' (2010) 1(1) *Journal of International Dispute Settlement*, 98.

140 Rudolf Dolzer, 'The Impact of International Treaties on Domestic Administrative Law' (2006) 37 *International Law and Politics*, 953.

the doctrine of necessity to defend certain restrictive actions undertaken by the government in response to the nation's economic and financial crisis from 1999 to 2001.[141]

One may be tempted to think that the discourse on sovereignty diminution is a recent phenomenon. Krasner thinks that the claim that globalisation is undermining sovereignty is exaggerated and historically myopic.[142] He believes that the control of the State has always been challenged and as such not a recent problem. He argues that capital is one area in which discussions around globalisation and sovereignty erosion have often been remarked on and that international capital markets are hardly a new one; he goes further to examine the sixteenth century where financial and trading groups operated around the world; in fact, to him, the movement of capital around the world is not a new thing.[143] What Krasner, however, failed to acknowledge is that the liberalisation of the investment regime, trade, and services has grown far beyond the time in his case in point. He fails to acknowledge that the consequent enactment and proliferation of investment treaties to regulate the movement of capital which he touched upon have exacerbated the sovereignty problems he identifies, albeit on a minor scale.

Nonetheless, it is pertinent to question if the discussions on sovereignty should even be paid attention to in the first place seeing that treaties are by their nature voluntary. If we are to go by this argument, one may risk ignoring an important point about developing States having no other choice but to enter into treaties because it was just the "proper thing to do".[144] Economic globalisation exerts a strong influence on the outcomes of BITs: "for many of the worlds weakest and most dependent States, the inclusion of ICSID clauses within BITs is not so much of a choice than a requirement".[145] Signing investment treaties was just a way to advance the calculability of western business in foreign States; and, since developing States did not envision a sudden outflow of capital towards the developing world, investment treaties represented asymmetric consensus and therefore were unequally extended to developing States.[146]

Opponents of the view on the delimitation of the nation-State hegemony in the aftermath of foreign investments believe that large corporations and State governments are potentially useful to each other even though they have features that are

141 Elizabeth A. Martinez, 'Understanding the Debate over Necessity: Unanswered Questions and Future Implications of Annulments in the Argentine Gas Cases' (2012) 23 *Duke Journal of Comparative and International Law*, 149.

142 Stephen D. Krasner, 'Globalization and Sovereignty' in David A. Smith, Dorothy J. Solinger & Steven C. Topik (eds), *State and Sovereignty in the Global Economy* (Taylor & Francis Group 1999) 34.

143 *ibid.*

144 Adaeze Aniodoh, 'Host States Monetary Sovereignty within the Construct of Bilateral Investment Treaties' (2021) 65(1) *Journal of African Law*, 20.

145 Todd Allee & Clint Peinhardt, 'Delegating Differences: Bilateral Investment Treaties and Bargaining over Dispute Resolutions Provisions' (2010) 54 (1) *International Studies Quarterly*, 23.

146 Nicolas M. Perrone, 'The Governance of Foreign Investment at a Crossroad: Is an Overlapping Consensus the Way Forward? (2015) 15(1) *Global Jurist*, 3.

antagonistic to each other.[147] To them, States that have even the most ineffectual government also have the unequivocal authority to block the entrance of any foreign investor that is not welcomed. In most instances, it is the foreign investors that turn to the host government for assistance and not the other way round.[148] It is important to acknowledge that the host States have significant leverage against foreign investors. They are sovereigns and this connotes that they have power to regulate within their sovereign territory as well as the monopoly on the legitimate use of force. If the host State ultimately decides to pass laws that are adverse to investments, the foreign investor has no way of resisting them since the MNCs must have completed the initial capital investment and the hosts States may no longer need the capital sunk as much as it did at the outset.[149] Therefore, a government can force a foreign investor to leave by either tightening regulatory controls or raising the costs of doing business amongst other things; and, with respect to foreign investors/MNCs, the sanction of nationalisation to accept hard demands from States. To this extent, MNCs serve as means for government to exert and enhance national power; they affirm sovereignty rather than diminish it.

Governments have used their power to integrate their States into the global economy and admit foreign investors because internationalisation and strong economic performance are statistically intertwined. If integration is chosen rather than imposed; where then lies the issue of States being rendered powerless by foreign investors? Because the State has the supreme decision-making authority, it is rarely affected by external factors.[150] Treaties derive their power from the explicit consent of contracting States. Consent can be revoked, and, since a State retains the power to decide on an issue or choose a policy, the ultimate power resides with them. In rare occasions where exit from treaties is intended by parties to be expressly barred, the delegation of power by States can either be revoked or renegotiated as a matter of international law. Therefore, treaty membership where revocable represents the acceptance of temporary limits on the exercise of sovereign powers, but it does not implicate sovereignty.[151]

What is however clear from these differing opinions is that, where an international investment agreement or formal treaty enshrines its member's commitment to a certain set of policies, any change in those policies will have domestic ramifications and constitute a breach of international obligations. Thus, by signing an international treaty on FDI, a sovereignty cost is activated.[152] The obligations imposed by these treaties are by their nature legally binding and raise the costs and

147 *ibid.*

148 Foster (n 13) 370–371.

149 Foster (n 13).

150 Stephen D. Cohen, 'Multinational Corporations versus the Nation State' in Stephen D. Cohen (ed), *Multinational Corporations and Foreign Direct Investment* (Oxford University Press 2007) 243.

151 Kal Raustiala, 'Rethinking the Sovereignty Debate in International Economic Law' (2003) 6(4) *Journal of International Economic Law*, 847.

152 Jonathan Crystal, 'Sovereignty, Bargaining and the International Regulation of Foreign Direct Investment' (2009) 23(3) *Global Society*, 228.

difficulties of *ex post* commitment violations. There are not only threats of arbitration but failure to adhere to these treaty commitments will lead to reputational harm on contracting States; and as such will affect future engagement within the international law regime.[153]

It has been repeatedly stated that the basic bargain of both parties to an investment treaty is to derive benefits from one another; a promise to protect the investments of the nationals of a contracting State in return for the protection of its nationals' investment in the other State's territory. This basic bargain, however, does not appear to be plausible given that most contracting States are developed States and developing States whose nationals may have little prospect in the near future to invest abroad.[154] One may be constrained to question the gains of these developing States when they limit their own sovereignty by concluding treaties with the very purpose of limiting the freedom to take actions they find necessary to advance, in order to protect their national interests.[155] A plausible explanation for this is that developing States may have signed BITs as a means to liberalise their economy and thereby promote economic growth, thus jettisoning the 1980s economic model whereby developing States relied on State enterprises and heavy regulation of the private sector in favour of the neoliberal economic model otherwise known as the "Washington Consensus".[156] The current climate now primarily focuses on the private sector rather than on State corporations as the primary engine for economic growth, with much emphasis on the deregulation of economies and openness to international economic transactions through the medium of FDI.[157]

4.5 Sovereignty Reassertion through Exceptions and Safeguards

The partial relinquishment of State sovereignty to international laws and organisations was a bit uncontrolled at the onset of globalisation in the last quarter of the 20th century. Now States are rethinking this stance.[158] This is manifest in the constructive process whereby States are becoming cautious in delegating powers to rulers and organisations.[159] The increasing trend amongst States to include exceptions is perhaps a precursor to a reclamation of State sovereignty.[160] Other means of sovereignty preservation have been the limiting of access to domestic markets,

153 Racheal Brewster, 'Unpacking the State's Reputation' (2009) 50(2) *Harvard International Law Journal*, 232.

154 Jeswald W. Salacuse & Nicholas P. Sullivan, 'Do BITs Really Work?: An Evaluation of Bilateral Investment Treaties and Their Grand Bargain' (2005) 46(1) *Harvard International Law* 77.

155 Jeswald Salacuse, 'The Emerging Global Regime for Investment' (2010) 51(2) *Harvard International Law Journal*, 440.

156 *ibid*, 442–443.

157 *ibid.*

158 Georgios Dimitropoulus, 'National Sovereignty and International Investment Law: Sovereignty Reassertion and Prospects of Reform' (2020) 21 *Journal of World Investment and Trade*, 77.

159 *ibid.*

160 Martin Karas & Katarina Brockova, 'Investment Treaties and National Sovereignty: Latest Developments' (2021) 20(2) *Journal of International Trade Law and Policy*, 134.

limited adoption of treaties and the emphasis on domestic investments as means of generating wealth. In some cases, non-nationals are required, when permitted to invest, to become shareholders in a company that is established by national laws, and a domestic investor must contribute more than half of the capital of the company.[161] Exceptions, under international law, are justifications that exclude a State's conduct when it could have been considered a breach of an international obligation.[162] Exception clauses have taken different forms such as defences, circumstances precluding wrongfulness, and non-precluded measures (NPM).[163] The right to regulate is also becoming an increasing feature of State sovereignty reassertion in new model BITs. As a safeguard, it is an umbrella clause that legitimises public policy objectives and therefore operates as an affirmative defence to measures which would otherwise have been in breach of the treaty provisions. They may also serve as carveouts of regulatory space from the reach of a treaty provision.[164] Thus the belief that the new rules in global governance have done away with sovereignty is not correct. Claims by States that measures taken to protect public interest should not be considered as violation of treaty standards are pointers that States consider sovereignty as undergirding the law on the protection of investments.[165]

The use of exceptions as means of sovereignty reassertion recognises that States' authority to regulate can be achieved within the ambit of a bilateral or multilateral treaty framework. The NPMs are regarded as mediums to safeguarding the host State's right to regulate and balancing the protection of public interest and foreign investor's rights. These types of clauses are often regarded as general exceptions to protect public interests in treaties. They include, but are not limited to, provisions for the conservation of resources, culture, morals, peace, security, and human and animal life.[166] They generally limit the scope of a treaty obligation.[167] As an exception to a general rule, once invoked, the measure in issue would be regarded as a lawful measure, meaning that no host State can incur liability for the adoption of such measure.[168] Thus the tribunal considers whether such a measure falls within the ambit of the NPM provision before examining whether they have breached a BIT provision.[169]

161 Dimitropoulus (n 158) 78.

162 Gabriele Gagliani, 'The Interpretation of General Exceptions in International Trade and Investment Law: Is a Sustainable Development Interpretative Approach Possible?' 2015 43(4) *Denver Journal of International Law and Policy*, 561.

163 *ibid* 561–562.

164 Vera Korzun, 'The Right to Regulate in Investor-State Arbitration: Slicing and Dicing Regulatory Carve-outs' (2017) 50(2) *Vanderbilt Journal of Transnational Law*, 380.

165 Muthucumaraswamy Sornarajah, *The International Law on Foreign Investment* (Cambridge University Press 2021) 47.

166 Wei Wang, 'The Non-Precluded Measure Type Clause in International Investment Agreements: Significances, Challenges, and Reactions' (2017) 32(2) *ICSID Review*, 447.

167 Prabhash Ranjan, '"Necessary" in Non-Precluded Measures Provisions in Bilateral Investment Treaties: The Indian Contribution' (2020) 67 *Netherlands International Law Review*, 474.

168 Wang (n 166) 450.

169 Ranjan (n 167).

Some of these measures when clearly worded provide a cushion to governments while providing clarity and predictability to foreign investors.[170] Also, the exclusion of certain economic zones or activities from the scope of investment obligations are often regarded as carveouts or safeguards necessary to address policy concerns. This means has become a frequent feature in recent international investment agreements as it allows governments to favour local production above foreign investors.[171] This method may, however, not be the most appropriate for achieving the intended purpose of public space protection. Promoting discriminatory practices could lead to favouritism and the creation of powerful domestic monopolies. In this context, it is not clear how the exemption of abusive measures makes an argument for public interest protection.[172] It is the case that these clauses will create a paradigm shift from the way investors' rights have always been interpreted. However, the new treaty provisions may not fully address all the criticisms of ISDS, as the concerns also involve the more general arbitral competence to review governmental policies as such and the lack of arbitral deference in doing so.[173] It is therefore important that arbitral bodies consider the developmental condition of the State adopting a contentious measure and the effect of the measure itself.[174]

Specifically, and in relation to the subject matter of this book, capital transfers in BITs raise issues of practical significance for State sovereignty. Foreign investor's right to transfer capital in the form of profits, interest on loans, royalties, dividends, etc is very important in the transnational investment process. The stakeholders often have conflicting interests at some points, and those junctures raise considerable issues of law, and sovereignty.[175] For example, an investor would want an assurance from the host State that he would be able to repatriate his capital which could take any form; but in a State where the economy is volatile or fragile, the right to repatriation of capital will be considered detrimental to such an economy as it may lead to the depletion of the State's foreign exchange (for details, see Chapter 3). Transferring capital may be viewed as a source of fiscal instability and, beyond that, generate resentment from domestic investors who may loathe the idea of preferential treatment accorded to foreign investors[176]

The conflicting interest of the foreign investor and the host State in relation to repatriation concerns is now addressed in new BITs through exceptions and

170 Safeguarding Policy Space in Investment Agreements, 5. By Simon Lester & Bryan Mercurio. Available on https://www.cato.org/sites/cato.org/files/articles/lester-mercurio-iiel-issue-brief-december-2017.pdf [Accessed on 4 December 2024].

171 *ibid.*

172 *ibid* 8.

173 Klara Polackova Van Der Ploeg, 'Protection of Regulatory Autonomy and Investor Obligations: Latest Trends in Investment Treaty Design' (2018) 51(1) *The International Lawyer*, 119.

174 Gabriele Gagliani, 'The Interpretation of General Exceptions in International Trade and Investment Law: Is a Sustainable Development Interpretative Approach Possible?' 2015 43(4) *Denver Journal of International Law and Policy*, 562.

175 Thomas Walde & Abba Kolo, 'Investor-State Disputes: The Interface between Treaty-Based International Investment Protection and Fiscal Sovereignty' 2007 35(8–9) *Intertax*, 435.

176 *ibid* 435, 436.

safeguards to retain sovereign rights of the host State.[177] Thus, the transfer of funds clause is now written to include exceptions which can be seen as restrictions in cases of balance of payments issues or currency crises.[178] The next chapter discusses, in detail, the proclivity of economically challenged countries to preserve sovereignty through its transfer of funds clause. The Morocco-Nigeria BIT, considered in detail, for example, contains innovative provisions that safeguard a State's right to enact laws and impose obligations on foreign investors, thus illustrating the growing density of reforms that are aimed at centring host State's interests.[179]

To this end, assessing the efficacy of an exception and its ability to have a competitive advantage over another treaty provision will require the establishment of its link to non-investment obligations and threats to State concerns.[180] For example, climate change may be a proximate and powerful threat to national security, and, although the impact of the predicted threat to national security varies within and between States, the link between climate change and national security is undeniable. And since States are likely to apply climate-related measures which may run contrary to foreign investors' interest, it may seek to defend its position by relying on exceptions if they are available in the applicable treaty.[181]

4.5.1 Reflections from the Argentine Economic Crises

Argentina's emergency response to its economic crisis in the early 2000s raises significant questions about State sovereignty on public policy implementation and the scope of foreign investment protection. In the case of *CMS Gas Transmission v Argentine Republic*,[182] CMS claimed that Argentina's emergency measures during its economic crisis violated the US-Argentina BIT. The arbitral tribunal did not concur on the specific necessity provisions in the BIT, nor under customary international law. While it did accept that an economic crisis can preclude a State from fulfilling its obligations under the BIT, it nonetheless ruled that Argentina had contributed to the crisis and could not therefore rely on BITs and customary international law.[183] In the case of *LGE V Argentina*,[184] with similar facts and applicable

177 Nigeria-Morocco BIT and Nigeria-Singapore BIT. Available on http://investmentpolicyhub.unctad.org/Download/TreatyFile/1382 [Accessed on 4 December 2024].

178 *ibid.*

179 Olabisi D. Akinkugbe, 'Africanization and the Reform of International Investment Law' (2021) 53(1) *Case Western Reserve Journal of International Law*, 20, 21.

180 Rawan Al-Louzi, 'Bilateral Investment Treaties as Tools for Enhancing Foreign Investment Climate and Increasing Competitiveness' (2017) 14(1) *Manchester Journal of International Economic Law*, 87.

181 *ibid.*

182 *CMS Gas Transmission Co. v. Argentine Republic* (2005) ICSID Case No. ARB/01/8.

183 *CMS Gas Transmission Co. v. Argentine Republic* (2005) ICSID Case No. ARB/01/8.

184 *LGE V Argentina* ICSID Case No. ARB/02/01.

laws to the *CMS* case, another tribunal ruled that Argentina was not liable for breach of its treaty obligations.[185]

Discordant legal interpretation of similar thematic issue on economic crises raises issues of legal significance. It has spawned discussions on the relationship between the State and the market on the one hand, and the role of regulation on the other. As evidenced in most cases, there is a strong desire by the State to use law or even expand regulations to deal with market failures that show up as economic crisis.[186] In some cases, the role of the State in managing the crisis is questioned as well as the tools employed to manage such a crisis. Textual dissimilarity has implications for the exception scope. It may be regarded as either self-judging or non-self-judging. In cases where it is self-judging following the use of the words such as "considers" or "determines", an arbitral tribunal will look at whether a State via its conduct has acted reasonably and in good faith. And when a provision is non-self-judging, the host State's action will be scrutinised in greater detail.[187]

The arbitral decisions from the Argentine economic crisis are the first cases to examine the effect of the self-judging clauses. One tribunal states that a State which adopts a self-judging clause should be the sole arbiter of the scope and application of a treaty provision, while another states that, pursuant to such clauses, each party will determine whether the situation requires measures of the type that were anticipated under the treaty, subject to the decision of the tribunal on whether they have been made in good faith.[188] One of the contentions in the Argentine cases was, to what extent can the degree of protection offered to the foreign investor be withdrawn in emergencies in order to preserve essential security interests.[189] Argentina had contended that Article XI of the US-Argentina BIT was self-judging, in the sense that it allowed Argentina to determine whether the measures it took were necessary without interfering with international responsibility, and free from arbitral review. [190]The tribunal in this case and other similar cases ruled that self-judging clauses must be expressly framed to reflect such intention; in which case the State would have the discretion to determine the scope of its application.[191]

185 Stephan W. Schill, 'International Investment Law, and the Host State's Power to Handle Economic Crises-Comment on the ICSID Decision LG&E v Argentina' (2007) 24(3) *Journal of International Arbitration*, 265.

186 Ioannis Glinavos, 'Regulation and the Role of Law in Economic Crisis' (2010) 21(4) *European Business Law Review*, 540.

187 *ibid* 88.

188 Michael D. Nolan & Frederic G. Sourgens, 'The Limits of Discretion? Self-Judging Emergency Clauses in International Investment Agreements' *Michael Nolan & Karl Sauvant eds*, in *Yearbook of International Investment Law and Policy* (Oxford University Press, 2011) 362.

189 S. R. Subramanian, 'Too Similar or Too Difficult: State of Necessity as a Defence under Customary International Law and the Bilateral Investment Treaty and their Relationship' (2012) 9(1) *Manchester Journal of International Economic Law*, 68–67.

190 Stephan Schill & Robyn Briese, '"If the State Considers": Self-Judging Clauses in International Dispute Settlement' (2009) 13 *Max Planck Yearbook of United Nations Law*, 72.

191 *ibid* 73.

It is apparent that arbitral tribunals are willing to recognise the utility of self-judging clauses once established. However, these clauses cause tensions between international cooperation and unilateralism, in the sense that, a State invoking it *ex post* dispute may use its discretion unwittingly, and beyond what was anticipated by both contracting parties in the first place. This means that instead of being an exit-valve from an international cooperation regime, they do in some cases become destructive to international cooperation.[192] In addressing disputes that concerns the application of self-judging clauses, it is important that there is need to balance such clauses by the application of very robust standards of review so as to prevent the arbitrary use of such clauses and respect the discretion that such clauses bestow on a State.[193] Although host States have the right to regulate for domestic constituents in relation to public interest and, since the protection of foreign investment is not the sole purpose of a treaty, there should be a counterbalance between the interests of the contracting parties to a treaty.[194] This is because there are few incentives for States to be cautious when dealing with economic crises if they know that they can transfer risks to foreign investors during economic crises upon a successful invocation of a defence measure.[195] It is thus recognised that States can solve sovereignty concerns by establishing exceptions. The divergent arbitral awards from the Argentine cases make clear the need for States to have flexibility to specifically deal with economic crises rather than the reliance on customary international law on 'essential interest' which is traditional understood as physcial security. [196] The recommendations proposed in Chapter 6 suggest that such exceptions should not be self-judging so as to create a leeway for treaty appliers to consider the "essentials of treaty interpretation" and find a balance between the competing interests of parties to a treaty. One example would be the need to consider the end of a crisis and the risk-sharing mechanism framework for when a State has, through its negligence, contributed to economic crisis.

4.6 Conclusion

BITs, as mechanisms for investment liberalisation, have undoubtedly increased the costs associated with implementing government policies. As economic globalisation intensifies, the sovereignty of host States is increasingly jeopardised.

192 *ibid 64.*

193 Robyn Briese & S. Schill, 'Djibouti v. France: Self-Judging Clauses before the International Court of Justice' (2009) 10(1) *Melbourne Journal of International Law*, 310.

194 Joseph Thaliath, 'Bilateral Investment Treaties and Sovereignty: An Analysis with Respect to International Investment Law' (2016) 5(2) *Christ University Law Journal*, 5.

195 Alberto Alvarez-Jimenez, 'International Investment Law, Time, and Economics: Fixing the Length of Economics Crises as a Costs Allocation Tool between Host States and Foreign Investors' (2020) 19 *World Trade Review*, 93.

196 Dillon Fowler, 'Is this Really Necessary?: The Scope of Necessity in 21st Century Investment Treaties' (2017) 9(1) *Creighton International and Comparative Law Journal*, 3–4.

The proliferation of investment treaties raises the potential for conflicts between host States and foreign investors, highlighting the need to protect regulatory space and mitigate related costs. Reevaluating the terminology and framework of BITs is crucial, particularly as many foreign investors seek global profits, a pursuit that does not always align with the interests or economic development goals of host States. While BITs often reflect the existing imbalances in political and economic power amongst signatory States, recent trends indicate a shift towards incorporating features that enhance sovereignty in newer agreements. Given the growing inconsistencies in how arbitral tribunals interpret treaty rights, it is essential for States to remain vigilant. They must strategically carve out policy space within investment treaties to re-regulate cross-border finance and safeguard the remnants of their sovereignty.

5 Sovereignty vs. Globalisation

The Contemporary Investment Treaty Landscape

5.1 Introduction

It is often said that the obligations in an agreement reflect how much value a government places on retaining its sovereignty. A government willing to cede some sovereignty will prioritise its partner's welfare when making policy decisions, while a government seeking to maintain full sovereignty will focus on maximising its own perceived interests.[1] However, globalisation, with its increasing international relations, has rendered the concept of absolute sovereignty obsolete. It is no longer accurate to claim that States possess full sovereignty if they are bound by external rules and procedures.[2] BITs often overlook economic sovereignty, prioritising the extensive rights granted to foreign investors, which host States are invariably bound to uphold.[3] By signing BITs, States trade some degree of sovereignty for enhanced credibility, as international investment law not only imposes significant restrictions on their regulatory conduct but also subjects it to compulsory international adjudication mechanisms.[4] However, not all regulatory measures taken by host States that negatively affect foreign investors arise from opportunistic motives; some are enacted in good faith to address unforeseen contingencies. Unfortunately, these non-discriminatory, good-faith measures have, in certain instances, been found to violate BITs,[5] leading to widespread criticism of the international investment regime.

Criticisms of the investment regime is also partly derived from the differential treaty texts applications by tribunals who have arrived at divergent findings on liability. Instead of creating the certainty that is required for a functional investment regime, the process of resolving investment disputes through arbitration is creating

1 Martin Richardson & Frank Stahler, 'International Agreements, Economic Sovereignty and Exit' (2019) 120 *European Economic Review*, 2.

2 Arthur L. Goodhart, 'Rule of Law and Absolute Sovereignty' (1958) 106(7) *University of Pennsylvania Law Review*, 951.

3 George Forji Amin, 'All that Glitters is not Always Gold or Silver: Typical Bilateral Investment Treaties (BITs) Clauses as Peril to Third World Economic Sovereignty' (2020) 6(3) *Athens Journal of Law*, 318.

4 Anne van Aaken, 'International Investment Law between Commitment and Flexibility: A Contract Theory Analysis' (2009) 12 (2) *Journal of International Economic Law*, 508.

5 *ibid* 521.

DOI: 10.4324/9781003611714-5

uncertainty about the meaning of rights enshrined in BITs.[6] Harmonisation, predictability, and consistency are much desired traits in investment law and policy. Thus the absence of these is usually unsettling.[7] The phrase "legitimacy crisis" is often heard in this regard.[8] Commentaries and complaints such as this fail to take into consideration the structural framework of the regime. Often the reasons for the legitimacy crisis may be the complexity and imprecision of treaty texts that warrant the attention of investment arbitrators in the first place, as well as the modalities for the text interpretations which have wider implications on policy issues.[9]

Criticisms of the international investment regime, highlighted above and expatiated upon in previous chapters, are credited to the widespread concerns amongst governments, the public and other relevant stakeholders in the investment regime about the potential biases and shortcomings in BITs. They have served as an awakening for governments to assess whether the system is true to its purpose. The criticism has contributed to States starting to remedy certain shortcomings through the introduction of more transparency and third-party participation, clarification of international investment agreement standards, and tighter control mechanisms.[10] States are beginning to reappraise their stance on BITs. In 2007, Bolivia terminated the International Centre for Settlement of Dispute Resolution (ICSID) Convention.[11] Following closely, Venezuela arguing reasons of national sovereignty denounced the ICSID Convention and terminated[12] nine BITs with other States.[13] South Africa has terminated its treaties with Luxembourg, Belgium, the Netherlands, Spain, Switzerland, Austria, Denmark, Argentina, and Germany, and has, furthermore, proceeded to replace these treaties with domestic legislation that caters to foreign investors.[14] Ecuador, Bolivia, and Venezuela have denounced

6 Susan D. Franck, 'The Legitimacy Crisis in Investment Treaty Arbitration: Privatizing Public International Law through Inconsistent Decisions' (2005) 73(5) *Fordham Law Review*, 1523.

7 Andrea K. Bjorklund, 'Practical and Legal Avenues to Make Substantive Rules and Disciplines of International Investments Coverage' in Roberto Enchandi & Pierre Sauve (eds), *Prospects in International Investment Law and Policy: World Trade Forum* (Cambridge University Press 2013) 175.

8 Yas Banifatemi, 'Consistency in the Interpretation of Substantive Investment Rules: Is It Achievable?' in Roberto Enchandi & Pierre Sauve (eds), *Prospects in International Investment Law and Policy: World Trade Forum* (Cambridge University Press 2013) 200.

9 *ibid.*

10 Stephen Schill, 'In Defence of International Investment Law' in Bungenberg Marc, Christoph Herrmann, Markus Krajewski & Jorg Philipp Terhechte (eds), *European Yearbook of International Economic Law* (Springer International Publishing 2016) 337.

11 Nicolette Butler & Surya Subedi, 'The Future of International Investment Regulation towards a World Investment Organisation?' (2017) 64(1) *Netherlands International Law Review*, 44.

12 It is pertinent to note that, despite the termination of these BITs, they have not been fully dismantled as most of them contain survival clauses. This clause makes it possible for foreign investors to bring a claim against a State in relation to an investment that was made when the BIT was still in force.

13 Dickson Moses Oruaze, 'Rebalancing International Investment Agreements in Favour of Host States' (2018) 60(2) *International Journal of Law and Management*, 453.

14 George K. Foster, 'Investors, State and Stakeholders: Power Asymmetries in International Investment and the Stabilizing Potential of Investment Treaties' (2013) 17(2) *Lewis & Clark Law Review*, 366; Engela C. Schlemmer, 'An Overview of South Africa's Bilateral Investment Treaties and

some of their BITs,[15] while others have instead developed a new model BIT practice aimed at balancing investment protection and the host State's right to regulate for her sovereignty.[16] These marathon denunciations and terminations signify one and one thing only: a rethinking of the costs and benefits of BITs within the context of preserving the policy space following the gradual erosion of State sovereignty. The increase in arbitration has shown the need to adjust treaty texts;[17] it is an indicator that the institution is simply reacting to external developments.[18] Thus the proliferation of treaty negotiations, treaty consents and recourse to treaty agreements in resolving conflicts arising between foreign investors and host States, combined with the growing awareness amongst stakeholders in the international investment regime about the possibility of claims against States for breaches of investment treaty protections, will shape further discussions.

This chapter examines the international investment climate and the potential impact of traditional BITs on economic sovereignty. It analyses the linkages and overlaps between BITs signed by developing and developed countries, enhancing discussions on contemporary international practices that prioritise public policy in balancing State and private interests. The discussion includes an examination of Nigerian BITs, emphasising their shortcomings, particularly regarding fund transfer clauses in the context of modern international investment law. These BITs are reassessed as part of a comprehensive system of 21st-century global economic governance, with suggestions for improvements aimed at reducing regulatory costs and addressing the legitimacy crisis in the international investment regime.

To provide context, the chapter explores whether treaty clauses strike an appropriate balance between a host State's need for regulatory discretion and the principles of investment protection, or if additional reforms are necessary. It highlights both the procedural and substantive shortcomings of the treaty clauses on the transfer of funds, assessing the extent to which a recalibration of these clauses is needed

Investment Policy' (2016) 31(1) *ICSID Review*, 189; Srikar Mysore & Aditya Vora, 'Tussle for Policy Space in International Investment Norm Setting: The Search for a Middle Path' (2016) 7(2) *Jindal Global Law Review*, 138, 140; Leila Choukroune, 'Judging the State in International Trade and Investment Law: Why, How and What For?' in Leila Choukroune (ed), *Judging the State in International Trade and Investment Law: Sovereignty Modern, the Law and Economics* (Singapore: Springer 2016) 3.

15 *ibid.*

16 Prabhash Ranjan & Pushkar Amand, 'The 2016 Model Indian BIT: A Critical Deconstruction' (2017) 38(1) *Northwestern Journal of International Law and Business*, 6.

17 Roberto Echandi, 'Be Careful with What You Wish: Saving Developing Countries from Development and the Risk of Overlooking the importance of a Multilateral Rule-Based System on Investment in the 21st Century' in Bungenberg Marc, Christoph Herrmann, Markus Krajewski & Jorg Philipp Terhechte (eds), *European Yearbook of International Economic Law* (Springer International Publishing 2016) 235.

18 Margrete Stevens, 'ICSID at the Crossroads: Some Thoughts and Recommendations for Improving the Dispute Settlement System' in Sauve Pierre & Echandi Roberto (eds), *Prospects in International Investment Law and Policy: World Trade Forum* (Cambridge University Press 2013) 253.

to address modern realities. The chapter concludes by emphasising the need for BITs to be reconciled with other international legal principles.

5.2 Regulatory Approaches to Fund Transfers

Recently, treaties between developing and developed economies are increasingly tailored to align with sustainable development goals, particularly regarding the conditions under which fund transfers can be limited or delayed, especially during economic crises. Some BITS exemplify this trend. The Angola-Japan BIT stipulates that a party may delay or prevent a transfer by applying its laws and regulations in an equitable, non-discriminatory, and good-faith manner, especially those concerning: bankruptcy, insolvency, or the protection of creditor rights; the issuance, trading, or dealing in securities, futures, options, or derivatives; criminal or penal offences; the reporting or record-keeping of currency or other monetary instrument transfers as needed to assist law enforcement or financial regulatory authorities; or ensuring adherence to orders or judgments in legal proceedings.[19]

This qualification indicates a significant shift from norms where BITs provide unfettered commitments to foreign investors. Some BITs signed by Nigeria include minor modifications to the general guarantees on fund transfers. They are a bit nuanced, some touching on balance of payment concerns, while some focus on other minor issues. For instance, the Nigerian-Algerian BIT[20] introduces an exception regarding the right to transfer funds. Article 7 of the Treaty asserts the unconditional right to transfer funds, stating that such transfers will be conducted in accordance with the internal laws of the host State; the laws should not impose compromising conditions, and their application must be prompt and unimpeded. However, Paragraph 4 of Article 7 of the Treaty outlines an exception: the provisions on fund transfers do not apply to Algerian or Nigerian nationals who have obtained permanent residency in either country. Furthermore, Article 5 specifies that any restrictions mentioned in Paragraph 4 will be automatically lifted once they are rescinded by the internal laws of Algeria or Nigeria, as applicable.[21] In regard to the preservation of the economic sovereignty of a host State, the treaty remains silent on potential financial crises or balance of payment problems mitigation.

A more nuanced exception to the general rule on fund transfers is illustrated in Article 8(3) of the Nigeria-United Arab Emirates BIT.[22] This provision permits a contracting party to temporarily restrict a transfer through the equitable, non-discriminatory, and good-faith application of its laws relating to (a) bankruptcy and insolvency, including the protection of creditors' rights, or (b) criminal

19 Angola-Japan BIT. Available on https://investmentpolicy.unctad.org [Accessed on 5 December 2024].

20 Nigeria-Algeria BIT. Available on https://investmentpolicy.unctad.org [Accessed on 5 December 2024].

21 *ibid.*

22 Nigeria-UAE BIT. Available on https://investmentpolicy.unctad.org [Accessed on 5 December 2024].

offences. The Nigeria-Canada BIT extends this approach by integrating equitable, non-discriminatory, and good-faith measures to restrictions aimed at upholding the safety, soundness, integrity, or financial responsibility of financial institutions. Importantly, these restrictions must be consistent with those established under the WTO Agreement.[23] Additionally, the exception in the Nigeria-Romania BIT permits derogation from the general right to transfer funds during exceptional financial or economic circumstances, provided that such restrictions comply with the host State's national laws and regulations.[24]

While these agreements are commendable for their distinctive features, they also highlight a central issue: some BITs fail to adequately address balance of payments concerns with sufficient clarity. For example, the Romania Agreement conflicts with the national laws it references, as those domestic laws do not permit any derogation of the right to transfer funds. Additionally, the concept of "good-faith application" presents challenges, as "good faith" can be interpreted in various ways and is not a fixed term; its meaning can vary significantly depending on the context.[25] Some treaties are, however, direct in addressing balance of payment problems, which are of often a feature of economic crisis. The Nigeria-Singapore BIT takes a sophisticated approach to issues related to the transfer of funds. Article 7 allows for the free and prompt transfer of all funds related to an investment in and out of the host State. However, Article 8 introduces an exception that may initially seem conclusive; it allows for temporary safeguard measures. This article permits contracting parties to maintain restrictions on fund transfers related to investments, particularly when balance of payments difficulties necessitates such restrictions for economic development. Additionally, it mandates that the application of these measures aligns with the Articles of Agreement of the International Monetary Fund.[26] Similarly, while the Nigeria–Morocco BIT recognises the rights of a foreign investor to transfer funds relating to investments such as profits, capital, and loan repayments, it nonetheless subjects them to restrictions. First, Article 11 provides that any delay with regards to funds transfer must be made in good faith and be non-discriminatory. Article 12 further provides that the host State may make some restrictions in the event of serious balance of payment difficulties and to ensure the integrity of a party's financial system.[27] This article does provide a balance between the foreign investor's right to transfer funds and the host State's

23 Nigeria-Canada BIT. Available on https://investmentpolicy.unctad.org [Accessed on 5 December 2024].

24 Nigerian-Romanian BIT. Available on https://investmentpolicy.unctad.org [Accessed on 5 December 2024].

25 Paul S. Davies, *The Law of Contract* (2nd edn, Oxford University Press 2018) 285.

26 Investment Policy Hub. Available on https://investmentpolicy.unctad.org [Accessed on 5 December 2024].

27 Nigeria–Morocco BIT. Available on https://investmentpolicy.unctad.org [Accessed on 5 December 2024].

regulatory power; it is, however, not clear which circumstances qualify as serious balance of payment difficulties.[28]

5.3 Exploring the Justifications for Differences in Treaty Language

Some BITs, as previously noted, exhibit significant textual variation, reflecting a range of obligations and exceptions influenced by the dynamics of economies, negotiating power, and leverage. In some instances, key issues may be overlooked, likely due to negotiators' inability to anticipate all potential risks that could affect either the State or foreign investors. While some treaties clearly outline the limitations on specific obligations, others remain ambiguous. Some incorporate public interest measures, while others do not. However, certain exceptions are drafted in ways that may not align with the developmental objectives and priorities of the contracting States. When considered in this context, these exceptions—permitting derogation from general norms—can serve to uphold a State's sovereignty. However, if their analytical foundations are uncertain and weak, they risk constraining rather than preserving the regulatory space of contracting States. One interesting feature observed in several of the treaties is the absence of safeguards related to balance of payments crises. This may be due to the rarity of States negotiating BITs during economic crises. If they did so more often, it would likely become evident from a domestic perspective that unqualified free-transfer clauses in BITs could pose significant challenges. In extreme circumstances, balance of payment safeguards could offer crucial flexibility.[29]

Recent developments in BITs reflect efforts to address possible issues on economic crises, by recognising States' rights to regulate for public purposes.[30] The introduction of carve-out clauses to shield States from claims by foreign investors in unforeseen circumstances, as seen in the Morocco–Nigeria BIT, is a notable trend. Some other Nigerian BITs materially depart from textual components that hitherto permit unrestricted guarantees. Presumably, because such provisions do not accommodate the use of foreign exchange restrictions during economic crises or times of balance of payment problems. By incorporating safeguard clauses or exceptions to general provisions, a host State in this instance aims to mitigate potential claims related to legitimate public interest measures while enhancing the relationship between domestic regulatory actions and their international obligations. Host States, now more than ever, protect their regulatory space by including provisions that explicitly affirm their right to regulate, exclude liability when

28 Okechukwu Ejims, 'The 2016 Morocco–Nigeria Bilateral Investment Treaty: More Practical Reality in Providing a Balanced Investment. Treaty' (2019) 34(1) *ICSID Review*, 74.

29 Andrew Yianni & Carlos de Vera, 'The Return of Capital Controls' (2010) 73(5) *Law and contemporary Problems*, 365.

30 Alison Giest, 'Interpreting Public Interest Provisions in International Investment Treaties' (2017) 18(1) *Chicago Journal of International Law*, 325.

necessary, and clarify treaty language.[31] For instance, countries such as Brazil, Mozambique, Indonesia, and India have revised their treaty models and adopted less ambitious facilitation agreements.[32]

BITs should, nonetheless, be designed to be optimal from both *ex ante* and *ex post* perspectives, encouraging contracting parties to invest in the relationship at the time of treaty conclusion to maximise anticipated mutual benefits, while also ensuring value maximisation once unforeseen uncertainties are resolved. Given that these goals can conflict—since future events may render contractual commitments impracticable—exceptions, in addition to safeguards become a justified tool. Moreover, unexpected circumstances may lead to the costs of fulfilling a promised investment exceeding the value that a party initially expected to derive from the treaty.[33]

5.4 Deconstructing the Morocco–Nigeria Bilateral Investment Treaty: A Critical Perspective

The Morocco–Nigeria BIT provides substantive and procedural protections to foreign investors while also imposing obligations on them, such as conducting environmental and social impact assessments, adhering to international corporate governance and social responsibility standards, protecting human rights and labour, and applying the precautionary principle. The clause on fund transfers is notable for addressing balance of payments difficulties, marking a departure from older Nigerian BITs.[34]

The Morocco–Nigeria BIT is acknowledged for its ingenuity and significant textual differences compared to traditional Nigerian treaties. However, it could be argued that the treaty was primarily introduced by the Kingdom of Morocco, as evidenced by its ratification by Morocco on 30 August 2017, while Nigeria has yet to ratify it. Given that Nigeria has not moved swiftly to ratify the treaty since its signing, it may be reasonable to conclude that the much-praised innovation did not originate from the Nigerian government. Furthermore, this is the only treaty Nigeria has signed that reflects a notable shift towards balancing the interests of the State with those of foreign investors. Additionally, the "model BIT" has served

31 Camille Martini, 'Avoiding the Planned Obsolescence of Modern International Investment Agreements: Can General Exception Mechanisms be Improved, and How?' (2018) 59(8) *Boston College Law Review*, 2881.

32 India has a new (2015) model BIT. The BIT is almost four times longer than most of its existing BITs. The length is said to provide greater precision of the investment protections provided. It also creates a very complex framework that defines exceptions to key terms which may result in inconsistent interpretations and unintended consequences. Grant Hanessian & Kabi Duggal, 'The 2015 Indian Model BIT: Is this Change the World Wishes to See?' (2015) 30(3) *ICSID Review*, 730.

33 Anne van Aaken, 'Perils of Success? The Case of International Investment Protection' (2008) 9(1) *European Business Organization Law Review*, 12.

34 Rethinking the Promotion and Protection of Foreign Investments: The 2015 South Africa's Protection Investment Act, p.3. By Tarcisio Gazzini. Available on https://papers.ssrn.com/sol3/papers.cfm?abstract_id=2960567 [Accessed on 4 December 2024].

as the template Morocco used to conclude investment agreements with Mali, Guinea-Bissau, Rwanda, and Ethiopia, reinforcing the view that this may indeed be Morocco's model BIT.[35] Nonetheless, the treaty's new provisions aim to balance the interests of foreign investors and contracting States, responding to criticisms of the investment regime. While these innovative clauses are important for protecting host State sovereignty, there are concerns that they could enable protectionist measures or limit regulatory flexibility for public policy. The clause on the transfer of funds presents several theoretical and interpretative challenges, as it is not free from the complexities often associated with treaty drafting.

Although these innovative clauses are recognised as crucial for protecting host States' sovereignty, there are concerns that they may empower host States to adopt protectionist measures or fail to provide the necessary regulatory flexibility for managing public policy. The fact that arbitral tribunals often acknowledge and incorporate the "host State's right to regulate" when interpreting traditional protection standards could render these clauses redundant and ineffective,[36] creating uncertainty in investment disputes. It is argued that the innovative features, while ambitious, lack the clarity needed to guide tribunals effectively. The deficiencies are discussed further below, with proposed solutions to be explored in the next chapter.

5.4.1 Prospects and Pitfalls: The Unruly Public Policy Horse

The overarching theme of the newly modelled BIT is "sustainable development", a phrase that appears three times in the preamble and is referenced numerous times throughout the operative provisions. Article 24 on Corporate Social Responsibility stipulates that "investors make the maximum feasible contribution to the host State and local community".[37] The definition of "investment" in the treaty is qualified to include a condition that the investment contributes to the host State's sustainable development. This means that the host State has the capacity to raise objections regarding sustainable development in any dispute, even at the jurisdictional stage. The treaty further reaffirms the right of a State to regulate in line with sustainability. It provides that a host State has "the right to take regulatory or other measures to ensure that development in its territory is consistent with the goals and principles of sustainable developments and with other legitimate social and

35 Investment Policy Hub. Available on https://investmentpolicy.unctad.org [Accessed on 4 December 2024].

36 Camille Martini, 'Avoiding the Planned Obsolescence of Modern International Investment Agreements: Can General Exception Mechanisms be Improved, and How?' 2018 59(8) *Boston College Law Review*, 2883.

37 The Morocco–Nigeria BIT. Available on https://investmentpolicy.unctad.org/international-investment-agreements/treaties/otheriia/3711/morocco---nigeria-bit-2016- [Accessed on 5 December 2024].

economic objectives".[38] This provision is quite commendable and is a re-affirmation of the policy objectives advanced by the United Nations Conference on Trade and Development (UNCTAD).[39]

The right to repatriate capital and transfer profits clarifies that treaty obligations do not extend to actions that fall within the scope of its exceptions. Legally, these exceptions can be characterised either as limitations on the scope of investment protection provided by the treaty or as affirmative defences that justify actions that would otherwise be prohibited by the treaty.[40] The BIT seeks to accommodate legitimate and democratic policymaking, recognising that FDI cannot be entirely separated from public policy considerations. This approach is well-founded, as the integration of public policies into investment regulation is essential; elements of public policy significantly influence how treaty texts are drafted and interpreted. The prioritisation of public policy over market forces is evident in treaty clauses, such as non-precluded measures and exceptions to general guarantees, which allow a contracting State to implement protective measures for sovereign interests and public policy, even when these measures conflict with other core treaty obligations. Public policy is further reflected in treaty language, such as "in accordance with the laws", in the definition of "investment", and in various other sections of investment treaties.[41] Thus the autonomy a foreign investor enjoys is an important public policy concern.

In contextualising public policy issues, Article 11 of the Morocco–Nigeria BIT allows for free transfer of funds, while Article 12 provides for exceptions to the general rule. Article 12, regarded as a temporary safeguard measure, provides that: a party may implement restrictions on payments or transfers related to investments in cases of serious balance of payments issues or to safeguard its financial system. Such restrictions are recognised as necessary during economic development to maintain adequate financial reserves. These restrictions are required to be confined to what is necessary for the specific circumstances, temporary, and phased out gradually as conditions improve. They must be applied in a non-discriminatory manner, ensuring equal treatment for the other party in comparison to non-parties. Additionally, any restrictions or modifications must be communicated to the other party without delay, and consultations should be conducted to review the measures implemented.[42]

38 The Morocco-Nigeria BIT: a new breed of investment treaty? By Thomas Reuters. Available on http://arbitrationblog.practicallaw.com/the-morocco-nigeria-bit-a-new-breed-of-investment-treaty/ [Accessed on 5 December 2024].

39 Investment Policy Framework on Sustainable Development. By UNCTAD. Available on https://unctad.org/en/PublicationsLibrary/diaepcb2015d5_en.pdf [Accessed on 5 December 2024].

40 Caroline Henckels, 'Should Investment Treaties Contain Public Policy Exceptions?' (2018) 59(8) *Boston College Law Review*, 2825.

41 Nartnirum Junngam, 'Public Policy in International Investment Law: The Confluence of the Three Unruly Horses' (2016) 51(1) *Texas International Law Journal*, 91–92.

42 Morocco–Nigeria BIT (2016) Available on https://investmentpolicyhub.unctad.org/IIA/State/153/treaty/3711 [Accessed on 5 December 2024]

The Nigeria–Morocco BIT stipulates those measures must serve the public interest, benefit, or purpose.[43] The preamble reaffirms "the right of a State to regulate and to introduce new measures relating to investments in their territories in order to meet national policy".[44]This preamble gives validity to the exception enunciated in Article 12. It gives a meaning and context for the justification of whatever measures that may be taken under the article. Academic writers largely concur on the need for the legality of this requirement though they don't seem to see it as so much of a big task for States. This is because the requirement of public policy for an action to be lawful is not much of a limitation in modern times.[45] It is very easy for States to couch an action in terms of public purpose; and investment tribunals have been reluctant to second guess the sovereign determination of public purpose. This could perhaps be attributable to the concept of public purpose being very broad and not subject to effective re-examination by other States.[46]

These provisions are noteworthy for their emphasis on preserving a State's regulatory rights. However, while Article 12 outlines protective measures for a State's sovereign and public policy rights, the specifics of what constitutes public policy remain ambiguous. Even if the treaty parties had a mutual understanding of the concept during the drafting process, the vagueness and generality of the terms could lead to their misuse, potentially allowing the host State to invoke public policy abusively.[47] Although there is a broad consensus on the concept of public policy, stakeholders in international investment law often hold conflicting views on its applicability and the specific categories of public policy that should be recognised.[48]

The conceptualisation of Article 12 reflects an ongoing debate about a host State's right to regulate. However, the Article remains vague regarding which measures are deemed legitimate in response to economic crises.[49] This ambiguity may hinder tribunals in determining how to balance competing interests and assess the extent to which the host State's actions should be scrutinised. For instance, the phrasing of exceptions related to "serious balance of payments and external financial difficulties, or threats thereof" lacks clarity. It is uncertain what situations would qualify as balance of payments difficulties[50] and how much regulation is necessary to protect the economy. The exceptions fail to provide clear criteria for navigating the complex relationship between legitimate State actions and foreign

43 *ibid.*

44 *ibid.*

45 August Reinisch, 'Legality of Expropriations' in August Reinisch (ed), *Standards of Investment Protection* (Oxford University Press 2009) 179.

46 *ibid.*

47 Nartnirum Junngam, 'Public Policy in International Investment Law: The Confluence of the Three Unruly Horses' (2016) 51(1) *Texas International Law Journal*, 92.

48 *ibid* 55.

49 Aikaterini Titi, *The Right to Regulate in International Investment Law* (Normos Verlagsgesellschaft 2015) 55.

50 Okechukwu Ejims, 'The 2016 Morocco–Nigeria Bilateral Investment Treaty: More Practical Reality in Providing a Balanced Investment. Treaty' (2019) 34(1) *ICSID Review*, 75.

investor expectations, potentially undermining the very purpose for which these provisions were established.

While there seems to be a consensus that the term "public policy" aims to promote a State's economic interests, political objectives, and essential social agendas, its precise definition remains elusive. As it stands, "policy space" is vague and often subject to politicisation The content of BITs needs to be accompanied by a *clarification of key concepts*, interrelationships, and investor's responsibilities.[51] Article 12 does not offer much clarity and transparency as to the nature of its commitment; and the importance of clarity cannot be overstated. Since lawmakers and treaty negotiators cannot anticipate every situation or address them comprehensively, the variability, subjectivity, and unpredictability inherent in public policy raise a crucial question: what precisely defines public policy?

The famous quote from Burroughs J, in *Richardson v Mellish*, best elucidates the problems inherent in determining public policy:

> Public Policy—it is an unruly horse, and when once you get astride it, you will never know where it will carry you. It may lead you from the sound law. It is never argued at all but when other points fail.[52]

The fluidity of public policy makes it necessary to define parameters one must consider in legitimising States actions.

Capital control, when referenced in the context of Article 12, can create a policy dilemma and result in contentious outcomes. This is underpinned from two theoretical approaches; first is that a government has two essential interests: the desire to maintain State autonomy and the desire to retain its constituents' interests. The first interest leads the government to prefer the maintenance of capital controls to liberalisation—the use of policy autonomy to reduce the risk of currency and financial crisis—while the latter leads governments to satisfy the dictates of their constituents, which is the operation of a liberalised economy, one that does not require capital controls. These two interests, though complementary, are often in conflict, presenting a policy dilemma for the State that may desire to rein in their economic problems.[53] The global financial crisis has shown that we live in a world where the financial markets are susceptible to herding, panics, and contagion, and capital controls will always feature as a desirable mechanism because economic crisis can have negative effects on a domestic economy.[54]

51 The Evolving International Investment Law and Policy Regime by Karl P. Sauvant, p.7. Available on http://www3.weforum.org/docs/E15/WEF_Investment_Law_Policy_regime_report_2015_1501.pdf [Accessed on 6 December 2024].

52 Florentine Sneij, 'Are IIAs old-fashioned? How Consistency in the Use of Public Policy Fosters the Object and Purpose of Investment Agreements' (2016) 21(2–3) *Uniform Law Review*, 203.

53 Quan Li & Dale L. Smith, 'The Dilemma of Financial Liberalization: State Autonomy and Societal Demands' (2002) 65(3) *The Journal of Politics*, 765.

54 Andrew Yianni & Carlos de Vera, 'The Return of Capital Controls' (2010) 73(1) *Modern Legal History of Sovereign Debt*, 359.

Capital controls when employed to excercise policy autonomy in crisis moments risk being abused. Exchange controls are distortionary, and there is likelihood that there would be special, if not discriminatory, arrangements for different people to agree to special concessions. In some cases, it can become a source of corruption: because it is discretionary, there is no way to monitor its application. Some economists believe that, when an exchange control period is extended for a long period, it works badly.[55] Article 12 (1) of the Morocco–Nigeria BIT does not specify the restrictions that are necessary in balance of payment difficulties. It mentions "the use of restrictions to ensure the maintenance of a level of financial reserves adequate for the implementation of its programme of economic development". It does not specify whether limitations of current payments, limitations of capital transfers, currency redenomination, or prudential measures to stabilise the financial sector or intermediaries will apply as a measure. Restrictions can take many forms, and if a desired form is not explicitly specified for addressing economic anomalies, it may be susceptible to abuse by any contracting party. Additionally, an investment arbitral tribunal may have the discretion to make a determination that does not accurately reflect the original intent of the parties at the time of contracting. This is amidst the growing concern that some developing countries may attempt to manipulate their exchange rate to benefit the domestic exporting sector.[56]

Furthermore, economic measures aimed at enhancing the stability of financial services, or fiscal policies designed to increase public spending in strategic industries while favouring domestic institutions as the primary recipients of capital injections, may inadvertently create a distinction that disadvantages foreign investors both in practice and under the law. . These measures could be poorly designed and potentially violate the Fair and Equitable Treatment (FET) provision, allowing foreign investors to raise concerns about discrimination. Other standards of treaty protections, such as the prohibition of indirect expropriation and national treatment, could be contended.[57] A BIT establishes the principle of national treatment for foreign investors, which is assessed in the context of non-discrimination. Non-discrimination is a recognised standard of protection in international law. In the investment context, discrimination occurs when investors or investments in similar situations are treated differently without a valid reason. The non-discrimination standard does not require uniform treatment but does demand that any differential treatment be justified by reasonable grounds. Essentially, the main restriction is that foreign investors cannot be discriminated against based on race or nationality.[58] Article 12 when operative could become contentious since non-discrimination attempts to neutralise the protectionist tendency of States to protect domestic

55 *ibid.*

56 Adam Feibelman, 'The IMF and Regulation of Cross-border Capital Flows' (2015) 15(2) *Chicago Journal of International Law*, 424.

57 Giorgio Sacerdoti 'BIT Protections and Economic Crises: Limits to Their Coverage, the Impact of Multilateral Financial Regulation and the Defence of Necessity' (2013) 28(2) *ICSID Review*, 359.

58 Bogdan Biris, 'Investor Protection and Bilateral Investment Treaties: An Overview of the Main Provision' (2015) 5(1) *Perspectives of Business Law Journal*, 210.

investors' producers from competition. Its analysis often requires identifying the appropriate comparator against which to measure any alleged less favourable treatment. If the claimant (in this case likely to be foreign investor), is not "in like circumstances" with the more favourably treated entity, then the claim of national treatment will fail.[59] Foreign investors who operate in the same economic ecosystem with domestic investors and who now find themselves at the receiving end, as they are the ones likely to repatriate their capital or profits to their home States, may feel discriminated against.

Therefore, policy measures, even if they do not violate the provisions of Article 11 and 12 on transfer of funds, may attract a liability under other investment treaty commitments, on the basis that these other guarantees proscribe discriminatory conduct by signatory States. Due to the absence of certainty on the scope of "fair and equitable treatment" in arbitral jurisprudence,[60] care must be taken in the drafting of a transfer of funds clause. Also, the fact that a measure is temporary and triggers loss but is then removed does not erase legal liability. What is most important is that a foreign investor suffered loss in the economic value of his investment or assets, albeit in a discriminatory fashion. The obligation to accord national treatment will cover instances of both de jure (in law) and de facto (in fact) discrimination.[61] The latter covers measures that may not be distinguishable on the basis of nationality but pose a greater adverse risk to the foreign investors in the host State.[62] Ultimately, the question of breach may require whether there is evidence of malign governmental purpose, particularly in cases of de facto discrimination.

There are cases that have explored whether differentiation between the foreign investors and the States are justifiable based on legitimate policy grounds or impermissible because they confer special protection to domestic actors. For example, economic measures employed by the Czech Republic to cushion the domestic financial crisis in the late 1990s were ruled to be in breach of its investment treaty obligations.[63] Since national treatment rests on the legitimacy of State's conduct, there is a conundrum on when, how, or who should demonstrate this legitimacy. Little guidance is left for tribunals to weigh competing State and foreign investor's interests and to what extent the State's interests should be scrutinised.[64] In the context of the Argentine financial crisis, arbitral tribunals have addressed a State's essential security interests, highlighting the need for precise wording in treaties.[65]

59 August Reinisch, *Standards of Investment Protection* (Oxford University of Press 2009) 30.

60 Jean Kalicki & Suzana Medeiros, 'Fair, Equitable and Ambiguous: What is Fair and Equitable Treatment in International Investment Law?' (2007) 22(1) *ICSID Review*, 24–25.

61 Anne Van Aaken & Jurgen Kurtz, 'Will State Emergency Measures Trigger International Investment Disputes' (2009) 1(3) *Transnational Corporations Review*, 13.

62 *ibid.*

63 *ibid* 14.

64 Alison Giest, 'Interpreting Public Interest Provisions in International Investment Treaties' (2017) 18(1) *Chicago Journal of International Law*, 336.

65 William W. Burke-White, 'The Argentine Financial Crisis: State Liability under BITs and the Legitimacy of the ICSID System' (2008) 3(1) *Asian Journal of WTO and International Health Law and Policy*, 200–201.

This raises the question of whether the measures implemented during the crisis can be justified by the circumstances at the time. Ultimately, this illustrates that exceptions to a host State's conduct in cases of liability for breaches of fair and equitable treatment may be self-judging. In instances where they are not, many treaties provide for a role for investment arbitral adjudicators in applying such exceptions.

5.4.2 Duration of Capital Controls

Article 12 (2) provides no specific period in which exchange controls should work. The times for which the restrictions are supposed to lapse are not clear cut. Article 12(1) states the circumstances that may necessitate temporary safeguards while paragraph (2) merely states that restrictions should not exceed those necessary to deal with the circumstances described in the paragraph and that the restrictions should be temporary and phased out progressively as the situation specified in paragraph 1 improves. The open-ended timeline for the application of exchange control works to enable abuse and unconscionable conducts that may affect the viability of foreign investments. For it is not ordinary that the IMF Fund Agreement permits the use of capital controls when necessary and only for a very limited time because the restrictions are derogations.[66] The 2005 French Model BIT, for example, contains both a funds-transfer clause and a balance of payment safeguards. It does not guarantee free convertibility at market exchange rates. The model treaty not only provides for quite a number of items that are guaranteed, but it also goes further to specify that:

> [w]hen, in exceptional circumstances, capital movements from or to third countries cause or threaten to cause a serious disequilibrium to its balance of payment problems, each Contracting Party may temporarily apply safeguard measures to the transfers, provided that these measures shall be strictly necessary, would be imposed in an equitable, non-discriminatory and in good faith basis and shall not exceed in any case *a six months period*[67]

It may be essential to establish a time frame for the application of policy measures to prevent potential arbitrary actions by host States that could undermine the interests of foreign investors.

5.4.3 Margin of Appreciation

The extent to which a contracting party should bear the risks associated with measures taken to address an economic crisis remains unclear. This is particularly relevant when a State's governance has contributed to the crisis. Additionally, it

66 Anne van Aaken, 'Perils of Success? The Case of International Investment Protection' (2008) 9(1) *European Business Organization Law Review*, 18.

67 Andrew Yianni & Carlos de Vera, 'The Return of Capital Controls' (2010) 73(1) *Modern Legal History of Sovereign Debt*, 365.

raises the question of whether the appropriateness of restrictions, as assessed by relevant authorities, should be self-judging or subjected to international scrutiny by supranational authorities and treaties, such as the Articles of Agreement of the IMF, GATT, and the GATT rules. The Morocco–Nigeria BIT does not clarify the issue of when a host State has negligently contributed to an economic crisis due to poor governance, particularly when such negligence undermines the practicality of Article 11 and restricts the foreign investor's rights or significantly diminishes their economic interests. In this context, should the defence measures outlined in Article 12 still be applicable?

The case of *Vincent v. Lake Eric Transportation*[68] exemplifies the loss of a privilege to act out of necessity because of a defendant's imprudence. This case involves a boat owner, the defendant, who secured a boat to a dock owned by the plaintiff during a severe storm instead of taking out the boat and its crew. The plaintiff's property was damaged because the boat was secured to its property during the storm. The plaintiff sued and recovered damages.[69] This case embodies the principle that a defendant who acts out of necessity must pay for the harm suffered by the plaintiff because of his actions. It eliminates inefficiencies that could arise if the defendant caused damage(s) with impunity. It forces the defendant to internalise the costs and benefits of his decisions or actions. This legal rule may require the loss of the privilege to act out a necessity if one's own negligence contributes to the condition of necessity.[70]

Although this legal principle originates from tort law, it can still be applied to international investment law, as economic crises and balance of payments issues can arise, often resulting in comparable circumstances, even if they are not explicitly defined as such. Exigent circumstances may suspend or eliminate the fulfilment of treaty obligations, or they may allow for the derogation of a State's commitments under treaties or customary international law. In the Morocco–Nigeria BIT, the circumstances that allow for exceptions to the general right to transfer funds are clearly outlined. However, drawing from the Vincent case, one might question whether Article 12 of the treaty should be rendered inoperative if the host State acted imprudently in creating the "exigent circumstances". Should the foreign investor-plaintiff bear the consequences of such imprudence? This issue is particularly relevant in light of the *Sempra Energy International v. Argentine Republic* case. The ICSID tribunal in applying customary international law found that Argentina had not acted out of "necessity", not only because the measures undertaken were not the only available ones to it, but because they had also contributed to creating the situation that led to the alleged state of necessity. Even though this decision was later annulled, the annulment was only based on the technicalities of law, the conflation of both the customary international law and the articles

68 Vincent v. Lake Erie Transp. Co., 109 Minn. 456, 124 N.W. 221.
69 Alan O. Sykes, 'Economic "Necessity" in International Law' (2015) 109 *The American Journal of International Law*, 298.
70 *ibid* 291.

of the Argentine BIT.[71] Thus the structure of a treaty and its provisions have great implication for the allocation of burden of proof between the parties to the treaty—the claimant, the respondent—and for regulatory autonomy, particularly in cases that involve complex economic transactions and analysis. Hence ambiguous, or insufficient, evidence can lead to a ruling against the party who bears the burden of proof.[72]

It is also important to consider how the provision on the freedom to transfer funds should interact with relevant provisions of the IMF Articles of Agreement and whether the two norms should be applied concurrently. Simply put, how should a conflict between the two rules be resolved? This is an often-considered point in international law.[73] Answering such questions is not just important for theoretical purpose, but also for practical reasons. This issue was raised in the Iran-United States claims tribunals for acts which occurred in 1979.[74] Foreign investors had challenged the measures taken during the economic crisis which adversely affected them. Although the claims were based on the BITs between the host State and the home State, the respondents relied on it, amongst other rules such as the IMF Fund Agreement.[75]

Even when a BIT's capital transfer provision explicitly mandates that host State measures align "consistently" with the IMF Fund Agreement, determining the meaning of "consistency" can be problematic. Should the arbitral tribunal defer to the IMF, making the Fund's opinions dispositive in such cases? In other words, should the Fund's assessments be considered final? Addressing these questions is crucial, as similar issues have arisen in GATT cases involving private parties and the consistency of various exchange restrictions with the Fund Agreement.[76] While Article 12 does not directly address these concerns, it is essential to discuss them due to the potential for future occurrences.

The reason why international norms are examined is because violations of international obligations are often considered under State responsibility in international law. The customary rules on State responsibility to aliens contemplate weighing the respective interests of sovereigns and investors as part of determining whether a substantive guarantee has been breached.[77] The State can assert its

71 Sempra Energy International v. Argentine Republic: ICSID Case No. ARB/02/16; Bart M. J. Szewczyk, 'Sempra Energy International v. Argentine Republic' (2011) 105(3) *The American Journal of International Law*, 558.

72 Bradly J. Condon, 'Treaty Structure and Public Interest Regulation in International Economic Law' (2015) 17(2) *Journal of International Economic Law*, 336.

73 Abba Kolo, 'Transfer of Funds: The Interaction between the IMF Articles of Agreement and Modern Investment Treaties: A Comparative Law Perspective' in Stephan Schill (ed), *International Investment Law and Comparative Public Law* (Oxford University Press 2010) 356.

74 John R. Crooks, 'Applicable Law in International Arbitration: The Iran-US Claims Tribunal Experience' (1983) 83(2) *The American Journal of International Law*, 279–280.

75 *ibid* 308.

76 *ibid*.

77 Suzanne A. Spears, 'The Quest for Policy Space in a New Generation of International Investment Agreements' (2010) 13(5) *Journal of International Economic Law*, 1056.

regulatory power to justify a conduct if recourse to the interpretation of a treaty fails in its favour. It may resort to an independent first order defence (for example, "necessity" as a circumstance precluding wrongfulness under Article 25 of State Responsibility) or the notion of regulatory freedom as an independent customary norm of international law. These defences could work either way, by eroding culpability of States or substantially mitigating the ultimate value of compensation that a State may pay for incurring liability through the International Investment Agreement breach.[78] Consequently, the repercussions of State violations are typically assessed in line with the International Law Commission's Articles on the Responsibility of States for Internationally Wrongful Acts, commonly referred to as the ILC Articles. Article 31 of the Articles stipulates that States that breach international obligations must provide reparations for any harm caused.[79]

Whether as a result of a desire to respond to or prevent crises, the imposition of capital control raises, amongst BITs, a host of other international considerations such as the International Monetary Fund (IMF) Articles of Agreement[80] and the World Trade Organisation (WTO) General Agreement on Trade in Services (GATS) and Annex on Financial Services.[81] The relation can be viewed in terms of BITs representing *lex specialis*, or, better still, those agreements being the framework in which BITs operate requiring systematic interpretation to coordinate them.[82] Article 31(3) (c) of the Vienna Convention on the Law of Treaties (VCLT) allows for consideration of other international treaties that are concluded by contracting parties.

Thus in considering the IMF Articles of Agreement, which the Nigerian government is signatory to, Article VIII 2(b) provides that:

> Exchange contracts which involve the currency of any member, and which are contrary to the exchange control regulations of that member maintained

78 Diane A. Desierto, 'Public Policy in International Investment and Trade Law: Community Expectations and Functional Decision Making' (2015) 26 *Florida Journal of International Law*, 125.

79 Irngard Marboe, 'State Responsibility and Comparative State Liability for Administrative and Legislative Harm to Economic Interests' in Stephan Schill (ed), *International Investment Law and Comparative Public Law* (Oxford University Press 2010) 378.

80 Yianni & Vera, (n 67) 360. It is essential to highlight that the discussion of the IMF Articles is significant because BITs do not exist in isolation; they interact with other international norms, particularly when arbitral tribunals face the challenge of interpreting treaty provisions. The interplay between BITs and other international frameworks can shape their application and influence decision-making. Moreover, both Morocco and Nigeria are signatories to the IMF. Nigeria became a member on 30 March 1961, while Morocco joined on 25 April 1958. As members of the IMF, both countries are legally bound by the Fund's regulations and obligations, which must be taken into consideration when analysing their BIT commitments and resolving disputes. IMF Fund Agreement. Available on https://www.imf.org/en/Countries [Accessed on 10 December 2024].

81 Giorgio Sacerdoti, 'BIT Protections and Economic Crises: Limits to Their Coverage, the Impact of Multilateral Financial Regulation and the Defence of Necessity' (2013) 28(2) *ICSID Review*, 351.

82 *ibid.*

or imposed consistently with this agreement shall be unenforceable in the territories of any member[83]

This suggests that States possess the inalienable right to set terms regarding the use of their currency. However, if an IMF Member State enters into an agreement that contradicts the exchange control regulations of the IMF, then they will be unenforceable in such State.[84] The IMF Articles of Agreement is considered in this context because it is a multilateral treaty whose rules on capital and exchange controls in their historic and political context show that they are located at the intersection of international trade, investment, and monetary law.[85]

IMF clauses are relevant in this instance because they provide regulations on the right to transfer of funds within a definite period. The IMF Articles of Agreement recognises exchange control in three parts, namely Article VI (3), Article VIII (2) (a), and Article XIV. An ideal BIT should combine the expectations and commitments of the IMF with the unique characteristics of a State.

Conflicting rights and obligations under the IMF Articles and BITs are a real possibility; because the investment related transfers listed in and permitted under BIT provisions include both current transactions and capital movements. Disinvestments, bond issues, and debentures are capital transactions; while profits, interest, dividends and other returns, royalty payments, and management of other fees are current transactions.[86] Under IMF Article VIII 2(a), IMF members are prohibited from imposing restrictions on the making of payments and transfers for current international transactions without the approval of the Fund. The transfer provision of Nigerian BITs thereby raises many concerns in this regard.

The provisions in Article VIII of the IMF Articles ban restrictions on current transactions except with the approval of the IMF Fund, and unless the Member State chooses to resort to the transitional arrangements of Article XIV (2). In this instance, temporary and non-discriminatory exchange restrictions may be authorised by the Fund for balance of payment problems. With respect to capital transactions, under Article VI (3), IMF Members are free to make regulations as they deem fit, in so far as they do not restrict payment for current transactions.[87] Therefore any restriction on the making of payments and transfer for current international transactions not approved by the Fund Article VIII 2(a) or being maintained under the transitional provisions of Article XIV of the IMF Agreement constitutes a breach of the IMF Agreement. In general, the Fund Agreement recognises the need to impose capital controls as important mechanisms to fight against economic crises;

83 Bamford Colin, *Principles of International Financial Law* (2nd edn, Oxford University Press 2015) 55.
84 *ibid.*
85 Claus D. Zimmermann, 'The Promotion of Transfer-of-Funds Liberalisation across International Economic Law' (2011) 12(5) *The Journal of World Investment & Trade*, 725.
86 Anna De Luca, 'Transfer Provisions of BITs in Times of Financial Crisis' (2014) 23(1) *The Italian Yearbook of International Online*, 125.
87 *ibid.*

however, incompatibility mainly exists between the IMF Agreement and most bilateral agreements in this regard, as the IMF Agreement usually permit the imposition of transfer restrictions in a temporary and non-discriminatory manner for balance of payment reasons in the case of current transactions. Nonetheless, any incompatibility with the IMF Fund Agreement and a bilateral agreement cannot form a valid basis for a cause of action in any international or domestic court, but the inconsistency with the IMF Agreement (or any other regional agreement) does not seem desirable.[88]

5.5 Conclusion

This chapter has focused on the Morocco–Nigeria BIT, highlighting claims that its innovative elements strike a balance between the need for investment protection and the importance of preserving the State's legitimate public policy space. It appears to respond to the backlash against the investment regime, marking a significant departure from the drafting patterns of traditional BITs, which are often viewed as limiting host States' regulatory powers. In this BIT, contracting States are granted considerable latitude to deviate from substantial obligations to prioritise policy objectives.

However, the treaty requires further introspection and review, as it has not sufficiently reconciled itself with other conflicting international obligations. Additionally, the provisions related to the transfer of funds lack clear guidelines for arbitral review. This analysis is framed within the context of a "grand bargain"—the understanding that wealth maximisation through private foreign direct investment is the primary purpose of foreign investment protection. Given that the goal of contemporary international investment law is to promote economic development through FDI by enhancing the security of such investments, there is a need for a flexible interpretation of treaty texts that serves the common interests of both parties to a BIT. It is crucial that States evaluate and, if necessary, reconsider BITs that weaken their regulatory authority. Without such action, contracting States may face challenges in enacting legitimate regulatory measures designed to promote the public interest, as the corporate advantages afforded to foreign entities could be undermined. In the following chapter, we will examine how to strike a fair balance that protects the interests of both host States and foreign investors.

88 Qiao Liu, 'Transfer of Funds in China-US BIT Negotiations: Comparing the Articles of Agreement of the IMF' (2012) 11(1) *Journal of International Trade Law and Policy*, 7.

6 Balancing Competing Interests in Treaty Rights' Application and Interpretation

6.1 Introduction

First, it is easy to identify that, possibly, the diminution of State sovereignty could arise from the commitments made by States which sometimes overreach any of the contracting parties legitimate expectation.[1] Secondly, there is the expansive interpretation of foreign investors' protections by tribunals,[2] which are often unanticipated and inconsistent, having its root from investment treaty claims against public policy measures.[3] These reveal problems in a BIT's architecture, as most BITs show a discord between preserving sovereignty and attracting foreign investments, as well as concerns over the scope of treaty obligations.[4] Given the impact of the COVID-19 pandemic and other world events such as the wars in Ukraine and Palestine, consequent regulatory actions may have adverse effects on foreign direct investment. Regulatory actions such as economic rescue packages and deposit guarantees for local investors, but not foreign businesses, could lead to foreign investor claims against States for actions taken to protect national economies.[5]

Jurisprudence on investment law is discordant because it is largely built by reference to academic opinions and other tribunal awards.[6] This disconnect alienates treaty parties from the interpretative process, which increases prospects for dissonance between States and tribunals[7] That several States are terminating their BITs and even renouncing the International Centre for Settlement of Dispute Resolution (ICSID) is a testament to the bifurcation of the legitimacy crisis in the investment

1 Bernard Hanotiau, 'Are Bilateral Investment Treaties and Free Trade Drafted with Sufficient Clarity to Give Guidance to Tribunals' (2016) 5(3) *American University Businesses Law*, 314.

2 Asha Kaushal, 'Revisiting History: How the Past Matters for the Present Backlash Against Foreign Investment Regime' (2009) 50(2) *Harvard International Law Journal*, 492.

3 Andrew D. Mitchell & James Munro, 'Someone Else's Deal: Interpreting International Investment Agreements in the Light of Third-Party Agreements' (2017) 28(3) *The European Journal of International Law*, 669–670.

4 Kaushal (n 2) 495.

5 Therese Wilson, Yuri Banens & Shanayah Sharif, 'ISDS and States' Ability to Deal with Financial Crisis' 2023 40(3) *Journal of International Arbitration*, 247.

6 Anthea Roberts, 'Power and Persuasion in Investment Treaty Interpretation: The Dual Role of States' (2010) 104(2) *American Journal of International Law*, 179.

7 *ibid.*

DOI: 10.4324/9781003611714-6

ecosphere. A perception of bias will work against the system as stakeholders may feel the need to abandon the system if they feel prejudiced by it.[8] If a BIT omits important public policy considerations or forseeable circumstances, an investment tribunal will play a part in its interpretation or cure the lacuna in the law.[9] Arbitrators in cases of dispute may be left with the task of harmonising and administering a cacophony of details. Where investment arbitration becomes operative due to government actions from an economic policy perspective, different lines of enquiry emerge. It is however important to note that the mere existence of economic crises does not impact a host State's liability in international investment arbitration, save for where such a host State, in reaction to an economic crisis, implements regulatory measures that interfere adversely with a foreign investor's rights.[10] The likelihood that international investment disputes could emanate from linked actions between economic crises and governmental interventions in the market process which are desirable if considered from a socialist welfare perspective[11] makes a call for holistic investment regime reappraisal.

When a State fails to clarify treaty texts, they risk having the treaty interpreted in favour of foreign investors and at the expense of the host State. This practice is not unusual due to the precedence of public welfare disregard in the language of investment treaties.[12] This situation is further exacerbated by the ongoing unpredictability of standard concepts in investment law, as arbitral decisions often endorse a broad *ex post facto* approach characterised by a subjective, "I will know it when I see it". In practice, however, tribunals have not consistently demonstrated that they truly "know it". [13] There is also considerable concern that investment tribunals frequently craft vague standards of international investment regime in the limited context of investment claims and without engagement with other bodies of international law. Investment tribunals in this regard are perceived as a threat to the effectiveness of other international legal regimes.

Thus a careful approach to treaty adoption is necessary because a State's conduct can have serious economic implications and legal consequences on foreign investments within jurisdictions.[14] Emergency measures taken to protect the economy

8 Giovanni Zarra, 'The Issue of Incoherence in Investment Arbitration: Is there Need for a Systemic Reform' (2018) 17(1) *The Chinese Journal of International Law*, 141–142.

9 Robert D. Sloane, 'On the Use and Abuse of Necessity in the Law of State Responsibility' (2012) 106(3) *American Journal of International Law*, 557.

10 Christian Bellak & Markus Leibrecht, 'Do Economic Crises Trigger Treaty-Based Investor-State Arbitration Disputes' (2021) 24 Journal of International Economic Law, 129.

11 *ibid.*

12 Alison Giest, 'Interpreting Public Interest Provisions in International Investment Treaties' (2017) 18(1) *Chicago Journal of International Law*, 331.

13 Benedict Kingsbury & Stephen Schill, 'Public Law Concepts to Balance Investors' Rights with State Regulatory Actions in the Public Interest: The Concept of Proportionality' in Schill S. (ed), *International Investment and Comparative Law* (Oxford University Press 2010) 76.

14 Susan D. Franck, 'Considering Recalibration of International Investment Agreements: Empirical Insights' in Jose E. Alvarez & Karl P. Sauvant (eds), *The Evolving International Investment Regime: Expectations, Realities, Options* (Oxford University Press 2011) 73.

may well be adjudged against a host State and may require such State to incur a cost for an otherwise permissible conduct, if only a BIT had been carefully drafted.[15] Obviating this would require a reform of existing model BITs, a redefinition of treaty standards, and the introduction of appropriate exceptions that preserve a policy space and protect public interest, which could be helpful in finding a balance between investment and non-investment concerns. As rightly stated by the South African ambassador to the World Trade Organisation in Geneva: "rebalancing the relationship between investor protection and government's right to regulate in the public interest has moved to the centre of the debate on the future of international investment agreements".[16]

This chapter suggests mechanisms for interpreting treaties, regarding the right to repatriate capital and transfer profits, aimed at effectively addressing the challenges and impacts of globalisation while balancing the competing interests of the contracting parties. This will be achieved by providing a theoretical framework that aims to harmonise existing techniques on treaty interpretation and general principles of international law, with emphasis on the symbiotic relationship that ought to exist in treaty negotiations and ratification in the first place. It prescribes hard exceptions for public policy goals which signal that negotiators have grappled with multiple concerns and competing objectives. By nudging adjudicatory choices, this sort of flexibility extends assurances to States that public regulation, properly tailored and implemented, will not trigger State responsibility under the treaty regime at issue.[17] Striking a sustainable balance between investment liberalisation and protection and a set of defined public values through exceptions will go a long way in shoring up weakening stakeholders' confidence in the investment regime. These value propositions are based on the premise that balancing foreign investors' rights and States' rights can be resolved within a BIT framework and that a recalibration of substantive texts is therefore imperative. It considers how the recalibrated texts should be interpreted and the guidance for arbitral tribunals when reviewing a host State's conduct. Furthermore, UNCTAD expressly encourages States, as contracting parties to BITs, to be more proactive in asserting their interpretative authority to guide tribunals towards a proper and predictable reading of investment agreement provisions.[18]

The mechanisms proposed in this context should be interpreted as the level of deference an international adjudicator extends to national decision-makers. They

15 Stephen Schill, 'In Defense of International Investment Law' in Marc Bungenberg, Christoph Herrmann, Markus Krajewski & Jorg Philipp Terhechte (eds), *European Yearbook of International Economic Law* (Springer International Publishing 2016) 311.

16 Sunya P. Subedi, *International Investment Law: Reconciling Policy and Principle* (3rd edn, Hart Publishing 2016) 20–21.

17 Jurgen Kurtz, *The WTO and International Investment Law. Converging Systems* (Cambridge University Press 2016) 170.

18 Ciaran Cross & Christian Schliemann-Radbruch, 'When investment Arbitration Curbs Domestic Regulatory Space: Consistent Solutions through Amicus Curiae Submissions by Regional Organisations' (2013) 6(2) *Law and Development Review*, 69.

are considered as mediums for coherence, consistency, and predictability, and are desirable in narrowing the chasm between a foreign investors' right to transfer of funds and a host State's right to regulate for her sovereignty. This is because a treaty language may hinder the development policy of a State.[19]

It is argued that the much-needed clarity can be achieved if treaty expressions provide arbitrators with better analytical insights to adjudicate disputes that involve competing policy objectives, for example, by clarifying investments that are capable of protection. This represents an attempt to proactively shape the substantive content of investment treaties in order to obviate any significant uncertainty or generate any form of arbitration. This strategy is not unprecedented as other States who are parties to the North American Free Trade Agreement (NAFTA) have used interpretative powers to exercise reasonable control over treaty interpretation by making submissions to tribunals when cases are brought against any of the NAFTA parties.[20]

Additionally, the importance of involving public international lawyers and experienced economists as amicus curiae and relevant stakeholders in the decision-making process is explored. Their participation is essential when decisions impact public interest. Discussions aim to enable interpretations that are responsive to legitimate claims of the host State to regulate in furtherance of essential development policy objectives and to also prevent the expansive interpretation of a host State's conduct. Investment arbitration is considered in this context because it is a spectrum of the investment landscape given the role they play in the interpretation of treaties. More so, treaty parties are supreme when creating laws, but tribunals are (more) supreme when interpreting them. Thus investment tribunals play a critical role in treaty interpretation, hence developing investment treaty law. Amicus curiae participation is proposed as an important element of investment arbitration and as part of the solution to the lack of clarity likely to arise from interpreting treaties because governments may not be able to harmonise conflicting objectives and interests. Hence, they augur well for canvassing important elements of public policy which are usually present in investor-State claims. Also, their participation can bring additional specific information and expertise which can be factual as well as legal and ought to be taken into consideration.[21]

19 Rawan Al-Louzi, 'A Coherence Review of Investment Protection Under Bilateral Investment Treaties and Free Trade Agreements' (2015) 12(3) *Manchester Journal of International Economic Law*, 271.

20 Jesse Coleman, Lise Johnson, Lisa Sachs & Kanika Gupta, 'International Investment Agreements 2015–2016. A Review of Recent Trends and Approaches' Jin Sachs L. E. & Johnson L. (eds) in Yearbook on International Investment Law & Policy 2015–2016 (Oxford University Press 2018) 49.

21 Laurence Boisson De Chazournes, 'Transparency and Amicus Curiae' (2004) 5(2) *The Journal of World Investment and Trade Law*, 335.

6.2 Revisiting the BIT Framework

Although both developing and developed States need a secure and stable legal environment for international investment, they do not see this same fundamental goal from the same standpoint. Developed States are interested in protecting their citizens' investment whereas developing States seek to attract investment while maintaining their regulatory rights. This has led to the unsystematic development of international investment law.[22] A typical BIT nomenclature is framed primarily around the objective of one interested party. Although important premises are evaluated, the end goal remains the same as with the traditional investor protection model, purportedly designed to promote FDI.[23] BITs are susceptible to power dynamics. Home States (in most cases developed States who are involved in capital exportation) consistently pursue their universal design preferences, leading to treaties that typically conform to their wishes, provided that their relative bargaining power is sufficient.[24] Treaties from these home States have strong enforcement provisions to protect the interests of their investors.[25] They are asymmetric given that only foreign investors may bring claims under them and thus only foreign investors benefit from the protection they provide.[26] Increased regulation has led to concerns about Investor-State Dispute Settlement (ISDS) and the potential impact that it has in giving foreign businesses greater legal rights than domestic businesses and constraining governments in their policy-making abilities.[27]

The global increase of BITs has corresponded with a significant increase in investor-State disputes in international investment law where a wide range of regulatory measures such as monetary policies and tax laws have been challenged by foreign investors as potential breaches of BITs.[28] At the centre of those disputes lies the friction between national sovereignty and property rights of foreign investors. The extraordinary magnitude in the history of arbitration whereby more than 60 States have faced investment treaty arbitration poses the problem of having to pay compensations exceeding the State's possibilities.[29] With regard to States that have recently experienced an economic crisis and have signed BITs with no

22 Silvia Karina Fiezzoni, 'Striking Consistency and Predictability in International Investment Law from the Perspective of Developing Countries' (2012) 7(4) *Frontiers of Law in China*, 526.

23 Richard C. Chen, 'Bilateral Investment Treaties and Domestic Institutional Reform' (2017) 55(3) *Columbia Journal of Transnational Law*, 550.

24 Todd Alle & Clint Peinhardt, 'Evaluating Three Explanations for the Design of Bilateral Investment Treaties' (2014) 66(1) *World Politics*, 62.

25 *ibid* 61.

26 Camille Martini, 'Avoiding the Planned Obsolescence of Modern International Investment Agreements: Can General Exception Mechanisms Be Improved, and How?' (2018) 59(8) *Boston College Law Review*, 2878.

27 Jeonogho Nam, 'Model BIT: An Ideal Prototype or a Tool for Efficient Breach?' (2017) 48(4) *Georgetown Journal of International Law*, Summer, 1280–1281.

28 Prabhash Ranjan & Pushkar Amand, 'The 2016 Model Indian BIT: A Critical Deconstruction' (2017) 38(1) *Northwestern Journal of International Law and Business*, 3.

29 Antonio Pastor Palomi, 'Emergency Economic Intervention and the Rights of Foreign Investors: US-Argentina Practice' (2009) 20(1) *Journal of Interdisciplinary Economics*, 170.

public policy measures, there is currently no evidence of claims brought under the "transfer of funds" clause. A plausible explanation to this could be the difficulties in proving damages or the use of gaps in the existing global network of BITs. It may also be too early to make a conclusive remark as the crisis remains relatively recent. Despite the dearth of claims under financial crises, the subject has attracted widespread commentary;[30] it is however expected that such claims may materialise in the very near future. In a world characterised by an ever-increasing global economic interaction and cooperation and a recurring economic and financial insecurity, it can only be expected that the transfer of funds clause which remains the central focus of this book will be increasingly put to test in the future, and it will be interesting to see the role arbitral tribunals will play when balancing State functions and international obligations. However, previous claims against regulatory measures taken by States have created a backlash against the international investment dispute system. The textual indeterminacy of BITs has resulted in divergent and inconsistent legal conclusions by investment treaty arbitration.[31] Critics of the investment arbitration posit that arbitral tribunals use vague standards of protection to intrude into the regulatory space of host States and this invariably leaves arbitral tribunals as the ultimate commander of public policy decisions.[32]

Coherence and consistency are highly expedient for both the source and destination of foreign investments because both developed and developing States rely on treaty templates, otherwise known as model BITs, to negotiate consistent investment treaties. These model BITs are expressions of what a State may consider to be ideal standards of investment protection. Thus making deviations from the models in or during negotiations is highly undesirable. Often any change to a model BIT is driven by those in a position with more leverage: the capital-exporting States.[33] Not-so-pleasant arbitral outcomes influence changes in successive treaties to reflect increased legal precision.[34] Invariably, most (capital exporting) States do not quit

30 Jeffrey P. Commission, 'The Global Financial Crisis and International Investment Regimes' (2010) 104 *American Society of International Law*, 445.

31 Ranjan & Amand (n 28) 5.

32 Stephan Schill, 'Deference in Investment Treaty Arbitration: Reconceptualising the Standard Review' (2012) 3(3) *Journal of International Dispute Settlement*, 578.

33 Developing countries are beginning to conclude BITs between themselves, and, as a direct result, these countries have been placed in the unexpected and uncomfortable position of being sued by foreign investors. During the early years when developed economies like Germany, the United Kingdom, France, and the Netherlands were encouraging developing countries to sign BITs with capital-exporting countries as a precursor to international development, there was little or no controversy in developed countries. No question was raised on the propriety or otherwise of the regime as a means of guaranteeing respect for investment treaty commitments; Armand De Mestral, 'Investor-State Arbitration between Developed Democratic Countries' (2015) 1 *Investor-State Arbitration Series*, 4.

34 Precision, in this sense, relates to narrowing the scope for reasonable interpretation by being specific about the nature of State commitments. Precise language explains how third parties should interpret State actions; Mark S. Manger & Clint Peinhardt, 'Learning and the Precision of International Investment Agreements' (2017) 43(6) *International Interactions*, 922; Mark A. Clodfelter, 'The

signing treaties; rather they redefine the content of treaties to reduce ambiguity in order to avoid outcomes that contradict their interest.

The development of a model BIT has witnessed three eras. The first era ran from the late 1950s until the end of the 1980s.[35] This was a period when developed States prepared model BITs that they used for negotiation with developing States, with the aim being simply to protect foreign investments against specific injurious actions by host States. It was during this era that BIT provisions which are common today were adopted; developed countries cornered developing countries into signing the BITs because they believed that they had no choice since they hoped for foreign investment that would aid their national economies.[36] Such treaties, it was believed, constituted a grand bargain in which sovereignty was surrendered in exchange for prosperity.[37] However, fewer treaties were concluded than developed countries wished due to the suspicious view of foreign investments by some countries.[38] The second era was the period when developing countries abandoned their scepticism of foreign investment and began to conclude more BITs. These developing States prepared their own model BITs, which they used as counter drafts or templates to negotiate with other States. The substance of these model BITs did not differ much from those utilised by developed States due to the belief that a weakened BIT would be a less effective inducement for investment. Thus model BITs prepared by developing States were based on the traditional models.[39] The third era was triggered by a growing backlash against economic globalisation following economic crises in Asian economies in the 1990s, most notably the East Asian Crises that began in Thailand in 1997 despite the sound economic policies she had pursued, thus showing the volatility of investment flows in a world of integrated markets and the increase in investor-State arbitration under the BITs in the mid-1990s.[40]

Some new models BITs are driven by different ideological factors; China has redrafted its current model treaty to be more accommodating to investors and investment protection partly because they have become a significant capital exporter. But this new consciousness is not just fuelled by the dynamics of interest or circumstances but largely by the substantive obligations that BITs entail and the new dimensions to the risk inherent in the earlier generation of BITs.

The United States was motivated to reconsider its BITs as the pre-2000 agreements were primarily with countries that had minimal investment in the US. The negotiations surrounding NAFTA's investment chapter prompted the US to place

Adaptation of States to the Changing World of Investment Protection through Model BITs' (2009) 24(1) *ICSID*, 167.

35 Kenneth J. Vandevelde, 'Model BIT: The Way Forward' (2011) 18(1) *Southwestern Journal of International Law*, 307.

36 *ibid.*

37 *ibid.*

38 *ibid.*

39 *ibid.*

40 *ibid* 308.

greater emphasis on risk management, particularly because Canada, as a partner, represented the second-largest source of inward investment into the US.[41]

This new awareness is a direct response to investment arbitration, which has highlighted the risks associated with the interpretation of substantive provisions that can be applied in various ways, and the way investment arbitration tribunals which held States to obligations that they had not previously considered to exist. It also underscores the circumstances under which investor-State arbitration procedures may be invoked.[42]

Most contemporary model BITs have significantly evolved in both substance and form, resulting in increased complexity and greater precision in the substantive standards of treatment. Traditional protection standards have been enhanced with interpretative clauses that clarify the contracting parties' intentions regarding the normative content of specific protections. As a result, these agreements have become more detailed and sophisticated.[43] Nonetheless, BITs share a common set of standardised language. They revolve around the same common principles, norms, rules, and decision-making process. As a result of this relative homogeneity, most investment agreements virtually consist of highly standardised text and reoccurring treaty language. For example, the right to transfer funds appears virtually in all BITs. Several reasons can be adduced for this: firstly, States rely on treaty templates (model BITs) to negotiate consistent investment treaties; any variation of these standardised texts are indicative of the intended level of investment protection that the framers hope to confer on themselves.[44] If at any point there are deviations from the norm, such deviations are likely to imply that a concession has been made or there is simply a change in the normative contents. Secondly, for capital-importing States, consistent treaty provisions make a breach of investment standards less likely since they observe uniform commitments across board. And, for the capital-exporting States, maintaining such a practice is important because it creates a level playing field of investment protection across varying countries. Thirdly, while lexical variations are assets in literary documents, they are liabilities that lawyers guard against. Effective legal interpretation requires a consistent use of treaty terms.[45] Finally, when negotiators choose to use different language, they typically do so with caution. Treaty negotiators tend to favour clarifying existing terms rather than introducing new and uncertain concepts.[46] For stakeholders in the investment regime, the advantage of consistent language supported by clarification clauses or annexes is that it can reveal a discernible pattern, indicating when deviations have occurred or should occur.

41 Mark A. Clodfelter, 'The Adaptation of States to the Changing World of Investment Protection through Model BITs' (2009) 24(1) *ICSID*, 167.

42 *ibid.*

43 *ibid* 170.

44 Wolfgang Alschner & Dmitriy Skougareviskiy, 'Mapping the Universe of International Agreements' (2016) 19(3) *Journal of International Economic Law*, 566.

45 *ibid.*

46 *ibid* 566–567.

Many States that have developed model BITs have historically been capital-exporting countries. Their status as capital exporters gives them a strategic advantage in the treaty-making process, allowing them to influence negotiations and establish their own rules for investment treaties.[47] Negotiations are often based on these model BITs.[48] However, some developing States are becoming active participants in treaty drafting: for example, the Indian Cabinet approved a new model text for India's BITs in December 2015 as all prior BITs were cancelled.[49] India has to rely on the new model text when negotiating or renegotiating BITs. Even as India intensifies efforts to attract foreign investors, it has also narrowed the rights and protections it is willing to offer them when disputes arise.[50] This act signifies a fundamental rethink of some of the principles underpinning today's international investment regime following the resort to international arbitration when there is a dispute on the applicability of treaty texts. In the landmark case of *White Industries Australia Ltd. (WIAL) India*, WIAL asserted that India's judicial delays breached the provisions of the India-Australia BIT. While the tribunal rejected several of WIAL's claims, it determined that India's failure to enable WIAL to enforce its rights was a violation of its treaty obligations.[51] Cases like this are not unique to India alone and are simply a pointer to the emerging struggles between foreign investors and States in economic spaces which are looking constricted in the face of uncertain economic prospects. States' ability to manage their economies during crises have run contrary to the rights granted to foreign investors.[52]

A brief examination of the United States' approach to its BIT programme since its inception in 1981 shows that its model BIT has been revised twice in eight years. The first review aimed to ensure that investment protections for foreign investors were not excessive, while the second, leading to the 2012 model BIT, focused on advancing public interests and balancing government regulatory autonomy with environmental and public welfare considerations.[53] This model treaty employs a three-pronged strategy to address regulatory concerns, incorporating public interest exceptions into its preambles and various sections to guide States in regulation, companies in investment, and tribunals in assessing compliance with the treaty.[54] The US model treaty reflects increased concern for regulation and now serves as the template for investment treaties between the US and other States. The Office of the United States Trade Representative has the capacity to adjust the model; but

47 Aniruddha Rajput, 'Safeguarding India's Regulatory Autonomy: Analysis of the New Model Bilateral Investment Treaty' (2017) 14(3) *Manchester Journal of International Economic Law*, 280.

48 *ibid.*

49 *ibid* 279–280.

50 Premila Nazareth Satyanand, 'Once BITten, Forever Shy: Explaining India's Rethink of Its Bilateral Investment Treaty Provisions' (2016) 16(1) *AIB Insights*, 17.

51 *ibid* 18.

52 Biswajit Dhar, Reji Joseph & TC James, 'India's Bilateral Investment Agreements: A Time to Review' (2012) 42(52) *Economic & Political Weekly*, 114.

53 *ibid* 115.

54 Giest (n 12) 337–338.

any derogation from the model would require a two thirds approval from the US Senate.[55]

With the exception of NAFTA, US treaties generally do not include a balance-of-payments exception like the GATS. However, they do feature a prudential exception akin to that in the GATS Annex on Financial Services (0. This allows a party to adopt or maintain measures related to financial services for prudential reasons, such as protecting investors, depositors, policyholders, or anyone to whom a fiduciary duty is owed by a financial services provider and ensuring the integrity and stability of the financial system. Such measures must not be employed to evade the party's commitments or obligations under the treaty.[56]

The term "prudential reasons" specifically refer to: "the maintenance of the safety, soundness, integrity, or financial responsibility of individual financial institutions or cross-border financial service suppliers".[57] This therefore means that macroprudential regulations of capital inflows do not apply to US treaties. The absence of capital account regulatory provisions in US treaties has become a sticking point for other contracting States. In a Free Trade Agreement (FTA) with Chile and Singapore, the US was able to negotiate what can be termed a "cooling off period"—whereby an investor in the US cannot file a claim for a period of one year after the provisions have been deployed. This "cooling off" period is based on the rationale that a host State may have a need to address a financial crisis and should therefore not be subject to litigation in the middle of such actions. A cooling off period invariably permits a foreign investor to institute action (only after the cooling off year) for damages related to capital controls measures taken during the cooling off year. It is pertinent to note that this cooling off period is not mutually applicable as it applies *only to those foreign investors filing a claim against a party other than the United States*.[58] The IMF has expressed strong concerns that the US BITs and FTA do not provide adequate flexibility to regulate a capital account; it further criticised the lack of mention by US BITs of the ability of the IMF to recommend capital control as part of a financial programme, as it had argued that BITs should have temporary derogations for balance-of-payment difficulties and that the cooling off period was not adequate. The limitations posed by these agreements are likely to create challenges for the management of capital flows.[59]

55 *ibid.*

56 Andrew D. Mitchell, Jennifer K. Hawkins & Neha Mishra, 'Dear Prudence: Allowances Under International Trade and Investment Law for Prudential Regulations in the Financial Services Sector' (2016) 19 *Journal of International Economic Law*, 789, 792; Kevin P. Gallagher, 'Trading Away Financial Instability: Reconstructing Capital Account Liberalization as Trade and Investment Policy' in Kevin P. Gallagher (ed), *Emerging Markets and the Reregulation of Cross-Border Finance* (Cornell University Press 2015) 181.

57 Kevin P. Gallagher, 'Trading Away Financial Instability: Reconstructing Capital Account Liberalization as Trade and Investment Policy' in Kevin P. Gallagher (ed), *Emerging Markets and the Reregulation of Cross-Border Finance* (Cornell University Press 2015) 181.

58 *ibid.*

59 *ibid* 182.

Unlike the United States, major capital exporting nations such as the EU States, Japan, Canada and China provide for capital account regulation for the mitigation of economic crisis. BITs and FTAs of these States contain a broad balance-of-payments safeguard exception or controlled-entry exception to enable States to deploy their domestic laws towards the management of capital flows.[60] At this juncture, it is pertinent to state that the focus is not on India nor the United States as a case study but to draw parallels on why a treaty model clause on transfer of funds has become imperative in light of today's realities. More and more States are reconsidering their international commitments in BITs, all of which are motivated by the need to protect themselves against the litigatory reach of standard BIT provisions which can be triggered by a sudden legislative change, revocation, or refusal to grant a permit and a cancellation of an investment contract.[61] The outstanding and huge sums of money from arbitral awards make it all the more obvious why developing States who suffer from resource constraint should make their interests in the investment regime unequivocal. Recommendations proposed sooner do not exaggerate the protection conferred on foreign investors to the detriment of parties' mutual economic relations. They are simply tailored in such a way so as not to trigger State responsibility under the treaty regime nor substantially diminish the prospects of the foreign investor. Balancing public policy and foreign investors' interests will lead to the adoption of a proportionate approach. This limits arbitrators to examining the suitability, necessity, and proportionality of a State regulation when making decisions in an investment case.

6.3 Guiding Arbitral Tribunals with Purposive Treaty Interpretation Guidelines

In the complex transnational environment where foreign investments are made and where investment treaties play a fundamental role, the importance of treaty interpretations is self-evident and cannot be over emphasised. Succinctly stated:

> the importance [of the rules on interpretation] and their centrality to the ability of the regime of international agreements cannot be overstated, for no matter how much care parties may take in expressing with precision their commitments, the predictability of their commitment depends upon commonly accepted rules of interpretation and equally important, correct application of those rules by those called upon to construe the commitments in question.[62]

60 Policy Space to Prevent and Mitigate Financial Crises in Trade and Investment Agreements. By Kevin P. Gallagher. https://unctad.org/system/files/official-document/gdsmdpg2420101_en.pdf [Accessed 17 October 2024].

61 Satyanand (n 50) 17.

62 Tarcisio Gazzini, *Interpretation of International Investment Treaties* (Hart Publishing 2016) 1.

Rules on interpretation presuppose that a text embodies a wide range of possible meanings amongst which any interpreter has a choice to make. Proposed guidelines draw from Article 31 of the Vienna Convention on the Law of Treaties (VCLT), which is deeply rooted in public international law and is useful for ambiguous texts. When consent is legitimised in a treaty and when claims relate to treaty violation, the rhetoric of Article 31 helps to structure the debate.[63] The ability of the rules on interpretation to have a centripetal effect will not only be determined by their precision and specificity but also by their interplay with other rules of international law and the normative background of the investment treaty.[64] One important aspect of Article 31 is that it requires sequencing in reasoning.[65] One can purpose the Vienna Convention both on logic and inherent morality. Where parties have made commitments which they hope to be bound by in a set of words, those words are to be construed in the context of the entire instrument in which they appear. Theinstrument also reveals the shared objectives and intents of the parties. It is only when this exercise is futile that one can look at other circumstances that redacts the text.[66] Thus it is important to restate the provisions of Article 31 in two paragraphs:

> *A treaty shall be interpreted in good faith in accordance with the ordinary meaning to be given to the terms of the treaty*
> *in their context and in light of its object and purpose*[67]

What is obvious from this rule is that recourse should be made to the object and purpose of the treaty. Since the VCLT is the first port of call in treaty interpretation, it may well serve the purpose of providing insight on what may or may not be relevant in treaty construction. Tribunals are first likely to take a review of the preambular recitals of a BIT in identifying the objective of States in economic relations. This is, however, neither a dominant methodology nor a full representation of approaches in arbitral jurisprudence. For other tribunals are likely to consider the protections, the exclusive telos of the system or, disturbingly, suggest it as the dominant purpose. Conversely, Article 32 of the VCLT permits additional rules of interpretation for two alternative reasons: (1) to confirm a meaning which originates from the application of Article 31, and (2) to determine a meaning when

63 Herve Ascensio, 'Article 31 of the Vienna Convention on the Law of Treaties and International Investment Law' (2016) 31(2) *ICSID Review*, 369.

64 *ibid* 368.

65 Mahnoush Arsanjani & Michael Reisman, 'Interpreting Treaties for the Benefit of Third Parties: The "Salvors and the Use of Legislative History in Investment Treaties' (2010) 104(4) *American Journal of International Law*, 601.

66 *ibid.*

67 United Nations, *Vienna Convention on the Law of Treaties*, 23 May 1969, United Nations, Treaty Series, vol. 1155, p. 331, Available on https://www.refworld.org/docid/3ae6b3a10.html [Accessed on 6 December 2024].

Article 31 interpretation "leaves the meaning ambiguous or obscure" or leads to a result which is manifestly noisome or unreasonable.[68]

The VCLT appears to have provided definitive guidelines, effectively settling longstanding debates on the rules of interpretation. However, it also allows considerable room for distinctive interpretative approaches, all within the framework established by its broad principles.[69] Articles 31 and 32 provide reasonable delineations for a treaty applier, yet despite this clarity "treaty appliers'" liberal methodologies could still subvert the unitary system of treaty interpretations. For example, in the case of *Continental Casualty Company v. Argentina*, the ICSID tribunal interpreted Article XI of the Treaty between Argentina and the United States by examining GATT and WTO case law to clarify the scope of essential security interests. Given that Article XI is based on the formulation of Article XX of GATT 1947, the tribunal deemed it more relevant to reference GATT and WTO jurisprudence regarding the doctrine of necessity in relation to economic measures that deviate from GATT obligations, rather than focusing on the necessity conditions established under customary international law.[70]

In addition to incorporating distinct legal frameworks like GATT and the WTO, the tribunal utilised the concept of necessity under customary international law as a supplementary means of interpreting Article XI. This approach expanded its interpretative sources in a way that deviated from the clear boundaries set by Articles 31 and 32 of the VCLT. The tribunal disagreed with the view that the treaty had become inextricably linked to the customary law standard regarding the conditions for the necessity of States. Its interpretation of Article XI of the US-Argentina BIT establishes a concerning precedent for how similarly worded provisions in non-precluded measures in other BITs or ambiguously drafted treaties may be interpreted.[71]

It is for this reason that further discussions propose guidelines to help legitimately engage with the host State and foreign investor's interests.

6.3.1 Redefining Investments Capable of Protection

The provision on the transfer of funds of most BITs provide for a free transfer of funds related to investment;[72] this means that the BIT definition of "investment" plays an integral role in the determination of the scope of rights and obligations

68 Diane A. Desierto, 'Necessity and "Supplementary Means of Interpretation" for Non-Precluded Measures in Bilateral Investment Treaties' (2010) 31(3) *University of Pennsylvania Journal of International Economic Law*, 829.

69 Michael Waibel, 'Demystifying the Art of Interpretation' (2011) 22(2) *European Journal of International Law*, 573.

70 *ibid.*

71 *ibid* 832.

72 Ardeshir Atai, 'Iranian Bilateral Investment Treaties: Substantive Principles and Standards' (2013) 14(3) *Journal of World Investment and Trade*, 412.

under a treaty and the establishment of the ISDS tribunal jurisdiction.[73] The definition of "investment" in a BIT is important in comprehending the struggle for space and the right to regulate. The definition determines to a large extent the scope of investment protection, the forms of interest that are protected, and the extent of State liability in terms of any arbitration claim.[74] In the case of *Continental Casualty Company v. Argentina*, in deciding whether a breach of Article V of the Argentine-US BIT had occurred, the tribunal had to first determine whether Continental's hypothetical transfer in the absence of Argentina's restrictions on the transfer of funds fell within the "transfer related to an investment" which parties to the BIT undertook to permit "freely and without delay into or out if its territory".[75] In addition to determining the scope of rights and obligations, the term investment also serves as a requisite for obtaining guarantees or a criterion defining competencies.[76]

Yet the framework relating to ICSID, and most BIT protections, remains deliberately silent with regard to the very meaning of "investment". Article 25 of ICSID merely provides that ICSID tribunals' jurisdiction extends to any legal dispute "arising directly out of an investment between a contracting State and a national of another".[77] As a result of the omission of the definition of investment, host States on some occasions have tried to escape investment disputes on the basis that certain economic activities do not qualify as investment and as such do not fall under the jurisdiction of ICSID tribunals.[78] Thus the scope of investment plays an important role in ensuring the legitimacy and effective functioning of the entire network of the treaty instruments. Although investment treaty protection of tangible property is often cited with credibility, the status of less tangible contractual rights and entitlements remains contentious. Financial assets are somewhat nuanced, as they do not fit neatly into the category of tangible property. Within this realm, rights with economic value have sparked significant debate in arbitral practice.[79]

Debates on the definition of investment are primarily shaped by a conflict between subjectivist and objectivist theorists.[80] The objective test implicit in Article 25 (1) of the ICSID Convention requires that an investment must show a commitment of resources, a certain duration, an element of risk, and a contribution

73 Ranjan & Amand (n 28) 19.

74 Srikar Mysore & Aditya Vora, 'Tussle for Policy Space in International Investment Norm Setting: The Search for a Middle Path' (2016) 7(2) *Jindal Global Law Review*, 143.

75 Alejandro Turyn & Facundo Perez Aznar, 'Drawing the Limits of Free Transfer Provisions' in Michael Waibel (ed), *The Backlash Against Investment Arbitration: Perceptions and Reality* (Kluwer Law & Business 2010) 68.

76 Jan Asmus Bischoff & Richard Happ, 'The Notion of Investment' in Marc Bungenberg, Jorn Griebal, Stephan Hobe & August Reinish (eds), *International Investment Law* (Hart Publishing 2015) 497.

77 Antoine Martin, 'Definition of "Investment": Could a Persistent Objector to the Salini Tests Be Found in ICSID Arbitral Practice?' (2011) 11(2) *Global Jurist*, 1.

78 *ibid.*

79 Mavluda Sattorova, 'Defining Investment Under ICSID Convention and BITs: Of Ordinary Meaning, Telos and Beyond' (2012) 2(2) *Asian Journal of International Law*, 268.

80 *ibid* 269.

to the economic development of the host State.[81] In the case of *Salini v. Morocco*, which addressed the ICSID jurisdictional requirement for investment, the tribunal distinguished between the definition of investment in the relevant investment treaty and the concept of investment as a jurisdictional matter under Article 25(1) of the ICSID Convention. While the disputed asset had the potential to generate economic benefits, the tribunal concluded that the parties' agreement to classify the contentious assets as an investment was insufficient to meet the jurisdictional requirement of "investment" as defined in Article 25.[82] The objectivist theory posits that Article 25(1) of the ICSID Convention inherently limits the jurisdiction of arbitral tribunals by providing a clear definition of what constitutes an "investment". According to this theory, the jurisdictional requirement of a qualifying investment cannot be altered or waived by the parties' consent, meaning that States cannot unilaterally expand ICSID's jurisdiction through bilateral agreements. This approach emphasises that the criteria for an investment are fixed and cannot be manipulated by the preferences or agreements of the involved States.[83] Thus assets qualifying as investments in a BIT must meet the objectivist test as set out in the jurisdictional conditions of Article 25.

The decision in Salini's case has had a significant impact on subsequent arbitral practice and has drawn considerable criticism due to a competing subjectivist theory that prioritises the definition of investment in BITs. Given that these treaties often include open-ended, asset-based definitions of investment, a key issue emerges regarding how to reconcile them with the implicit definition of investment in the ICSID Convention—particularly when parties to a BIT have explicitly identified what they consider to be protectable investments. The Morocco-Nigeria BIT and the Singapore-Nigeria BIT (explored in the previous chapter),[84] describe investment mainly from the perspective of an asset having proprietary value. Both treaties define investment capable of protection:

> as an enterprise within the territory of one State established, acquired, expanded or operated, in good faith, by an investor of the other State in accordance with the law of the party in whose territory the investment is made taken together with the asset of the enterprise which contribute sustainable development to that Party and has the characteristics of an investment involving a commitment of capital or other similar resources, pending profit, risk-taking and certain duration.[85]

81 *ibid*, Salini Costruttori S.P.A v Kingdom of Morocco [I] ICSID Case No. ARB/00/4; Alex Grabowski, 'The Definition of Investment under the ICSID Convention: A Defence of Salini' (2014) 15(1) *Chicago* Journal of International Law, 290.

82 *ibid*.

83 Michail Deskastros, 'Portfolio Investment: Reconceptualising the Notion of Investment under the ICSID Convention' (2013) 14(2) *The Journal of World Investment & Trade*, 290.

84 Investment Policy Hub. Available on https://investmentpolicy.unctad.org/international-investment-agreements/countries/153/nigeria [Accessed on 5 March 2021].

85 Morocco-Nigeria BIT. Investment Policy Hub. Available on https://investmentpolicy.unctad.org/international-investment-agreements/countries/153/nigeria [Accessed on 5 March 2021].

This definition of investment is so open-ended that a variety of meanings could be read into it. The language in the text of the treaties is accommodative of portfolio investments which is very much controversial given its spatial temporality, speculative effects, and the impact it has in an economy.

Some investment disputes illustrate the practical applicability of BITs for portfolio investments.[86] One example of an unsuccessful case of portfolio protection is the 1999 dispute between *Gruslin v. Malaysia (II)*. A Belgian investor sought compensation for losses on securities listed on the Kuala Lumpur Stock Exchange, following foreign exchange controls introduced by Malaysia in 1999. The investor claimed that these controls had devalued his assets. However, the claim was dismissed by a sole arbitrator, who ruled that portfolio investments were not covered by the Belgium-Luxembourg Economic Union (BLEU)-Malaysia BIT of 1979.[87]

In contrast, the 1996 *Lanco v. Argentina* case resulted in a successful admission of the dispute. The US-based investor sought compensation for an alleged breach of a concession agreement related to a port terminal. The arbitration tribunal accepted the case, noting that the broad definition of "investor" in the 1991 Argentina-United States BIT applied to the investor, even though they did not control the company's operations. The tribunal emphasised that control over a company's management is not necessary for BIT protection.[88]

Typically, States have considerable discretion in determining which instruments they consider appropriate for facilitating portfolio investments in the BITs they negotiate.[89] The challenge of integrating portfolio investments into the framework of investment protection is likely to reflect the same attitudinal issues that influence the definition of a protected investment.[90] It is suggested that portfolio investments should be largely excluded from the protection offered by BITs due to the varying perspectives that arbitrators bring to their decisions. Some arbitrators are willing to interpret the treaty language in ways that extend beyond the original intentions of the parties, while others resist using legal instruments to pursue a specific vision of investment protection.[91]

Portfolio investments are usually defined as freely circulating instruments which indicate interests in assets of companies but do not involve the owner such to participate, manage or enter the State in which such assets are put to productive use.[92]

86 Stefan Eichler & Jannik Andre Nauerth, 'Bilateral Investment Treaties and Portfolio Investment' (2014) 91 101918, *Journal of International Financial Markets, Institutions and Money*, 2–3.

87 ICSID, 2000. Gruslin v. Malaysia (II) – Award. ICSID Arbitral Tribunal, Case No ARB/99/3, 27 November 2000; *ibid.*

88 ICSID, 1998. Preliminary Decision: Jurisdiction of the Arbitral Tribunal ICSIC Case No. ARB/97/6 Lanco International Inc. v. The Argentine Republic. ICSID Arbitral Tribunal, Case No. ARB/97/6, 8 December 1998; *ibid.*

89 Deskastros (n 83) 289.

90 Muthucumaraswamy Sornarajah, 'Portfolio Investments and the Definition of Investment' (2009) 24(2) *ICSID Review*, 516.

91 *ibid.*

92 *ibid.*

The issue of whether portfolio investments should be considered as investments capable of protection is contentious as they are known to flee at the slightest sign of economic crisis. Cases have emerged on whether minority shareholdings should be considered as investments. In the case of *Enron v Argentina*, the tribunal proclaimed that there should be a limit at which investors should be precluded from bringing forth claims. Whether or not portfolio investment should be included or excluded from the definition of investment remains a moot point. Given these divergent views in academia, there is need for a thorough and analytical approach to be followed when delineating this term.[93]

Policy arguments for the inclusion of portfolio investment are such that, since capital flows are important for economic development, then it should not matter their forms; if they occur through portfolio investments, then they should be worthy of protection if it is likely to spur more inflow of foreign investment. This argument is weakened in light of the debate of whether BITs in reality promote foreign investments.[94]

Arguments for the exclusion of portfolio investments from protection are grounded in the belief that FDIs possess specific characteristics aimed at promoting economic development, which portfolio investments do not share. This perspective is bolstered by several policy considerations: first, the rapid movement of capital associated with portfolio investments does not contribute to sustainable economic development. Even with FDIs, a foreign investment that can be relocated at a moment's notice may not remain long enough to achieve meaningful economic growth. Furthermore, portfolio investments are primarily made with the objective of generating profit, and there is a clear intention to withdraw them if profitability appears to decline. Given these factors, it becomes challenging to align portfolio investments with the criteria established in *Salini v. Morocco* regarding contributions to economic development and the requirement for a certain duration.[95]

Transfer clauses are amongst the most crucial provisions in investment treaties and are a fundamental concern for foreign investors when deciding to invest.[96] An inconsistent definition of investment can prompt foreign investors—uncertain about the qualification of their transactions—to shy away from ICSID arbitration, thereby avoiding the uncertainty surrounding ICSID's *ratione materiae* jurisdiction. Conversely, such ambiguity may lead foreign investors to expand their understanding of what qualifies for protection beyond established limits. Therefore, defining investment is vital not only for the legal security it provides to both foreign investors and capital-importing States but also for theoretical clarity. Notably, a definition based on an enumerative approach, which is common in most international treaties (including Nigerian BITs), has never effectively constituted a

93 Deskastros (n 83) 303.
94 *ibid.*
95 *ibid.*
96 Carsten Kern, 'Transfer of Funds' in Marc Bungenberg, Jorn Griebel, Stephan Hobe & August Reinisch (eds), *International Investment Law* (Hart Publishing 2015) 871.

clear definition.[97] In the *White Industries* case, India's argument that the disputed transaction was merely a supply contract was rejected by the United Nations Commission on International Trade Law (UNCITRAL) arbitral tribunal. A key issue in India's arbitration case was the broad definition of investment in the India-Australia BIT, a common feature in many of India's other BITs. To address this concern, the 2015 Model BIT adopts more restrictive language to narrow the scope of investor protection.[98] While many BITs still utilise broad, open-ended definitions for investment protection, newer agreements,[99] including the Indian Model BIT, have shifted to an "enterprise-based" approach. This change aims to limit the scope of investments and reduce the likelihood of expansive claims.[100]

Portfolio investments do not meet the Salini Test criteria and the widespread economic benefits that are implicit in the political economic bargain of international investment agreements. In the event of an economic crisis, the volatility of portfolio flows could create serious problems for the financial and macroeconomic position of the State, thus complicating existing weaknesses. This is because the short-term economic nature of portfolio investments produces capital flights in economic crisis. FDI and portfolio investment are therefore in sharp contrast with the underlying economic benefits of capital flows. To subject both types of investment to the same legal treatment will undermine the political economic bargain that is the foundation of investment agreements.[101] It is recommended that portfolio investment be excluded when determining whether an asset should be protected under a BIT. Furthermore, assets which neither are of non-commercial nature nor used for non-business purposes should be excluded from investment protection; emphasis should be placed on investments which are incorporated or made according to a host State's domestic laws and make a substantial contribution to real economic development of the host State. Portfolio investments such as stocks and shares of companies which are acquired for speculative purpose and held for short-term benefits by foreign investors should be excluded from the purpose of protection offered by BITs. The definition of protected investments needs to be confined to what really needs to be covered so as to ensure a balance of protection of rights for foreign investments and the legitimate rights of regulation for host States. In this way, the interpretation of "investment" in accordance with Article 31 of the VCLT, which necessitates an objective standard, is met, while also giving defer-

97 Sebastien Manciaux, 'The Notion of Investment: New Controversies' (2008) 9(6) *The Journal of World Investment & Trade Law*, 6.

98 Bhagirath Ashiya, 'The Shift towards an Enterprise Based Definition of Investment: The Quagmire of the *Salini* Test and India's Model BIT' (2016) 7(2) *Jindal Global Law Review*, 263–277.

99 A risk to this type of definition is that local investors may channel their investment through foreign companies/investors in order to avail themselves of the protection that is inherent in BITs.

100 Mysore & Vora (n 74) 143.

101 Federico Lupo-Pasini, 'Monetary Policy Measures in Investment Law: The Uneasy Relationship Between Monetary Stability and Investment Protection' in Thomas Cottier, Lastrar Rosa & Christian Tietje (eds), *The Rule of Law in Monetary Affairs: World Trade Forum* (Cambridge University Press 2014) 582.

ence to the consent of parties under the applicable BIT. This can reconcile the varying jurisprudence concerning the investment criterion, which can in turn make investment protection more predictable.

6.3.2 *Systemic Integration of the Right to Transfer Funds with Other Obligations under International Law*

6.3.2.1 *Delineating the Scope of Necessity Defence under Customary International Law*

International investment law forms and interacts with other aspects of public international law. In the absence of express treaty provisions exempting States from liability, the necessity defence under customary international law can be relied on.[102] It is long recognised as a defence in customary international law which States can rely on to preclude liability for international wrongful acts in cases of necessity.[103]

The circumstances surrounding Argentina's claims after its economic crisis closely mirror one another, highlighting the customary law doctrine of necessity as a legitimate basis for justifying certain actions that may contravene international obligations. This connection underscores the interplay between international investment law, as a specialised regime, and general international law through the lens of necessity. Therefore, it is essential for interpreters to pursue a systemic integration of *lex specialis* and *lex generalis*. ICSID tribunals should consider not only the rules outlined in BITs but also relevant principles from customary international law.[104] The relationship between treaty rules and general international law is symbiotic and dynamic, rather than static. A State's customary obligations do not always align with those stipulated in treaties, nor can treaties be viewed in isolation from one another; in most cases, these obligations influence each other.[105] Consequently, it is essential to systematically integrate the customary international law doctrine of "necessity" into the substantive obligations outlined in investment treaties. In *Asian Agricultural Products Limited v The Republic of Sri Lanka*, the ICSID tribunal stated that a BIT:

> is not a self-contained closed legal system limited to provide for substantive material rules of direct applicability, but it has to be envisaged within a wider juridical context in which rules from other sources are integrated through implied incorporation methods, or by direct reference to certain

102 Suha Ballan, 'Economic Crises and Foreign Investors: Between Necessity and Reparation' (2018) 2(1) *International Comparative, Policy & Ethics Law Review*, 4.

103 *ibid.*

104 Palomi (n 29) 174.

105 Campbell McLaclilan, 'Investment Treaties and General International Law' (2008) 57(2) *International and Comparative Law Quarterly*, 364.

supplementary rules, whether of international law character or of domestic law nature.[106]

The significance of integrating customary international law with bilateral treaty provisions is illustrated by a 2001 NAFTA note clarifying that the concepts of fair and equitable treatment and full protection and security do not exceed the customary international law minimum standard for the treatment of foreign nationals. This clarification was made to prevent the broad interpretation of fair and equitable treatment, which could potentially include any adverse treatment of an investment.[107] In the same vein, the labour rights in the US model BIT are modelled in accordance with the international recognised labour rights while its fair and equitable treatment has been linked to the customary international law minimum standards of treatment of aliens.[108]

The relationship between BITs and other aspects of public international law is often contentious. BITs serve as specific agreements between two States, prevailing as *lex specialis* over the more general *lex generalis* of treaty law in cases of inconsistency. However, the imprecision in drafting these treaties can lead to ambiguities regarding specific provisions and the conditions under which general treaty law should apply.[109] This ambiguity often becomes apparent only when a treaty obligation is breached. Arbitral tribunals have varied in their endorsement of general international law, with some emphasising its importance in interpretation while others view it as a supplementary source to inform the meaning of investment treaties. This debate is particularly evident in cases involving utilities in Argentina.[110] States may choose to deviate from international norms, offering more favourable treatment or including special provisions for investments from particular countries.[111] Since international investment law provides only a broad framework, States have significant leeway to define their own *lex specialis* regarding foreign investments.

This section seeks to clarify the scope of customary international law and practices within the context of a proposed model treaty. In doing so, it enables States to structure their relationships through BITs and create effective frameworks for addressins. The defence of necessity can justify a State's non-compliance with treaty obligations when the treaty explicitly includes provisions addressing

106 *ibid* 370.

107 Surya P Subedi, *International Investment Law: Reconciling Policy and Principle* (Hart Publishing 2016) 118.

108 Giest (n 12) 347.

109 Tania Voon & Andrew D. Mitchell 'Denunciation, Termination and Survival: The Interplay of Treaty Law and International Investment Law' (2016) 31(2) *ICSID Review*, 414.

110 Bruno Simma & Dirk Pulkowski, 'Two Worlds, but Not Apart: International and General International Law' in Marc Bungenberg, Jorn Griebel, Stephan Hobe & August Reinisch (eds), *International Investment Law* (Hart Publishing 2014) 367.

111 Surya P Subedi, *International Investment Law: Reconciling Policy and Principle* (Hart Publishing 2016) 115.

necessity-like situations.[112] For example, Article XI of the US-Argentina BIT provides that:

> this treaty shall not preclude the application by either party of measures necessary for the maintenance of public order, the fulfilment of its obligations with respect to the maintenance of public order, the maintenance or restoration of international peace or security, or the protection of its essential security interest.[113]

States have some discretion in defining their essential security interests, but they cannot unilaterally interpret exception clauses, as these interpretations are subject to review by international bodies; otherwise they can encourage impunity. Therefore, international adjudicatory bodies are crucial in applying exception clauses, ensuring a balance between the legality of such actions and other international legal obligations.[114]

In this part, the elements of necessity defence under Article 25 of the International Law Commission (ILC) will be appraised and discussed with reference to its applicability in economic crisis. The reason for doing so is because the omission of necessity will not prevent States from relying on the defence. As adequately captioned by the special rapporteur of the ILC, Roberto Ago, necessity as a defence measure is deeply ingrained in the international community's consciousness, suggesting that even if it is formally rejected, it will re-emerge in other ways or forms.[115] Thus the presence or absence of balance-of-payments provisions will not prevent host States from invoking the defence to justify non-compliance with their transfer obligations under investment treaties, especially when States seek to derogate from their international commitments, potentially leading to wrongful actions. This necessitates a restrictive interpretation of derogation provisions, as the lack of investment law analysis regarding the necessity of State measures in economic crises is concerning. Allowing States broad discretion in defining "necessity" risks undermining foreign investor relationships.[116] The tribunal's decision in the *Continental Casualty* case, which derived its understanding of "necessity" from GATT/WTO case law, could hinder foreign investors' remedies in unforeseen

112 Alan O. Sykes, 'Economic "Necessity" in International Law' (2015) 109(2) *The American Journal of International Law*, 296.

113 How May Tribunals Apply the Customary Necessity to Rule to the Argentine Cases?, 29. By Javier El-Hage. Available on https://papers.ssrn.com/sol3/papers.cfm?abstract_id=2480059 [Accessed on 6 December 2024].

114 Ali Z. Marossi, 'Unilateralism and Power of Revision' in Ali Z. Marossi & Marisa R. Bassett (eds), *Economic Sanctions under International Law: Unilateralism, Multilateralism, Legitimacy, and Consequences* (Springer 2015) 169.

115 Christina Binder & August Reinisch, 'Economic Emergency Powers: A Comparative Law Perspective' in Stephen Schill (ed), *International Investment Law and Comparative Public Law* (Oxford University Press 2010) 505.

116 Abba Kolo & Thomas Walde, 'Economic Crises, Capital Transfer Restrictions and Investor Protection Under Modern Investment Treaties' (2008) 3(2) *Capital Markets Law Journal*, 164.

situations, ultimately counteracting the treaty's goal of promoting investments in developing countries.[117] This raises the question of what defences and supporting materials are reasonable and appropriate for resolving investment disputes. In other words, what rights do foreign investors truly have during economic crises?

The autonomy of contracting parties to define treaty provisions in public international law facilitates transnational commerce, but the lack of a cohesive supranational body overseeing the international investment regime leads to challenges, including compliance burdens with inconsistent laws and significant uncertainties. This section seeks to integrate the doctrine of necessity into treaty texts to clarify the meaning of the "transfer of funds" provision, aiming to enhance predictability and reduce reliance on ambiguous interpretations, thus providing a solid theoretical framework to support this approach.

6.3.2.1.1 THE DOCTRINE OF NECESSITY

Necessity as an exception to State responsibility in international economic relations can arise from both economic and non-economic causes. Domestically, it may stem from issues like monetary crises or trade disruptions, such as sudden import surges or high unemployment. Internationally, necessity can reflect conditions that require a response from external parties, such as famine, poverty, or natural disasters. In the realm of international economic law, this necessity is primarily addressed through bilateral and multilateral agreements, soft law, and the discretion of States, highlighting its relevance from both internal and external perspectives.[118]

According to Article 25 of the ILC, necessity can only be invoked under strict limitations and exceptional circumstances, justifiable only if a State's non-compliance with a BIT obligation is the sole means of protecting an essential interest. Additionally, all conditions outlined in Article 25 must be met cumulatively for necessity to apply.[119] For the necessity doctrine to preclude State wrongfulness, the act in question must be the only way to safeguard an essential interest from imminent danger, and the State must not have contributed to the necessity situation.[120] Thus it is crucial to explore the policy considerations available to States in this context.

6.3.2.2 Parameters for Defining an Economic Crisis and the Contributory Factors

This section examines the factors tribunals consider when evaluating breaches of the right to transfer funds, as well as the economic difficulties that may prompt host

117 Kathleen Claussen, 'The Casualty of Investor Protection in Times of Economic Crisis' (2009) 118 (7) *Yale Law Journal*, 1554.

118 Asif Qureshi, 'A Necessity in International Economic Law' in I. F. Dekker & E. Hey (eds), *Netherlands Yearbook of International Law* (Cambridge University Press 2010) 102.

119 *ibid.*

120 Roman Boed, 'State of Necessity as a Justification for Internationally Wrongful Conduct' (2003) 3(1) *Yale Human Rights and Development Law Journal*, 16–17.

States to deviate from their contractual obligations. It aims to establish a consistent threshold for such violations, particularly regarding how to determine if a State's actions represent the only viable response to a crisis—a notion referred to as the "only requirement" in customary international law—and whether the State played a role in creating the crisis.[121] Reconciling the state of necessity, as governed by international law, with a BIT clause that allows for emergency measures during an economic crisis can be challenging, particularly when there is a risk of prejudicing interests.[122]

The necessity requirement in both BITs and customary international law is not self-judging and is subject to arbitral inquiry. Analysis of case law indicates that necessity clauses in BITs have less stringent criteria than those found in customary international law.[123] Historically, States have used balance-of-payments measures to justify capital controls, as exemplified by India's invocation of this provision during a 1997 WTO dispute with the United States. The WTO panel, relying on information from the IMF, determined that India's monetary reserves were sufficient at the time, indicating that the imposition of controls was unnecessary.[124] Thus a problem for treaty drafters and adjudicators is to separate opportunistic behaviours of States from legitimate policies of host States who pursue them.[125] To obviate this, the violation of the legal obligation in question should be deemed at least theoretically avoidable in a situation where necessity is applicable.[126] Given the economic rationale for allowing host States to maintain some control over fund transfers, Article 12(b) of the Morocco-Nigeria BIT permits host States to temporarily restrict foreign investors' rights to transfer funds during serious balance-of-payments problems. While this provision aims to balance the interests of foreign investors and the regulatory autonomy of host States, it remains unclear what constitutes a serious balance-of-payments difficulty. The criteria for justifying derogations from the free transfer of funds are narrowly defined and inadequately articulated, raising questions about whether an equitable balance exists between the competing interests of treaty stakeholders.

To prevent the arbitrary imposition of controls, it is essential to clearly outline necessary constraints. This brings forth several important questions: are economic crises verifiable by arbitrators? What occurs when the circumstances necessitating the crisis subside? When is capital control the most appropriate public policy response when other measures might suffice? Should foreign investors be

121 Binder & Reinisch (n 115)148–149.

122 Sergey Ripinsky, 'Global Economic Crisis and the Danger of Protectionism: Does International Law Help?' (2009) (1)3 *Amsterdam Law Forum*, 6.

123 *ibid.*

124 *ibid* 3–4.

125 Anne Van Aaken & Jurgen Kurtz, 'Prudence or Discrimination? Emergency Measures, The Global Financial Crises and International Economic Law' (2009) 12(4) *Journal of International Economic Law*, 828.

126 Maria Agius, 'The Invocation of Necessity in International Law' (2009) 56(2) *Netherlands International Law Review*, 101.

compensated for losses incurred during this period? These questions can guide adjudicators in determining the extent to which legal obligations under customary international law and treaty provisions should apply or be set aside, addressing the tension between economic challenges and limiting opportunism by host States.

Given that economic crises can severely impact governments, corporations, and individuals, identifying early warning indicators of potential crises is vital. While economic crises are not new, statistical models can be developed to link their occurrence to lagged variables serving as early warning indicators.[127] Utilising these models can help identify serious economic threats and mitigate the perception that a host State's failure to prevent a crisis constitutes a "contribution" to the situation of necessity. Although these indicators may not predict all types of crises, they can provide a structured approach to recognising imminent economic dangers. It is recommended that parties to BITs and international tribunals utilise these early warning models to assess grave and imminent risks to host economies.

6.3.2.3 Reconciling BIT Provisions with Treaty Obligations

In times of emergency, host States must still adhere to their BIT and other international obligations.[128] Article VIII 2 of the IMF Articles of Agreement sets forth two important obligations that should regulate the conduct of external monetary affairs. It states that:

> (a) Subject to the provisions of Article VII, Section 3(b) and Article XIV, Section 2, no member shall, without the approval of the Fund, impose restrictions on the making of payments and transfers for current international transactions.
>
> (b) Exchange contracts which involve the currency of any member and which are contrary to the exchange control regulations of that member maintained or imposed consistently with this Agreement shall be unenforceable in the territories of any member. In addition, members may, by mutual accord, cooperate in measures for the purpose of making the exchange control regulations of either member more effective, provided that such measures and regulations are consistent with this Agreement.[129]

127 Matthieu Bussiere, 'Balance of Payments Crises in Emerging Markets: How Early Were the "Early" Warning Signals?' (2013) 45(12) *Applied Economics*, 1602; Alberto Alvarez-Jimenez, 'The Great Recession and the New Frontiers of International Investment Law: The Economics of Early Warning Models and the Law of Necessity' (2014) 17 *Journal of International Economic Law*, 517–550.

128 Diane Desierto, 'ICERSCR Minimum Core Obligations and Investment: Recasting the Non-Expropriation Compensation Model During Financial Crises' (2012) 44(3) *The George Washington International Law Review*, 481.

129 International Monetary Fund Agreement. Available on https://www.imf.org/external/pubs/ft/aa/index.htm [Accessed on 6 December 2024].

Article VIII makes exchange contracts that involve exchange restrictions that are maintained or imposed in a manner inconsistent with the IMF Fund Agreement to be unenforceable. BITs that require the protection of funds do not often differentiate between current and capital transfers, as mandated by the IMF Articles of Agreement, and restrictions on current transactions[130] are highly prohibited. BITs typically do not distinguish between current and capital transfers, as outlined by the IMF Articles of Agreement, and they generally prohibit restrictions on current transactions. To support the sovereignty of host States, it is recommended that BITs explicitly allow exceptions to this IMF provision, or exchange restrictions should specifically be stated to be on capital transfers.

Additionally, it is recommended that restrictions made on payments or transfers, where imposed using non-discriminatory, equitable and good faith measures, must not exceed in any case a six-month period. (For context, the IMF typically allows for a maximum of one year).[131] In this case, "non-discriminatory" means that measures should be confined to addressing the economic and financial aspects of the crisis. They should not disrupt the regular operations of foreign investors, and there should be no distinction made between domestic and foreign investors in their application.

To avoid conflicts with the IMF Fund Agreement, which most States are party to, it is recommended that a model treaty should explicitly exempt itself from other obligations under the IMF Articles. This would help resolve potential conflicts between BIT transfer clauses and IMF provisions. Additionally, the treaty could clarify that exceptions to the right to transfer funds—aimed at addressing balance of payments issues or public policy concerns—do not violate other treaty provisions. This would ensure that exercising these exceptions is not interpreted as indirect expropriation or a breach of treaty obligations.

6.4 Finding Consistency through Amicus Curiae Submissions

Vague treaty texts grant arbitrators a central role in exercising discretion over how the system should function.[132] This empowers arbitral tribunals to assess the legality of State conduct.[133] In the case that ambiguous texts in BITs are not eliminated, recourse can be made to interpretative guidelines from amicus curiae; they

130 Art XXX (d) of the Fund Agreement differentiates between capital and current account transactions by listing, in a non-exhaustive manner, examples of payments which do not qualify as capital account transactions; Stephan Schill, 'Transfer of Funds: The Interaction between the IMF Articles of Agreement and Modern Investment Treaties: A Comparative Law Perspective' in Abba Kolo (ed), *International Investment Law and Comparative Public Law* (Oxford University Press 2010) 349.

131 Article XXVII (Emergency Provisions) International Monetary Fund Agreement. Available on https://www.imf.org/external/pubs/ft/aa/index.htm [Accessed on 6 December 2024].

132 Gus Van Harten, 'Five Justifications for Investment Treaties: A Critical Discussion' (2010) 2(1) *Trade, Law and Development*, 27.

133 *ibid.*

are considered relevant in this context because they provide perspectives and relevant expertise different from those provided by the participating parties. They also increase transparency in investment arbitration by providing the public with insights into the investment arbitration process.[134] Although international law is principally engaged with inter-State relations, the role of non-State actors in international law is a reality that cannot be ignored.[135]

A defining characteristic of the BIT regime is the ability of foreign investors to make recourse to investor-State arbitration by invoking broadly defined treaty provisions without first exhausting judicial remedies available within the host-State. BITs are commonly characterised by their need for substantial and, in most cases, unpredictable interpretation. The interpretative function of tribunals furnishes arbitrators with a central role in the exercise of their discretion about what the system should be.[136] When BITs break down, treaty arbitration takes the centre stage. At this point, it becomes important that the process is watertight to forestall the failures that led to the breakdown of the treaty. Practically, it is not always the case that the arbitration process is watertight. The phenomenal growth of BITs is also accompanied with a fundamental paradox: the process is designed to protect foreign investors particularly in developing States. Yet, it is in those States that there is a growing suspicion of the process.[137] Host governments often feel pressured to engage in a process that is unfamiliar to them, leading to a sense of marginalisation. The same lawyers who draft the rules and conventions of international law and arbitration, and who may not grasp the unique characteristics of the region, are typically the ones representing these governments. This makes it difficult for developing States to adequately canvass the public interest purpose. This dynamic contributes to their discomfort and scepticism regarding the process. The result is total disillusionment in the arbitration process.[138]

Investor-State arbitration has implications for the ability of the public to control policy through its democratically elected leaders and the way those leaders allocate taxpayers funds. Investment claims are known to range from millions to billions of US dollars.[139] An arbitral award against a developing State is likely to have

134 Blackaby Nigel & Caroline Richard, 'Amicus Curiae: A Panacea for Legitimacy in Investment Arbitration?' In Michael Waibel (ed), *The Backlash Against Investment Arbitration: Perceptions and Reality* (Kluwer Law & Business 2010) 257.

135 State vs Non-State Actors: A Public International Law Perspective, 3. By Agata Kleczkowska. Available on https://www.hybridcoe.fi/wp-content/uploads/2020/07/Hybrid-CoE-Strategic-Analysis-20.pdf [Accessed on 6 December 2024].

136 Ciaran Cross & Christian Schliemann-Radbruch, 'When Investment Arbitration Curbs Domestic Regulatory Space: Consistent Solutions through Amicus Curiae Submissions by Regional Organisations' (2013) 6(2) *Law and Development Review*, 73.

137 Nudrat Majeed, 'Investor-State Disputes and International Law: From the Far Side' (2004) 98 *American Society of International Law*, 31.

138 *ibid.*

139 Susan D. Franck, *Arbitration Costs: Myths and Realities in Investment Treaty Arbitration* (Oxford University Press 2019) 160.

devastating consequences for its economy.[140] Arbitral awards can have a macro-economic effect and catastrophic effects on a State's budget.

Given that investor-State arbitration often challenges State measures aimed at achieving crucial public policy objectives, such as managing economic crises, it is essential to ensure high levels of public access to the dispute-settlement process. This transparency is vital for fostering public acceptance of the outcomes. Consequently, developing States should not rely solely on formal State institutions to advocate for their interests in investment disputes. Involving non-State actors—beyond just foreign investors—can provide valuable perspectives that neither contracting party may offer.[141]

International investment law is largely populated by lawyers. The legal constituency of those attributed to investment arbitration consists of those who have worked or work in commercial arbitration. These practitioners come with set ways of operating, without consideration of whether their methods are appropriate for dissolving disputes under a broadly worded treaty.[142] The adjudicatory flaw most often attributed by critics is a pro-investor bias. Many of the practitioners engage case law technically and doctrinally in order to minimise any area of conflict. Most times, little consideration is paid to disciplines other than law in order to probe the justifications for particular investment protections. These tendencies stand in contrast to the engagement of interdisciplinary insights (especially those of economists) in the working of the WTO.[143]

A new tool, amicus curiae participation, is perhaps vital, seeing that it recognises that investor-State arbitration belongs firmly in the public law sphere. This tool allows non-disputing parties to submit legal or factual perspectives on issues of public interest raised by disputants.[144] Given the limited resources available to developing States, these rules present a valuable and additional avenue to combat expansive interpretative trends in investment arbitration.[145] The importance of amicus curiae is recognised by the investment tribunal in the case of *Biwater v. Tanzania*[146] as a tool in "securing wider confidence in the arbitral process itself".[147] Thus amicus curiae are important elements in mitigating legitimacy concerns that

140 Assessing the Benefits of Allowing Amicus Curiae Briefs in Investor-State Arbitrations: A Developing State's Perspective, 7. By Kinyua Paul Kenneth. Available on https://www.researchgate.net/publication/255967036_Assessing_the_Benefits_of_Accepting_Amici_Curiae_Briefs_in_Investor-State_Arbitrations_A_Developing_State%27S_Perspective [Accessed on 7 December 2024].

141 *ibid* 8.

142 Jurgen Kurtz, 'The Shifting Landscape of International Investment Law and Its Commentary' (2012) 106(3) *American Journal of International Law*, 688.

143 *ibid* 689.

144 Cross & Schliemann-Radbruch (n 136) 79.

145 *ibid*.

146 Biwater Gauff (Tanzania) Ltd. v. United Republic of Tanzania, ICSID Case No. ARB/05/22.

147 Astrid Wiik, *Amicus Curiae before International Courts and Tribunals* (Hart Publishing 2018) 526.

arise from investment arbitration. They are non-parties to a dispute and are simply referred to as "friends of the court".[148]

The issue of legitimacy is one of the cornerstones for international adjudication. Legitimacy ensures that those who are affected by a decision should be eager to accept the outcome even if it does not reflect the desired outcome. Traditionally, courts have always recognised and accepted the intervention of amicus curiae in private litigation because those cases have involved issues of public interest and because decisions in those cases have the potential directly or indirectly to affect persons beyond those immediately involved as parties in the case.[149] Conversely, one could argue that most investment disputes possess a public dimension,[150] thereby justifying the involvement of amicus curiae in these forums. The international investment regime has a public and private international law underpinning. From one perspective, international investment law comprises of specialised objects of international investment law—involving a combination of different treaties; from another perspective, it is a specialised subject of international commercial arbitration, a series of business disputes based on treaty agreements and resolved by arbitral tribunals.[151] This hybridisation populates the investment regime with practitioners and academics with diverse professional and ideational backgrounds. While this combination of groups from public and private international law is fruitful in solving disputes, which are often factually and legally complex, it often results in a clash of epistemic communities as both groups operate on different philosophies and with different perspectives. While public international lawyers are more concerned with the specific responsibilities of a State to her sovereigns and the contribution of investment treaty arbitration to public objectives of the international community at large; the private international lawyers on the other hand are stressing the private nature of dispute settlement in resolving an individual dispute between two parties based on party autonomy and backed by confidentiality.[152]

Standards outlined in BITs help justify, legitimise, and sometimes explain modifications to the investment law regime. These standards are valuable for assessing how well contemporary investment law and arbitration practices align with internationally accepted norms. Beyond the customary international law and public international law practices, there exists a third set of standards:

148 S. Chandra Mohan, 'The Amicus Curiae: Friends No More?' (2010) *Singapore Journal of Legal Studies*, 353.

149 Jorge E. Vinuales, 'Amicus Intervention in Investor-State Arbitration' (2007) 61(4) *Dispute Resolution Journal*, 76.

150 *ibid.*

151 Alex Mills, 'Antinomies of Public and Private at the Foundations of International Investment Law and Arbitration' (2011) 14(2) *Journal of International Economic Law*, 470.

152 Stephan Schill, 'Enhancing International Investment Law's Legitimacy: Conceptual and Methodological Foundations of a New Public Law Approach' (2011) 52(1) *Virginia Journal of International Law*, 71–72.

political, economic, and policy considerations that operate outside formal legal constraints.[153] For instance, in the case of *LG & E v. Argentine Republic*, the tribunal evaluated the Argentine economy against the backdrop of its gross domestic product, the drop in private consumption, the decline in prices and value of assets of companies in Argentina, the State's risk premium, and the liquidity of the Central Bank of Argentina's reserves. The tribunal also evaluated the poverty data and unemployment data from the relevant period as well as the prices of pharmaceutical products in Argentina.[154]

Amicus curiae are canvassed as desirable in this instance to enable both the host State and foreign investors to understand the practicalities of their case and to create the transparency that is much needed in the investment regime. Article 28(3) of the 2012 United States Model BIT is known to have expressly included the possibility of tribunals to accept amicus curiae submissions from a person or entity that is a non-disputing party. Similarly, Article 39 of the 2004 Canadian Model Foreign Investment Promotion and Protection Agreement not only provides for amicus curiae, but it goes further to provide conditions that amicus curiae submissions must meet before they are accepted by tribunals. Other treaties that have included the possibility of arbitral tribunals to accept amicus curiae submissions are Article 10.26 of the Chile-Hong Kong BIT, Article 18 of the 2015 Norway Model BIT, and Article 22.4 of the 2015 Indian Model BIT.[155]

If States expressly consent to the participation of amicus curiae in the dispute-settlement mechanism, then they are not removing themselves entirely from the equation.[156] Private actors, once recognised, may petition States or international organisations directly about the conformity of particular acts to international law. For example, following a side agreement in NAFTA, the North American Environmental Cooperation authorised private parties to submit allegations where there have been infractions on environmental laws by any of the participating States. Also private parties may participate directly with States in reviewing the implementation of an international agreement,[157] and this is a mechanism advanced in this discourse.

153 Eric De Brabandere, '(Re)Calibration, Standard-Setting and the Shaping of Investment Law and Arbitration' (2018) 59(8) *Boston College Law Review*, 2610.

154 Avidan K. Kent & Alexandra R. Harrington, 'A State of Necessity: International Legal Obligations in Times of Crises' (2012) 42(1) *Canadian Review of American Studies*, 70.

155 Eric De Brabandere, 'Amicus Curiae (Investment Arbitration)' in Hélène Ruiz-Fabri Max Planck (ed), *Encyclopedia of International Procedural Law* (Oxford University Press, 2019) 7.

156 Duncan B. Hollis, 'Private Actors in Public International Law: Amicus Curiae and the Case for the Retention of State Sovereignty' (2002) 25(2) *Boston College International and Comparative Law Review*, 253.

157 *ibid* 246.

6.4.2 Economists as Amicus Curiae

One key issue likely to bedevil tribunals, by their traditional designation, is whether they are truly equipped to assess when an investment has contributed to the economic development of a host State and to determine the economic parameters for identifying the presence or absence of an economic crisis. ICSID, along with other arbitration centres handling investor-State disputes, does not employ a dedicated economist. Instead, arbitration tribunals typically appoint administrative or legal secretaries who may lack the expertise to address complex economic issues effectively.[158] It is therefore astonishing that, unlike lawyers, economists are typically not appointed as investment arbitrators; after all, investment arbitration is mainly about putting a number on the losses inflicted on foreign investment by the host State. Foreign investors initiate claims to reclaim monetary losses and respondent States defend against these claims to prevent payment of taxpayers' money; since arbitration in this sense is a mechanism for the valuation of losses and claims with an economic nature,[159] it would be sensible to have economists supplement the lawyers who decide these cases. Thus economists would be canvassed as support systems but not a substitute for legal analysis and interpretation.

Economics must be refined through legal criteria while the interpretational sovereignty should lie with the legal interpreter.[160] This is exemplified in the case of *CMS v Argentina*, where the tribunal considered the viewpoints of leading economists from both parties to make a final determination regarding the necessity of the measures Argentina had taken.[161] The use of economists in investor-State arbitration would be useful to decipher investment transactions that require protection, taking into consideration the often-cited criteria of risk and contribution to economic development. Economists can offer help in determining the basic elements of Article 25 of the ILC Articles on State Responsibility which need to be met for the defence of necessity to be activated. Contracting parties in some of the Argentinian cases discussed previously are known to have submitted extensive economic evidence and brought in highly qualified economic experts.[162]

158 The Use, Non-use and Abuse of Economics in WTO and Investor-State Dispute Settlement, 15. By Joost Pauwelyn. Available on https://papers.ssrn.com/sol3/papers.cfm?abstract_id=2141357 [Accessed on 7 December 2024].

159 Wolfgang Alschner, 'Aligning Loss and Liability: Toward an Integrated Assessment of Damages in Investment Arbitration' in Marion Jansen, Joost Pauwelyn & Theresa Carpenter (eds), *The Use of Economics in International Trade and Investment Disputes* (Cambridge University Press 2017) 284.

160 *ibid.*

161 Sarah F. Hill, 'The Necessity Defense and the Emerging Arbitral Conflict in its Application to the U.S.-Argentina Bilateral Investment Treaty' (2007) 13(3) *Law and Business Review of the Americas*, 558.

162 Wolfgang Alschner, 'Aligning Loss and Liability: Toward an Integrated Assessment of Damages in Investment Arbitration' in Marion Jansen, Joost Pauwelyn & Theresa Carpenter (eds), *The Use of Economics in International Trade and Investment Disputes* (Cambridge University Press 2017) 17.

Outcomes of arbitration are decided by so many factors. Primarily, arbitrators decide whether a foreign investor or a State wins and the damages or compensation that needs to be awarded to a disputing party. However, foreign investors and States can contribute significantly to the outcome of arbitration.[163] They can decide to expressly acknowledge the role of economists as amicus curiae as an important element for interventions of complex and non-legal issues. In the case of *Aguas del Tunari v Republic of Bolivia*, an ICSID tribunal asserted that the "interplay of the ICSID Convention and the BIT, and the consensual nature of arbitration meant that the decision as to whether to accept the third-party submissions should be left to the parties themselves".[164] The tribunal in this case refused to accept an amicus submission because the parties were unwilling to accept them. Though the principle of party autonomy is embedded in the investment regime, this decision was fiercely criticised, because, where important issues of the public interest is at stake, the centrality of the role of party autonomy becomes objectionable. The ensuing criticism surrounding this decision led to the amendment of ICSID Rule 37, which now enables non-disputing parties to file an amicus brief and further establishes their criteria for participation.[165] This means that contracting States to a treaty and non-State actors can appoint amicus curiae in matters that concern public policies.

Amicus curiae are thus relevant to provide new perspective and information in a case, which in turn may lead to fairer decisions in the long run, especially in investment issues where public concerns are at stake.[166]

In general, an amicus curiae can be understood as a body which is not a party to the case but is relevant because it helps the decision maker to arrive at its decision by providing the decision maker with expertise and arguments that the contending parties may not have. The interest of the arbitral tribunal is that the amicus curiae will assist the tribunal in conducting a better hearing and safeguarding the due process.[167] Article 15 of the UNCITRAL Arbitration Rules gives a tribunal a large amount of discretion in terms of procedural rules and principles which is confined to only the principles of equality and party agreement.[168] However, it is appropriate in the spirit of reducing ambiguities to expressly incorporate the provision that enables third-party participation in the proceedings.

163 Duy Vu, 'Reasons Not to Exit? A Survey of the Effectiveness and Spill Over Effects of International Investment Arbitration' (2019) 47(2) *European Journal of Law and Economics*, 300–301.

164 Nicoletter Butler, 'Non-Disputing Party Participation in ICSID Disputes: Faux Amici?' (2019) 66 *Netherlands International Law Review*, 146.

165 *ibid* 147.

166 *ibid.*

167 Yen-Chiang Chang, 'How Does the Amicus Curiae Submission Affect a Tribunal Decision?' (2017) 30(3) *Leiden Journal of International Law*, 649.

168 Eric De Brabandere, 'NGO and the "Public Interest": The Legality and Rationale of Amicus Curiae Interventions in International Economic and Investment Disputes' (2011) 12(1) *Chicago Journal of International Law*, 99.

The basis for this proposition is because, in some cases, arbitral rules only require the admittance of amicus curiae as permitted by the operating treaty. Thus the following recommendations are proposed: (1) the recognition of amicus curiae as important elements in the treaty interpretation of issues that border on economic matters. Emphasis should be placed on the academic qualifications, experience, expertise, and impartiality of the amicus curiae; (2) The granting of permission to arbitral bodies to access material information sufficient enough to provide relevant and informed submission to merit the participation of amicus curiae; (3) The admittance of amicus curiae should be based on their ability to bring new arguments that give a different legal and factual perspective to the issue being adjudicated. Proposed procedural safeguards are the limitation of time and length constraints to a maximum period of six months from the inception of the arbitral proceedings so as not to unduly disrupt the proceedings and burden the main parties to the dispute.

When determining the expertise and independence of the amicus curiae, in drawing parallels from the case of Methanex,[169] it is imperative that the prospective amici provide information on their identity, legal status, and relationship with any of the disputing parties.[170] An amicus, in this context, need not have any expertise in international investment law; what is important is an expertise in the established area of work for which his presence is needed in the first place and, in this case, knowledge in economics should be sufficient.

6.5 Conclusion

The investment regime faces significant concerns regarding the potential limitations it places on State regulatory authority. The open-ended language of investors' rights can lead investment tribunals to undervalue the importance of general regulations intended to protect public interests. To mitigate these issues, States should proactively assert their interpretative authority through guiding tribunals towards a more predictable interpretation of treaty provisions. While precise textual clarity in BITs is essential, it may not always be achievable due to evolving norms requiring States to adapt their regulations. Even if precise language were possible, structural changes would still be necessary to ensure that arbitrators interpret treaties effectively. Past tribunal decisions might fill gaps, but there is often a lack of coherence in how investment tribunals adhere to their own precedents. Interpretations that stray from typical usage can harm non-party beneficiaries, including the contracting States themselves, who may have had little input in the drafting process. Thus it is acknowledged that parties to a BIT can renegotiate or withdraw from treaties, recognising that the international investment regime does not inherently promote efficiency. The argument is straightforward: well-crafted and interpretative guidance can address a variety of inefficiencies that might otherwise arise.

169 Methanex Corporation v United States of America UNCITRAL (1976)
170 Cross & Schliemann-Radbruch (137) 83.

7 Conclusion

7.1 Conclusion

The exponential growth of FDI has led to a proliferation of investment treaties, particularly BITs, which have become essential components of the international legal and economic framework. However, this network of BITs is now facing a significant backlash. This backlash stems primarily from the expansive interpretations of foreign investor protections by tribunals and the broad definitions of arbitrability by arbitrators. These interpretations often clash with the principles of State sovereignty and societal self-determination, raising concerns about the balance between protecting foreign investments and upholding domestic rights. Critics argue that the rules and principles enshrined in these investment treaties disproportionately favour capital-exporting States and foreign investors, igniting a debate about the desirability and effectiveness of the international investment protection regime.[1] This has led to increasing scrutiny regarding substantive bias, procedural shortcomings, and the political implications of the regime, particularly evident in investor-State disputes. These disputes highlight the tension between preserving State sovereignty and attracting investment, as well as the complexities surrounding treaty obligations.

It has been argued that each State has the freedom to establish and manage economic relations with other States, private individuals, or companies, and can unilaterally disrupt these relationships to assert its economic sovereignty. In such cases, the primary considerations for the State are the interests of its people and sublime political desires.[2] However, one aspect of International Economic Law that intensifies concerns about sovereignty is the regulation of relationships between States and foreign investors. A State cannot fully exercise its economic sovereignty without adhering to the established rights of foreign investors outlined in treaties or laws. This challenge arises from the dynamic inconsistency problem faced by States; their sovereign status allows them to change laws in their own interest but

1 Schill Stephan, *The Multilateralization of International Investment Law* (Cambridge University Press 2009) 7.

2 Adibi A. & Habibi H., 'The Challenge of the Economic Independence and the Sovereignty of States: A Review of the Problem of Legitimacy of Economic Sanctions in the Reality of the International Legal Order' (2017) 5(3) *Russian Law Journal*, 116.

DOI: 10.4324/9781003611714-7

a commitment mechanism such as a BIT can effectively bind both the host State and the foreign investor to a specific set of rules.[3] The Argentina cases, as shown in previous discussions, evidence a distinct willingness to implement nationalistic and populist economic policies, not minding if this alienates multinational organisations and discourages investment by foreign companies.[4]

States may face a challenge with devising a regulatory scheme which addresses *ex- ante* and *ex post* concerns or is considered appropriate by domestic policy law makers in order not to incur liability under international law and, invariably, not discourage foreign investments. This is because an open and unrestricted invitation of foreign investment, while increasing the amount of foreign capital in an economy, may lead to unbalanced development in some sectors of the economy. Also, excessive regulation can be quite discouraging in attracting foreign capital.[5] Developing States that sign investment treaties with developed States run many risks, some of which arise during negotiation process. Developing States do not have the same resources as their developed counterparts to evaluate the appropriateness and impact on their economy of the investment agreements they sign. Even in situations where they have enough resources to evaluate the impact of an investment treaty, many developed States employ draft templates that leave less room for manoeuvre during negotiations.[6]

These treaties are not only highly asymmetric in their foundational norms, but there is also concern regarding how tribunals interpret common provisions. Investment tribunals have established precedents that tend to prioritise the rights of foreign investors, often overlooking the role of foreign investment in the development policies of host States, particularly in developing countries.[7] Arbitral awards in this context overcompensate and empower foreign investors to effectively override legitimate State expectations, to the latter's detriment.[8] The right to repatriation of capital and transfer of profits granted to a foreign investor involves a legal process which places them on a pedestal in international law not usually afforded to non-State actors and sets BITs apart from other international agreements where access to dispute settlement is typically restricted to sovereign States. This leads

3 Natasha Marusja Saputo, 'Paradoxical Pacts: Understanding the BIT Phenomenon and the Rejection of a Multilateral Agreement on Investment' (2014) 41(1) *Ohio Northern University Law Review*, 136.

4 Charity L. Goodman, 'Uncharted Waters: Financial Crisis and Enforcement of ICSID Awards in Argentina' (2007) 28(2) *University of Pennsylvania Journal of International Economic Law*, 480.

5 Jane E. Cross, 'Foreign Investment Laws in Developing States' (1984) 6(1) *Michigan Journal of International Law*, 155.

6 Graham Mayeda, 'International Investment Agreements between Developed Countries and Developing Countries: Dancing with the Devil? Case Comment on the *Vivendi*, *Sempra* and *Enron* Awards' (2008) 4(2) *McGill International Journal of Sustainable Development*, 191.

7 *ibid.*

8 Frank J. Garcia, Lindita Cikoo, Apurv Gaurav & Kirrin Hough, 'Reforming the International Investment Regime: Lessons from International Trade Law' (2015) 18 *Journal of International Economic Law*, 870.

to what some may term "shared sovereignty",[9] in some cases erosion of State sovereignty,[10] and constraints on the policy choices of States.[11]

The extent to which investment agreements allow flexibility and a policy space for achieving developmental goals largely depends on the nature and scope of the substantive obligations outlined in the BITs. The core argument advanced so far is that poorly drafted provisions regarding the right to repatriate profits can increase the costs and liabilities for host States. Consequently, the precarious position of States in fostering economic growth through investment protection may seem minor when weighed against the sovereignty challenges they face, especially during capital flight in economic crises. Addressing investment challenges is complex, as discussed in Chapter 5. Issues of economic sovereignty, the need for States to deviate from treaty obligations, and populist policies that may alienate multinational corporations often discourage foreign investment and remain underexplored. Efforts to balance societal self-determination with the protection of foreign property create additional complications related to substantive bias and procedural shortcomings, further fuelling the backlash against the investment regime. The economic volatility of developing States requires that they move away from undue emphasis on foreign investment protection to their own detriment and start leaning towards the need to preserve their regulatory space to interfere with foreign investment regulations if need be. Since these treaties are voluntary in nature,[12] there is need for a re-visitation and re-negotiation of these treaties to address contemporary challenges in investment.

Rightfully, a BIT should be central purposed for the establishment of principles that are critical to institutional quality: one which opens economies to capital movement with no absolute guarantees through exceptions to BIT obligations. This way, there are mutual commitments to principles of good governance as the success of the investment regime is not measured by the quality of foreign investments it attracts but by the quality of the legal environment that is established.[13] It is for this reason that the recommendations in Chapter 6 are premised to strengthen the ambit of the host State as a regulator and limit the regulatory discretion of an investor-State arbitral tribunal.

Not all recommendations favour the host State as a regulator; some aim to limit the host State's regulatory autonomy for valid reasons. For instance, proposals

9 Kyla Tienhaara, 'Once BITten, Twice Shy? The Uncertain Future of "Shared Sovereignty" in Investment Treaty Arbitration' (2011) 30(3) *Policy and Society*, 185–186.

10 Mohammad Belayet Hossain, Asmah Laila Bt Yeon & Ahmad Shamsul, 'Sovereignty, National Interest & Security and the Bilateral Investment Treaties of Bangladesh and the Netherlands: A Comparison' (2019) 12(2) *African Journal of Legal Studies*, 193.

11 Dominic Dagbanja, 'Changing Pattern and Future of Foreign Investment Law and Policy in Ghana: The Role of International Investment Treaties' (2011–2012) 19 *African Yearbook of International Law*, 58.

12 Kasey L. McCall-Smith, 'Severing Reservations' (2014) 66(3) *International and Comparative Law Quarterly*, 600.

13 Kenneth J. Vandevelde, 'Sustainable Liberalism and the International Investment Regime' (1988) 19(2) *Michigan Journal of International Law*, 313.

to define economic parameters for determining economic crises are designed to prevent the abuse of power by host States. Overall, these recommendations seek to rebalance the obligations outlined in BITs. In this context, a systematic integration of (customary) international law with the substantive obligations of treaties is suggested as a guide for relevant stakeholders in the investment landscape. This integration is important because the relationship between general international law and treaty rules is symbiotic, and the diverse obligations arising from these treaties can hinder broader coordination of national policies affecting global capital flows. Many recommendations discussed in Chapter 6 emphasise the need for the investment regime to support viable economies. They advocate for prohibiting arbitrary exchange controls while allowing exceptions for balance of payments crises under appropriate circumstances. Ultimately, the central purpose of BITs should be to establish legal principles that enhance institutional quality, ensuring that host States can pursue legitimate public policy measures without undermining their ability to open their economies to capital movement.[14] Recommendations are considered not as authoritative principles but as essentials for effective treaty interpretation and as practices or guidelines that investment tribunals and States should consider if the much-desired transparency in the international investment regime is to be achieved. The existence of interpretative guidelines as a treaty mechanism is validated further by Article 31(3) of the Vienna Convention on the Law of Treaties (VCLT),[15] as it could be argued that contracting States have considered their positions in their agreement.

In summary, it is proposed that there should be a limitation of investments that are capable of protection. This is crucial because the definition of investment plays an integral role in determining whether a tribunal has jurisdiction to adjudicate on a matter relating to transfer of funds. The redefinition of concepts such as "investment" from an asset-based approach to an enterprise-based one that excludes portfolio investment would be indicative of sovereignty reassertion.

Secondly, in order to aid treaty drafting and interpretation, parties should contemplate what they understand the "end" of a crisis to mean. This should be considered pivotal in the design of an exception clause. This is because, in the issues that arise during an economic crisis, when the crisis ceases to exist is important as it has profound implication for both the host State and foreign investor. It extinguishes the special privileges that the host State enjoyed during the economic crisis and amplifies its international commitment to foreign investors in its entirety. It may not be necessary to identify or stipulate a particular date an economic crisis ends as this is a highly subjective decision to make. After all, the Argentinian cases were adjudicated without a determination of this nature; even when a date is identified, it does not signify the possibility of making a precise objective determination of a date when the economic crisis ended. Instead, the identification of a crisis-end

14 *ibid* 314.

15 Arwel Davies, 'Investment Treaty Interpretation, Fair and Equitable Treatment and Legitimate Expectations' (2018) 15(3) *Manchester Journal of International Economic Law*, 337.

date helps a tribunal to decide a case before it and give effect to the tribunal's judgment.[16]

Thirdly, this book contemplates and substantiates the important need for amicus curiae to restore legitimacy to the international investment regime. Seasoned economists beyond legal practitioners are considered because determining matters of economic nature requires professional economic expertise which often raises alternative measures and hypothetical occurrences.[17] In general, recommendations are three fold: redefinition of investments, recourse to other international commitments, and acknowledgement of economists alongside a model treaty that will correct some of the issues identified so far and reflect the recommendations made. Developing States need to consider these recommendation for a much-desired model BIT, because if they do not have a model treaty, they will find it difficult to change the terms and conditions of a model BIT proposed by developed States.[18] Although developed States are in an advantageous position as they are the ones who initiate the outward movement of capital, this should not preclude developing States from advancing their own model BITs. To do otherwise would be akin to short-changing themselves, as they may be unwittingly placing themselves in a position of merely accepting or slightly reacting to a model BIT prepared by their counterpart.[19] More so, as many developing States are now exporting capital to developed States such as Europe and the United States, the distinction between the capital-exporting States and the capital-importing States may lose its significance.[20] The power asymmetry between the States will thin away, making the duality of the roles of the host States and home States uncertain.

Thus, instead of a total withdrawal from the Investor-State Dispute Settlement (ISDS) or termination of BITs, investment concerns can be addressed within a framework of a BIT. A model treaty provides a quicker and more predictable pathway to form an agreement. Many States have developed their own model BITs which they present during negotiations such that, when there are deviations, it is only a reflection of the fact that concession has been made. Legal regimes in developed and developing States are becoming more sophisticated and enhanced, and it is difficult not to see that the rudimentary protections offered in BITs would significantly reduce the cost of capital. Thus the argument that States are ignorant of the consequences of signing a BIT is not convincing any more;[21] claiming

16 Alberto Alvarez-Jimenez, 'International Investment Law, Time and Economics: Fixing the Length of Economic Crisis as a Cost Allocation Tool between Host States and Foreign Investors' (2020) 19 *World Trade View*, 96.

17 Suha Ballon, 'Economic Crises and Foreign Investors: Between Necessity and Reparation' (2008) (2)1 *International Comparative Policy & Ethics Law Review*, 5.

18 Zeng Huaqun, 'Balance, Sustainable Development, and Integration: Innovative Path for BIT Practice' (2014) 17 *Journal of International Economic Law*, 303.

19 *ibid* 304.

20 Muthucumaraswamy Sornarajah, 'The International Law on Foreign Investment (Cambridge University Press 2021) 47.

21 Joost Powelyn, 'At the Edge of Chaos? Foreign Investment Law as a Complex Adaptive System, How it Emerged and How It Can be Reformed' (2014) 29(2) *ICSID Review* 374.

ignorance in today's context is no longer tenable. Although developing States are more likely to accept an unmodified model BIT from developed States due to their eagerness to attract FDI,[22] their own model BITs can serve as prototypes that may be fully adopted by both parties, or as foundations upon which contracting parties can negotiate or build.

22 Jeongho Nam, 'Model BIT: An Ideal Prototype or a Tool for Efficient Breach?' (2017) 48 *Georgetown Journal of International Law*, 1292.

Bibliography

Aaken A. V., 'Perils of Success? The Case of International Investment Protection' (2008) 9(1) *European Business Organization Law Review*, 1–27.
Aaken A. V., 'International Investment Law between Commitment and Flexibility: A Contract Theory Analysis' (2009) 12(2) *Journal of International Economic Law*, 507–538.
Aaken A. V., 'Smart Flexibility Clauses in International Investment Treaties and Sustainable Development' (2014) 15 *Journal of World Investment and Trade*, 827–861.
Aaken A. V. & Kurtz J., 'Prudence or Discrimination? Emergency Measures, the Global Financial Crises and International Economic Law' (2009) 12(4) *Journal of International Economic Law*, 859–894.
Aaken A. V. & Kurtz J., 'Will States Emergency Measures Trigger International Investment Disputes' (2009) 1(3) *Transnational Corporations Review*, 12–16.
Abba K. A., 'Investor Protection vs. Host States Regulatory Autonomy during Economic Crisis: Treatment of Capital Transfers and Restrictions under Modern Investment Treaties' (2007) 8(4) *The Journal of World Investment Treaties,* 459–503.
Abba K. A. & Walde T., 'Economic Crises, Capital Transfer Restrictions and Investor Protection under Modern Investment Treaties' (2008) 3(2) *Capital Markets Law Journal*, 154–185.
Adeleke F., *International Investment Law and Policy in Africa: Exploring a Huma Rights Based Approach to Investment Regulation and Dispute Settlement* (Routledge 2018).
Adeleke K. M., Olowe S. O. & Fasesin O. O., 'Impact of FDI in Nigeria Economic Growth' (2014) 4(8) *International Journal of Academic Research in Business and Social Sciences*, 234–241.
Adibi A. & Habibi H., 'The Challenge of the Economic Independence and the Sovereignty of States: A Review of the Problem of Legitimacy of Economic Sanctions in the Reality of the International Legal Order' (2017) 5(3) *Russian Law Journal*, 113–139.
Agenor P. R., 'Benefits and Costs of International Financial Integration: Theory and Facts' (2003) 26(8) *The World Economy*, 1089–1118.
Agius M., 'The Invocation of Necessity in International Law' (2009) 56(2) *Netherlands International Law Review*, 95–135.
Agrawal K., 'Bilateral Investment Treaties: A Developing History' (2016) 7(2) *Jindal Global Law Review*, 175–199.
Aisbett E., Busse M. & Nunnenkamp P., 'Bilateral Investment Treaties as Deterrents of Host State Discretion: The Impact of Investor-States Disputes on Foreign Direct Investment in Developing States' (2018) 154 *Review of World Economics*, 119–155.
Aisbett E., Karp L. & McAusland C., 'Compensation for Indirect Expropriation in International Investment Agreements: Implications of National Treatment and Rights to Invest' (2010) 1(2) *Journal of Globalization and Development*, 1–35.
Akinkugbe O. D., 'Africanization and the Reform of International Investment Law' (2021) 53(1) *Case Western Reserve Journal of International Law*, 7–34.

Al-Louzi R., 'A Coherence Review of Investment Protection Under Bilateral Investment Treaties and Free Trade Agreements' (2015) 12(3) *Manchester Journal of International Economic Law*, 270–286.

Al-Louzi R., 'Bilateral Investment Treaties as Tools for Enhancing Foreign Investment Climate and Increasing Competitiveness' (2017) 14(1) *Manchester Journal of International Economic Law*, 69–91.

Alexandrov S. A., 'On the Perceived Inconsistency in Investor-States Jurisprudence' in Jose E. Alvarez & Karl P. Sauvant (eds), *The Evolving International Investment Regime; Expectations, Realities, Options* (Oxford University Press 2011).

Alle T. & Peinhardt C., 'Evaluating Three Explanations for the Design of Bilateral Investment Treaties' (2014) 66(1) *World Politics*, 47–87.

Allee T. and Peinhardt C., 'Delegating Differences: Bilateral Investment Treaties and Bargaining Over Dispute Resolution Provisions' (2010) 54(1) *International Studies Quarterly*, 1–26.

Alschner W. & Skougareviskiy D., 'Mapping the Universe of International Agreements' (2016) 19(3) *Journal of International Economic Law*, 561–588.

Alvarez-Jimenez A., 'The Great Recession and the New Frontiers of International Investment Law: The Economics of Early Warning Models and the Law of Necessity' (2014) 17(3) *Journal of International Economic Law*, 517–550.

Alvarez-Jimenez A., 'International Investment Law, Time and Economics: Fixing the Length of Economic Crisis as a Cost Allocation Tool between Host States and Foreign Investors' (2020) 19 *World Trade View*, 91–108.

Amin G. F., 'All that Glitters is Not Always Gold or Silver: Typical Bilateral Investment Treaties (BITs) Clauses as Peril to Third World Economic Sovereignty' (2020) 6(3) *Athens Journal of Law*, 299–322.

Annacker C., 'Protection and Admission of Sovereign Investment under Investment Treaties' (2011) 10(3) *Chinese Journal of International Law*, 531–564.

Anthea R., 'Power and Persuasion in Investment Treaty Interpretation: The Dual Role of States' (2010) 104(2) *International and Comparative Law Quarterly*, 179–225.

Arato J., 'The Margin of Appreciation in International Investment Law' (2014) 54(3) *Virginia Journal of International Law*, 545–578.

Arcuri A. & Montanaro F., 'Justice for All: Protecting the Public Interest in Investment Treaties' (2018) 59(8) *Boston College Law Review*, 2791–2824.

Arthur L. G., 'Rule of Law and Absolute Sovereignty' (1958) 106(7) *University of Pennsylvania Law Review,* 943–963.

Ascensio H., 'Article 31 of the Vienna Convention on the Law of Treaties and International Investment Law' (2016) 31(2) *ICSID Review*, 366–387.

Ashiya B., 'The Shift towards an Enterprise Based Definition of Investment: The Quagmire of the *Salini* Test and India's Model BIT' (2016) 7(2) *Jindal Global Law Review*, 263–277.

Asiedu E., 'On the Determinants of FDI to Developing States: Is Africa Different?' (2002) 30(1) *World Development*, 107–119.

Atai A., 'Iranian Bilateral Investment Treaties: Substantive Principles and Standards' (2013) 14(3) *Journal of World Investment and Trade*, 397–433.

Azubuike E. C., 'The Place of Treaties in International Investment' (2013) 19 *Annual Survey of International and Comparative Law*, 155–196.

Bagheri M. & Jahromi M. F. J., 'Globalization and Extraterritorial Application of Economic Regulation: Crisis in International Law and Balancing Interests' (2016) 41(2) *European Journal of Law and Economics*, 393–429.

Ballon S., 'Economic Crises and Foreign Investors: Between Necessity and Reparation' (2008) 2(1) *International Comparative Policy & Ethics Law Review*, 1–36.

Banifatemi Y., 'Consistency in the Interpretation of Substantive Investment Rules: Is it Achievable?' in Roberto Enchandi & Pierre Sauve (eds), *Prospects in International Investment Law and Policy: World Trade Forum* (Cambridge University Press 2013).

Barth J., 'Reconstructing Mercantilism: Consensus and Conflict in British Imperial Economy in the Seventeenth and Eighteenth Centuries' (2016) 73(2) *The William and Mary Quarterly*, 257–290.

Beck H. & Prinz A., 'The Trilemma of a Monetary Union: Another Impossible Trinity' (2012) 47 *Intereconomics*, 39–43.

Beeson M., 'Sovereignty under the Siege: Globalisation and the States in Southeast Asia' (2003) 24(2) *Third World Quarterly*, 357–374.

Bellak C. & Leibrecht M., 'Do Economic Crises Trigger Treaty-Based Investor-State Arbitration Disputes?' (2021) 24 *Journal of International Economic Law*, 127–155.

Berg E. & Kuusk E., 'What Makes Sovereignty a Relative Concept? Empirical Approaches to International Society' (2010) 29 *Political Geography*, 40–49.

Berger A., Busse M., Nunnenkamp P. & Roy M., 'More Stringent BITs, Less Ambiguous Effects on FDI? Not a Bit!' (2011) 112(3) *Economic Letters*, 270–272.

Bergstrand J. H. & Egger P., 'What Determines BITs?' (2013) 90(1) *Journal of International Economics*, 107–122.

Bernardini P., 'Investment Protection Under Bilateral Investment Treaties and Investment Contracts' (2001) 2(2) *Journal of World Investment & Trade*, 7–247.

Bernardini P., 'Under Bilateral Investment Treaties and Investment Contracts' (2001) 2(2) *Journal of World Investment*, 235–248.

Bezuidenhout H. & Kleynhans E., 'Implications of Foreign Direct Investment for National Sovereignty: The Wal-Mart/Massmart Merger as an Illustration' (2015) 22(1) *Nigerian Journal of International Affairs*, 93–110.

Binder C. & Reinisch A., 'Economic Emergency Powers: A Comparative Law Perspective' in Stephen W. Schill (ed), *International Investment Law and Comparative Public Law* (Oxford University Press 2010).

Biris B., 'Investor Protection and Bilateral Investment Treaties: An Overview of the Main Provision' (2015) 4(1) *Perspectives of Business Law Journal*, 209–213.

Biswas R., 'Determinants of Foreign Direct Investment' (2002) 6(3) *Review of Development Economics*, 492–504.

Bjorklund A. K., 'Practical and Legal Avenues to Make Substantive Rules and Disciplines of International Investments Coverage' in Roberto Enchandi & Pierre Sauve (eds), *Prospects in International Investment Law and Policy: World Trade Forum* (Cambridge University Press 2013).

Blake D. J., 'Thinking Ahead: Government Time Horizons and the Legalization of International Investment Agreement' (2013) 67(4) *International Organisation*, 797–829.

Boed R., 'States of Necessity as a Justification for Internationally Wrongful Conduct' (2003) 3(1) *Yale Human Rights and Development Law Journal*, 1–44.

Brabandere E. D., '(Re)Calibration, Standard-Setting and the Shaping of Investment Law and Arbitration' (2018) 59(8) *Boston College Law Review*, 2607–2634.

Brabandere E. D., 'NGO and the "Public Interest": The Legality and Rationale of Amicus Curiae Interventions in International Economic and Investment Disputes' (2011) 12(1) *Chicago Journal of International Law*, 85–114.

Brand R. A., 'External Sovereignty and International Law' (1994) 18(5) *Fordham International Law Journal*, 1685–1697.

Brew R., 'Exception Clauses in International Investment Agreements as a Tool for Appropriately Balancing the Right to Regulate with Investment Agreement' (2019) 25 *Canterbury Law Review*, 205–242.

Brewster R., 'Unpacking the State's Reputation' (2009) 50(2) *Harvard International Law Journal*, 231–269.

Briese R., 'Djibouti v. France: Self-Judging Clauses before the International Court of Justice' (2009) 10(1) *Melbourne Journal of International Law*, 308–328

Broos M. & Grund S., 'The IMF's Jurisdiction Over the Capital Account: Reviewing the Role of Surveillance in Managing Cross-Border Capital Flows' (2018) 21 *Journal of International Economic Law*, 489–507.

Bubb R. J. & Rose-Ackerman S., 'BITs and Bargains: Strategic Aspects of Bilateral and Multilateral Regulation of Foreign Investment' (2007) 27(3) *International Review of Law and Economics*, 291–311.

Buckley R. P., 'International Capital Flows, Economic Sovereignty and Developing States' (1999) 4 *Yearbook of International Financial and Economic Law*, 17–46.

Burke-White W. W., 'The Argentine Financial Crisis: States Liability under BITs and the legitimacy of the ICSID System' (2008) 3(1) *Asian Journal of WTO and International Health Law and Policy*, 199–234.

Burke-White W. W. & Von Staden A., 'Investment Protection in Extraordinary Time: The Interpretation and Application of Non-Precluded Measures Provisions in Bilateral Investment Treaties' (2008) 48(2) *Virginia Journal of International Law*, 469–526.

Bussiere M., 'Balance of Payments Crises in Emerging Markets: How Early Were the Early Warning Signals?' (2013) 45(12) *Applied Economics*, 1601–1623.

Buthe T. & Milner H., 'Bilateral Investment Treaties and FDI: A Political Analysis' in K. P. Sauvant & L. E. Sachs (eds), *The Effect of Treaties on Foreign Direct Investment: Bilateral Investment Treaties, Double Taxation Treaties, and Investment Flows* (Oxford University Press 2009).

Butler N., 'Non-Disputing Party Participation in ICSID Disputes: Faux Amici?' (2019) 66 *Netherlands International Law Review*, 143–178.

Butler N. & Subedi S., 'The Future of International Investment Regulation towards a World Investment Organisation?' (2017) 64(1) *Netherlands International Law Review*, 43–72.

Cai C., 'Change of the Structure of International Investment and the Development of Developing States' BIT Practice: Towards a Third Way of BIT Practice' (2007) 8(6) *Journal of World Investment and Trade*, 829–848.

Cai C., 'International Investment Treaties and the Formation, Application and Transformation of Customary International Law Rules' (2008) 7(3) *Journal of International Law*, 659–680.

Calderon C. & Kubota M., 'Sudden Stops: Are Global and Local Investors Alike?' (2013) 89(1) *Journal of International Economics*, 122–142.

Calvert J., 'Constructing Investors Rights? Why Some States (Fail to) Terminate Bilateral Investment Treaties' (2018) 25(1) *Review of International Political Economy*, 75–97.

Chang J. & Grabel I., *Reclaiming Development. An Alternative Economic Policy Manual* (Zed Books Limited 2004).

Chang Y. C., 'How Does the Amicus Curiae Submission Affect a Tribunal Decision' (2017) 30(3) *Leiden Journal of International Law*, 647–660.

Chazournes L. B., 'Transparency and Amicus Curiae' (2004) 5(2) *The Journal of World Investment and Trade Law*, 333–336.

Chen R. C., 'Bilateral Investment Treaties and Domestic Institutional Reform' (2017) 55(3) *Columbia Journal of Transnational Law*, 547–591.

Chen S. & Chang M. J., 'Capital Control and Exchange Rate Volatility' (2015) 33(1) *North American Journal of Economics and Finance*, 167–177.

Chen W., Dollar D. & Tang H., 'Why is China Investing in Africa? Evidence from the Firm Level' (2018) 32(3) *The World Bank Economic Review*, 610–632.

Chernyak O., Khomicik V. & Chernyak Y., 'The Main Triggers of the Balance of Payment Crisis in the Eastern Europe' (2013) 8 *Procedia Technology*, 47–50.

Chidede T., 'Decolonising Investment Regimes for Development Purposes in Contemporary Africa' in Tapiwa Victor Warikandwa, Artwell Nhemachena, Nkosinothando Mpofu & Howard Chitimira (eds), *Gridlocked African Economic Sovereignty* (Langaa RPCIG 2019).

Chilton A. S., 'The Political Motivations of the United States' Bilateral Investment Treaty Program' (2016) 23(4) *Review of International Political Economy*, 614–642.
Cho S., Kim Y. K. & Lee C., 'Credibility, Preferences and Bilateral Investment Treaties' (2016) 11(1) *The Review of International Organization*, 25–58.
Choudhary B. & Kulkarni P., 'Re-Crafting Bilateral Investment Treaties in a Development Framework: A Comparative Regional Perspective' in Ashwini Deshpande (ed), *Capital Without Borders* (Anthem Press 2010).
Choukroune L., 'Judging the States in International Trade and Investment Law: Why, How and What For?' in Leila Choukrone (ed), *Judging the States in International Trade and Investment Law: Sovereignty Modern, the Law and Economics* (Springer 2016).
Clark W. R., Reichart U. N., Lomas S. L. & Parker K. L., 'International and Domestic Constraints on Political Business Cycles in OECD Economies' (1998) 52(1) *International Organization*, 87–120.
Claussen K., 'The Casualty of Investor Protection in Times of Economic Crisis' (2009) 118(7) *Yale Law Journal*, 1545–1556.
Clodfelter M. A., 'The Adaptation of States to the Changing World of Investment Protection through Model BITs' (2009) 24(1) *ICSID*, 165–175.
Cole T. & Vaksha A. K., 'Power-Conferring Treaties: The Meaning of Investment in the ICSID Convention' (2011) 24(1) *Leiden Journal of International Law*, 305–330.
Colen L., Persyn D. & Guariso A., 'Bilateral Investment Treaties and FDI: Does the Sector Matter?' (2009) 83(1) *World Development*, 193–206.
Colin B., *Principles of International Financial Law* (2nd edn, Oxford University Press 2015).
Collins D., 'National Treatment in Emerging Market Investment Treaties' in K. A. Sanders (ed), *The Principle of National Treatment in International Economic Law: Trade Investment and Intellectual Property* (Edward Elgar Publishing Limited 2014).
Commission J. P., 'The Global Financial Crisis and International Investment Regimes' (Proceedings 104th Annual Meeting) (2010) 104 *American Society of International Law*, 443–447.
Condon B. J., 'Treaty Structure and Public Interest Regulation in International Economic Law' (2014) 17(2) *Journal of International Economic Law*, 333–353.
Coric T., Simovic H. & Deskar-Skrbic M., 'Monetary and Fiscal Policy Mix in a Small Open Economy: The Case of Croatia' (2015) 28(1) *Economic Research-Ekonomska Istraživanja*, 407–421.
Coronna M. E., 'The Right to Repatriation of Capital and Transfer of Profits for Foreign Investors in Yugoslav Joint-Ventures' (1986) 12 *Review of Socialist Law*, 139–150.
Cottier T., Lastra R. M., Tietje C. & Satragno L., *The Rule of Law in Monetary Affairs* (Cambridge University Press 2014).
Cremon M., 'Who Can Make Treaties? The European Union' in Duncan B. Hollis (ed), *The Oxford Guide to Treaties* (Oxford University Press 2012).
Crooks J. R., 'Applicable Law in International Arbitration: The Iran-US Claims Tribunal Experience' (1983) 83(2) *The American Journal of International Law*, 278–311.
Cross C. & Schliemann-Radbruch C., 'When Investment Arbitration Curbs Domestic Regulatory Space: Consistent Solutions through Amicus Curiae Submissions by Regional Organisations' (2013) 6(2) *Law and Development Review*, 67–110.
Cross J. E., 'Foreign Investment Laws in Developing States' (1984) 6(1) *Michigan Journal of International Law*, 155–171.
Crystal J., 'Sovereignty, Bargaining and the International Regulation of Foreign Direct Investment' (2009) 23(3) *Global Society*, 225–243.
Dagbanja D. N., 'Changing Pattern and Future of Foreign Investment Law and Policy in Ghana: The Role of International Investment Treaties' (2011–2012) 19 *African Yearbook of International Law*, 83–142.

Dagbanja D. N., 'The Limitation on Sovereign Regulatory Autonomy and Internationalization of Investment Protection by Treaty: An African Perspective' (2015) 60(1) *Journal of African Law*, 56–82.

Danzman B. S., 'Contracting with Whom? The Differential Effects of Investment Treaties on FDI' (2016) 42(3) *International Interaction*, 452–478.

Denters E., 'Preferential Trade and Investment Treaties' in Tarcisio Gazzini & Eric De Brabendere (eds), *International Investment Law: The Sources of Rights and Obligations* (Martinus NIJHOFF Publishers 2012).

Desai M. A., Fritz C. F. & Hines Jr J. R., 'Capital Controls, Liberalization and Foreign Direct Investment' (2006) 19(4) *The Review of Financial Studies*, 1433–1464.

Desborded R. & Vicard V., 'Foreign Direct Investment and Bilateral Investment Treaties: An International Political Perspective' (2009) 37(3) *Journal of Comparative Economics*, 372–386.

Desierto D. A., 'Necessity and "Supplementary Means of Interpretation" for Non-Precluded Measures in Bilateral Investment Treaties' (2010) 31(3) *University of Pennsylvania Journal of International Economic Law*, 827–934.

Desierto D. A., 'ICERSCR Minimum Core Obligations and Investment: Recasting the Non-Expropriation Compensation Model during Financial Crises' (2012) 44(3) *The George Washington International Law Review*, 473–520

Desierto D. A., *A Necessity and National Emergency Clauses: Sovereignty in Modern Treaty Interpretation* (Martinus Nijhoff Publishers 2012).

Desierto D. A., 'Public Policy in International Investment and Trade Law: Community Expectations and Functional Decision Making' (2014) 26 *Florida Journal of International Law*, 51–150.

Deskastros M., 'Portfolio Investment: Reconceptualising the Notion of Investment under the ICSID Convention' (2013) 14(2) *The Journal of World Investment & Trade*, 286–319.

Devreux M. B. & Yetman J., 'Capital Controls, Global Liquidity Traps, and the International Policy Trilemma' (2014) 116(1) *The Scandinavian Journal of Economics*, 158–189.

Dhar B., Joseph R. & James T. C., 'India's Bilateral Investment Agreements: A Time to Review' (2012) 42(52) *Economic & Political Weekly*, 113–122.

Dhooge L. J., 'The Revenge of the Trailer Smelter: Environmental Regulation as Expropriation Pursuant to the North American Free Trade Agreement' (2001) 38(3) *American Business Law Journal*, 475–558.

Dieibold N. F., 'Standards of Non-Discrimination in International Economic Law' (2011) 60(4) *The International Law and Comparative Law Quarterly*, 831–865.

Dimitropoulus G., 'National Sovereignty and International Investment Law: Sovereignty Reassertion and Prospects of Reform' (2020) 21 *Journal of World Investment and Trade*, 71–103.

Diseierto D. A., 'Necessity and Supplementary Means of Interpretation for Non-Precluded Measures in Bilateral Investment Treaties' (2010) 31(3) *Journal of International Law*, 827–934.

Dolzer R., 'The Impact of International Treaties on Domestic Administrative Law' (2006) 37 *International Law and Politics*, 953–972.

Dolzer R. & Schreuer C., *The Principles of International Investment Law* (Oxford University Press 2012).

Douglas Z., 'The Hybrid Foundations of Investment Treaty Arbitrations' (2004) 74(1) *British Yearbook of International Law*, 151–289.

Duchesne M. S., 'The Continuous Nationality of Claim's People: Its Historical Development and Current Relevance to Investor States Investment Disputes' (2004) 36(4) *George Washington International Law Review*, 783–816.

Dukagjin L., 'Challenges of States Sovereignty in the Age of Globalisation' (2017) 13(2) *Acta Universitatis Danubius Journal*, 61–72.

Dumberry P., 'Are BITs Representing the New Customary International Law in International Investment Law' (2010) 28(4) *Penn State International Law Review*, 675–702.

Dunning J. H. & Lundan S. M., 'The Changing Political Economy of Foreign Investment: Finding a Balance between Hard and Soft Forms of Regulation' in Jose E. Alvarez & Karl P. Sauvant (eds), *The Evolving International Investment Regime: Expectations, Realities, Options* (Oxford University Press 2011).

Dunning W. A., 'Jean Bodin on Sovereignty' (1896) 11(1) *Political Science Quarterly*, 82–104.

Echandi R., 'Be Careful with What You wish: Saving Developing States from Development and the Risk of Overlooking the Importance of a Multilateral Rule-Based System on Investment in the 21st Century' in Marc Bungenberg, Christoph Herrmann, Markus Krajewski & Jorg Philipp Terhechte (eds), *European Yearbook of International Economic Law* (Springer International Publishing 2016).

Edwards S., 'Capital Mobility, Capital Controls and Globalization in the Twenty-First Century' (2002) 579(1) *The Annals of the American Academy*, 261–270.

Egger P. & Pfaffermayr M., 'The Impact of Bilateral Investment Treaties on Foreign Direct Investment' (2004) 32 *Journal of Comparative Economics*, 788–804.

Eichengreen B., *Capital Flow and Crises* (Massachusetts Institute of Technologies 2003).

Eichengreen B. & Rose A., 'Capital Controls in the 21st Century' (2014) 48 *Journal of International Money and Finance*, 1–16.

Eichler S. & Nauerth J. A., 'Bilateral Investment Treaties and Portfolio Investment' (2014) 91(101918) *Journal of International Financial Markets, Institutions and Money*, 1–26.

Eilmansberger T., 'Bilateral Investment Treaties and EU Law' (2009) 46 *Capital Market Law Review*, 383–429.

Ejims O, 'The 2016 Morocco-Nigeria Bilateral Investment Treaty: More Practical Reality in Providing a Balanced Investment Treaty' (2019) 34(1) *ICSID Review*, 62–84.

Ekwueme K. U. K., 'Nigeria's Principal Investment Laws in the Context of International Law and Practice' (2005) 59(2) *Journal of African Law*, 177–206.

El-Kady H. & De Gama M., 'The Reform of the International Investment Regime: An African Perspective' (2019) 34(2) *ICSID Review*, 482–495.

Elkins Z., Guzman A. T. & Simmons B. A., 'Competing for Capital: The Diffusion of BIT, 1960–2000' (2006) 60(4) *International Organization*, 811–846.

Elkins Z., Guzman A. T. & Simmons B. A., 'Competing for Capital: The Diffusion of Bilateral Investment Treaties, 1960–2000' in Beth A. Simmons, Frank Dobbin & Geoffrey Garnet (eds), *The Global Diffusion of Markets and Democracy* (Cambridge University Press 2007).

Engster D., 'Jean Bodin, Scepticism and Absolute Sovereignty' (1996) 17(4) History of Political Thought, 469–499.

Ezeani E. C., 'Economic and Development Policy-Making in Nigeria' (2012) 56(1) *Journal of African Law*, 109–138.

Farley R. & McGregor N. F., 'Heterogeneous Effects of Bilateral Investment Treaties' (2017) 153(4) *Review of World Economics*, 631–656.

Feibelman A., 'The IMF and Regulation of Cross-Border Capital Flows' (2015) 15(2) *Chicago Journal of International Law*, 409–451.

Fiezzoni S. K., 'Striking Consistency and Predictability in International Investment Law from the Perspective of Developing States' (2012) 7(4) *Frontiers of Law in China*, 521–552.

Foster G. K., 'Investors, States and Stakeholders: Power Asymmetries in International Investment and the Stabilizing Potential of Investment Treaties' (2013) 17(2) *Lewis & Clark Law Review*, 362–375.

Fowler D., 'Is This Necessary: The Scope of the Doctrine Necessity in 21st Century Investment Treaties' (2017) 9(1) *Creighton International and Comparative Law Journal*, 1–28.

Fox G., 'A Future for International Investment? Modifying BITs to Drive Economic Development' (2014) 46 *Georgetown Journal of International Law*, 229–259.

Franck S. D. & Wylie L. E., 'Predicting Outcomes in Investment Treaty Arbitration' (2015) 65 *Duke Law Journal*, 459–475.

Franck S. D., 'The Legitimacy Crisis in Investment Treaty Arbitration: Privatizing Public International Law through Inconsistent Decisions' (2005) 73(4) *Fordham Law Review*, 1521–1625.

Frank S. D., 'The Nature and Enforcement of Investor Rights under Treaties: Do Investment Treaties Have a Bright Future?' (2005) 12(47) *U.C Davis Journal of International Law and Policy*, 48–99.

Franck S. D., *Arbitration Costs: Myths and Realities in Investment Treaty Arbitration* (Oxford University Press 2019).

Franck S. S., 'Considering Recalibration of International Investment Agreements: Empirical Insights' in Jose E. Alvarez & Karl P. Sauvant (eds), *The Evolving International Investment Regime; Expectations, Realities, Options* (Oxford University Press 2011).

Gagliani G., 'The Interpretation of General Exceptions in International Trade and Investment Law: Is a Sustainable Development Interpretative Approach Possible' (2015) 43(4) *Denver Journal of International Law and Policy*, 559–588.

Gallagher K. P., 'The IMF, Capital Controls and Developing States' (2011) 46(19) *Economic and Political Weekly*, 12–16.

Gallagher K. P., Anderson S. & Viterbo A., 'Capital Flow Management and the Trans-Pacific Partnership Agreement' (2013) G-24 *Policy Brief No.* 79, 1–7.

Gallagher K. P., 'Contesting the Governance of Capital Flows at the IMF' (2015) 28(2) *An International Journal of Policy, Administration, and Institutions*, 185–198.

Gallagher K. P., 'Trading Away Financial Instability: Reconstructing Capital Account Liberalization as Trade and Investment Policy' in Kevin P. Gallagher (ed), *Emerging Markets and the Reregulation of Cross-Border Finance* (Cornell University Press 2015).

Gallagher K. P. & Tian Y., 'Regulating Capital Flows in Emerging Markets: The IMF and the Global Financial Crisis' (2017) 7(2) *Review of Development Finance*, 95–106.

Galvez C. C., 'Necessity, Investor Rights, and State Sovereignty for NAFTA Investment Arbitration' (2013) 46(1) *Cornell International Law Journal*, 143–163.

Garcia C., 'All the Other Dirty Little Secrets: Investment Treaties, Latin America, and the Necessary Evil of Investor-States Arbitration' (2004) 16(2) *Florida Journal of International Law*, 301–370.

Garcia F. J., Cikoo L., Gaurav A. & Hough K., 'Reforming the International Investment Regime: Lessons from International Trade Law' (2015) 18 *Journal of International Economic Law*, 861–892.

Garcia-Bolivar O. E., 'Sovereignty vs. Investment Protection: Back to Calvo' (2009) 24(2) *ICSID Review*, 464–488.

Garner G. G., 'Bilateral Investment Treaties: A Means for Liberalising Trade in Services' (1986) 9(1) *University of Chicago Legal Forum*, 194–219.

Gathli J. T. & Mbori H. O., 'Reform and Retrenchment in International Investment Law: Introduction to a Special Issue' (2023) 24 *Journal of World Investment & Trade*, 535–563

Gazzini T., *Interpretation of International Investment Treaties* (Hart Publishing 2016).

Gess K. N., 'Permanent Sovereignty over Natural Resources: An Analytical Review of the United Nations Declaration and its Genesis' (1964) 13(2) *International and Comparative Law Quarterly*, 398–449.

Ghouri A. A., *Interaction and Conflict of Treaties in Investment Arbitration* (Kluwer Law International 2015).

Giest A., 'Interpreting Public Interest Provisions in International Investment Treaties' (2017) 18(1) *Chicago Journal of International Law*, 321–352.

Ginsburg R., 'Political Risk Insurance and Bilateral Investment Treaties: Making the Connection' (2013) 14(1) *The Journal of World Investment and Trade*, 943–977.

Glinavos I., 'Regulation and the Role of Law in Economic Crisis' (2010) 21(4) *European Business Law Review*, 539–558.
Gold J., 'The Fund Agreement in the Court' (1989) 4 *International Monetary Fund*, 16–21.
Golub S. S., 'Measures of Restrictions on Inward Foreign Direct Investment for OECD States' (2003) 12(1) *Economics Faculty Works*, 88–122.
Goodman C. L., 'Uncharted Waters: Financial Crisis and Enforcement of ICSID Awards in Argentina' (2007) 28(2) *University of Pennsylvania Journal of International Economic Law*, 449–486.
Gordon K. & Pohl J., 'Investment Treaties over Time-Treaty Practice and Interpretation in a Changing World' (2015) 2 *OECD Woking Papers on International Investment*, 1–40.
Grabel I., 'Marketing the Third World: The Contradictions of Portfolio Investment in the Global Economy' (1996) 24(11) *World Development*, 1776–1996.
Grabel I., 'Capital Controls in a Time of Crisis' in Philip Arestis & Malcolm Sawyer (eds), *Financial Liberalisation: Past, Present and Future* (Palgrave Macmillan 2016).
Grabowski A., 'The Definition of Investment Under the ICSID Convention: A Defence of Salini' (2014) 15(1) *Chicago Journal of International Law*, 287–309.
Gulcur A, 'The Necessity, Public Interest, and Proportionality in International Investment Law: A Comparative Analysis' (2019) 6(2) *University of Baltimore Journal of International Law* 215–265.
Guntrip E., 'Self Determination and Foreign Direct Investment: Reimaging Sovereignty in International Investment Law' (2016) 65(4) *International and Comparative Law Quarterly*, 829–857.
Guzman A. T., 'Why LDCs Sign Treaties that Hurt Them: Explaining the Popularity of BITs' (1998) 38 *Virginia Journal of International Law*, 639–688.
Haftel Y. Z. & Thompson A., 'Delayed Ratification: The Domestic Fate of Bilateral Investment Treaties' (2013) 67(2) *International Organization*, 355–387.
Haftel Y. Z. & Thompson A., 'Why Do States Renegotiate Investment Agreements? The Impact of Arbitration' (2018) 13(1) *The Review of International Organizations*, 25–48.
Hamed El-Kady & Mustaqeem De Gama, 'The Reform of the International Investment Regime: An African Perspective' (2019) 34(2) *ICSID Review*, 482–495.
Hanessian G. & Duggal K., 'The 2015 Indian Model BIT: Is This Change the World Wishes to See?' (2015) 30(3) *ICSID Review*, 729–740.
Hanotiau B., 'Are Bilateral Investment Treaties and Free Trade Agreement Drafted with Sufficient Clarity to Give Guidance to Tribunals?' (2016) 5(3) *American University Business Law Review*, 313–333.
Harten G. V., 'Private Authority and Transnational Governance: The Contours of the International System of Investor Protection' (2005) 12(4) *Review of International Political Economy*, 600–623.
Harten G. V., 'Five Justifications for Investment Treaties: A Critical Discussion' (2010) 2(1) *Trade, Law and Development*, 19–58.
Henckels C., 'Protecting Regulatory Autonomy through Greater Precision in Investment Treaties: The TPP, CETA, and TTIP' (2016) 19(1) *Journal of International Economic Law*, 27–50.
Henckels C., 'Should Investment Treaties Contain Public Policy Exceptions' (2018) 59(8) *Boston College Law Review*, 2825–2844.
Hill S. F., 'The Necessity Defence and the Emerging Arbitral Conflict in its Application to the US-Argentina Bilateral Investment Treaty' (2007) 13(3) *Law and Business Review of the Americas*, 547–569.
Hirsch M., 'Explaining Compliance and Non-Compliance with ICSID Awards: The Argentine Case Study and a Multiple Theoretical Approach' (2016) 19 *Journal of International Economic Law*, 681–706.

Hollis D. B., ‘Private Actors in Public International Law: Amicus Curiae and the Case for the Retention of States Sovereignty’ (2002) 25(2) *Boston College International and Comparative Law Review*, 235–255.

Howarth D. & Sadeh T., ‘In the Vanguard of Globalization: The OECD and International Capital Liberalization’ (2011) 18(5) *Review of International Political Economy*, 622–645.

Huang C., ‘The States and Foreign Investment’ (1989) 22(1) *Comparative Political Studies*, 93–121.

Huaqun Z., ‘Balance, Sustainable Development, and Integration: Innovative Path for BIT Practice’ (2014) 17 *Journal of International Economic Law*, 299–332.

Hueckel J., ‘Rebalancing Legitimacy and Sovereignty in International Investment Agreements’ (2012) 61(3) *Emory Law Journal*, 601–640.

Hutchinson T., ‘The Doctrinal Method: Incorporating Interdisciplinary Methods in Reforming the Law’ (2015) 3 *Erasmus Law Review*, 130–138.

Ilene G., ‘The Rebranding of Capital Controls in an Era of Productive Incoherence’ (2015) 22(1) *Review of International Political Economy*, 7–43.

Jackson J. H., 'Reflections on International Economic Law' (1996) 17(1) *University of Pennsylvania Journal of International Economic Law*, 17–28.

Jaime M. L., ‘Relying Upon Parties Interpretation in Treaty Based Investor-States Dispute Settlement: Filling the Gaps in International Investment Agreements’ (2014) 46(1) *Georgetown Journal of International Law*, 261–313.

Jain S. C., ‘Permanent Sovereignty over Natural Resources and Nationalisation in International Law’ (1977) 19(3) *Journal of the Indian Law Institute*, 242–256.

James Thuo Gathli & Harrison Otieno Mbori, ‘Reform and Retrenchment in International Investment Law: Introduction to a Special Issue’ (2023) 24 *Journal of World Investment & Trade*, 535–563.

Jamieson S., ‘A Model Future: The Future of Foreign Direct Investment and Bilateral Investment Treaties’ (2012) 53(3) *South Texas Law Review*, 605–630.

Jandhyada S., Hemisc W. J. & Mansfield E. D., ‘Three Waves of BITs: The Global Diffusion of Foreign Investment Policy’ (2011) 55(6) *Journal of Conflict Resolution*, 1047–1073.

Johnson A. R., ‘Rethinking Bilateral Investment Treaties in Sub-Saharan Africa’ (2010) 59(4) *Emory Law Journal*, 919–967.

Jose A., ‘Book Review: Investment Treaty Arbitration and Public Law by Gus Van Harten’ (2008) 102(4) *American Journal of International Law*, 909–915.

Jung Y. & Han S. D., ‘What to Do with the Dilemma Facing the States of Necessity Defense Under the Investment Treaties and How to Interpret the NPM Clause’ (2011) 12(3) *Journal of World Investment and Trade*, 397–410.

Junngam N., ‘Public Policy in International Investment Law: The Confluence of the Three Unruly Horses’ (2016) 51(1) *Texas International Law Journal*, 45–117.

Kalb D., Land M., Staring R., Wilterdink N. & Steenbergen B. V, *The Ends of Globalization* (Rowman & Littlefield 2000).

Kalicki J. & Medeiros S., ‘Fair, Equitable and Ambiguous: What is Fair and Equitable Treatment in International Investment Law?’ (2007) 22(1) *ICSID Review*, 24–54.

Kaushal A., ‘Revisiting History: How the Past Matters for the Present Backlash Against the Foreign Investment Regime’ (2009) 50(2) *Harvard International Law Journal*, 491–534.

Kelley G., ‘Multilateral Investment Treaties: A Balanced Approach to Multinational Corporations’ (2001) 39(2) *Columbia Journal of Transnational Law*, 483–532.

Kent A. K. & Harrington A. R., ‘A States of Necessity: International Legal Obligations in Times of Crises’ (2012) 42(1) *Canadian Review of American Studies*, 65–81.

Kern C., ‘Transfer of Funds’ in Marc Bungenberg, Jorn Griebel, Stephan Hobe & August Reinisch (eds), *International Investment Law* (Hart Publishing 2015).

Kerner A., ‘Why Should I Believe You? The Costs and Consequences of Bilateral Investment Treaties’ (2009) 53(1) *International Studies Quarterly*, 73–102.

Kim J., 'Balancing Regulatory Interests through an Exceptions Framework under the Right to Regulate Provisions in International Investment Agreements' (2018) 50(2) *George Washington International Law Review*, 289–356.

Kingsbury B. & Schill S. W., 'Public Law Concepts to Balance Investors' Rights with State's Regulatory Actions in the Public Interest: The Concept of Proportionality' in Stephan W. Schill (ed), *International Investment Law and Comparative Public Law* (Oxford University Press 2011).

Kleinhersterkamp J., 'European Public Policy Space in International Investment Law' (2012) 27(2) *ICSID Review*, 416–431.

Kleinheisterkamp J., 'Investment Treaty Law and the Fear for Sovereignty: Transnational Challenges and Solutions' (2015) 78(5) *The Modern Law Review*, 793–825.

Kolo A., 'Investor Protection vs Host States Regulatory Autonomy during Economic Crisis: Treatment of Capital Transfers and Restrictions under Modern Investment Treaties' (2007) 8(4) *The Journal of World Trade Investment and Trade*, vii–508.

Kolo A., 'Transfer of Funds: The Interaction between the IMF Articles of Agreement and Modern Investment: A Comparative Law Perspective' in Stephen W. Schill (ed), *International Investment Law and Comparative Public Law* (Oxford University Press 2010).

Kolo A. & Walde T., 'Economic Crises, Capital Transfer Restrictions and Investor Protection under Modern Investment Treaties' (2008) 3(2) *Capital Markets Law Journal*, 154–185.

Kolo A. & Walde T., 'Capital Transfer Restrictions under Modern Investment Treaties' in August Reinisch (ed), *Standards of Investment Protection* (Oxford University Press 2019).

Korzun V., 'The Right to Regulate in Investor-State Arbitration: Slicing and Dicing Regulatory Carve-outs' (2017) 50(2) *Vanderbilt Journal of Transnational Law*, 355–414.

Krajewski M. & Hindelang S., 'Towards a More Comprehensive Approach in International Investment Law' in M. Krajewski & S. Hindelang (eds), *Shifting Paradigms in International Investment Law* (Oxford University Press 2016).

Krasner S. D., 'Globalization and Sovereignty' in David A. Smith, Dorothy J. Solinger & Steven C. Topik (eds), *States and Sovereignty in the Global Economy* (Taylor & Francis Group 1999).

Kriebaum U., 'The Relevance of Economic and Political Conditions for the Protection under Investment Treaties' (2011) 10(3) *The Law and Practice of International Courts and Tribunals*, 383–404.

Kudrle R., 'Governing Economic Globalisation: The Pioneering Experience of the OECD' (2012) 46(3) *Journal of World Trade*, 695–732.

Kulick A., *Public Interest in International Investment Law* (Cambridge University Press 2012).

Kurtz J., 'Adjudging the Exceptional at International Investment Law' (2009) 103 *American Society of International Law*, 489–491.

Kurtz J., 'Adjudging the Exceptional at International Investment Law: Security, Public Order and Financial Crisis' (2010) 59(2) *International and Comparative Law Quarterly*, 325–371.

Kurtz J., 'The Shifting Landscape of International Investment Law and Its Commentary' (2012) 106(3) *The University of Chicago*, 686–689.

Kurtz J., *The WTO and International Investment Law: Converging Systems* (Cambridge University Press 2016).

Kuus M. & Agnew J., 'Theorizing the States Geographically: Sovereignty, Subjectivity, Territoriality' in Kevin R. Cox, Murray Low & Jennifer Robinson (eds), *The Sage Handbook of Political Geography* (Sage 2007).

Laborde G., 'The Case for Host States Claims in Investment Arbitration' (2010) 1(1) *Journal of International Dispute Settlement*, 97–122.

Lange F., 'Challenging the Paris Peace Treaties, States Sovereignty, and Western-Dominated International: The Multifaceted Genesis of the Jus Cogens Doctrine' (2018) 31 *Leiden Journal of International Law*, 821–839.

Lantos J. S., *The Life and Death of International Treaties, Double Edged Diplomacy and the Politics of Ratification in Comparative Perspective* (Oxford University Press 2009).

Lauterpacht H., 'The Subject of the Law of Nations' (1947) 63(4) *Law Quarterly Review*, 439–460.

Lavoice M., 'The Eurozone Crisis: A Balance of Payment Problem or Crisis Due to a Flawed Monetary Design? A Reply to Sergio Cesaratto' (2015) 44(2) *International Journal of Political Economy*, 157–160.

Leckow R., 'The Role of the International Monetary Fund in the Liberalization of Capital Movement' (1999) 17(3) *Wisconsin International Law Journal*, 515–528.

Lee C. H., 'To Thine Self Be True: IMF Conditionality and the Erosion of Economic Sovereignty in the Asian Financial Crisis' (2003) 24(4) *University of Pennsylvania Journal of International Economic Law*, 875–904.

Li Q. & Smith D. L., 'The Dilemma of Financial Liberalization: States Autonomy and Societal Demands' (2002) 64(3) *The Journal of Politics*, 764–790.

Liu Q., 'Transfer of Funds in China-US BIT Negotiations: Comparing the Articles of Agreement of the IMF' (2012) 11(1) *Journal of International Trade Law and Policy*, 6–26.

Lowenfeld A. F., *International Economic Law* (Oxford University Press 2011).

L. R. De Mello, Jr. 'Foreign Direct Investment in Developing States: A Selective Survey' (1997) 34(1) *The Journal of Development Studies*, 1–34.

Luca A. D., 'Transfer Provision of BITs in Times of Financial Crisis' (2014) 23(1) *The Italian Yearbook of International Law Online*, 113–130.

Lupo-Pasini F., 'Monetary Policy Measures in Investment Law: The Uneasy Relationship Between Monetary Stability and Investment Protection' in Thomas Cottier, Lastrar Rosa & Christian Tietje (eds), *The Rule of Law in Monetary Affairs: World Trade Forum* (Cambridge University Press 2014).

MacFarlance P. J., 'The IMF's Reassessment of Capital Controls after the 2008 Financial Crisis: Heresy or Orthodoxy?' (2015) 19 *UCLA Journal of International Law and Foreign Affairs*, 167–212.

Majeed N., 'Investor-States Disputes and International Law: From the Far Side' (2004) 98 *American Society of International Law*, 30–33.

Manciaux S., 'The Notion of Investment: New Controversies' (2008) 9(6) *The Journal of World Investment & Trade Law*, vii–466.

Manger M. S. & Peinhardt C., 'Learning and the Precision of International Investment Agreements' (2017) 43(6) *International Interactions*, 920–940.

Mann F. A., 'Money in Public International Law' (1949) 26 *British Yearbook of International Law*, 259–293.

Marboe I., 'States Responsibility and Comparative States Liability for Administrative and Legislative Harm to Economic Interests' in Stephan W. Schill (ed), *International Investment Law and Comparative Public Law* (Oxford University Press 2010).

Marcoux J., 'Beyond Gold Reserves Inc v Bolivarian Republic of Venezuala: The Host States Capacity to Regulate Extractive Activities in Light of Canadian's Firms' Experience in International Investment Arbitration' (2014) 52 *The Canadian Yearbook of International Law*, 261–295.

Marossi A. Z., 'Unilateralism and Power of Revision' in Ali Z. Marossi & Marisa R. Bassett (eds), *Economic Sanctions under International Law* (Springer 2015).

Martin A., 'Definition of "Investment": Could a Persistent Objector to the Salini Tests Be Found in ICSID Arbitral Practice?' (2011) 11(2) *Global Jurist*, 1–19.

Martin A., 'Investment Dispute after Argentina's Economic Crisis: Interpreting BIT Non-Precluded Measures and the Doctrine of Necessity under Customary International Law' (2012) 29(1) *Journal of International Arbitration*, 49–70.

Martinez E. A., 'Understanding the Debate over Necessity: Unanswered Questions and Future Implications of Annulments in the Argentine Gas Cases' (2012) 23 *Duke Journal of Comparative and International Law*, 149–186.

Martini C., 'Avoiding the Planned Obsolescence of Modern International Investment Agreements: Can General Exception Mechanisms Be Improved, and How?' (2018) 59(8) *Boston College Law Review*, 2877–2898.

Mayeda G., 'International Investment Agreements between Developed States and Developing States: Dancing with the Devil? Case Comment on the *Vivendi, Sempra* and *Enron* Awards' (2008) 4(2) *The McGill International Journal of Sustainable Development*, 189–230.

McCall-Smith K. L., 'Severing Reservations' (2014) 66(3) *International and Comparative Law Quarterly*, 599–634.

McElhiney W. B., 'Responding to the Threat of Withdrawal: On the Importance of Emphasizing the Interests of States, Investors, and the Transnational Investment System in Bringing Resolutions to Questions Surrounding the Future of Investments with States Denouncing the ICSID Convention' (2014) 49(3) *Texas International Law Journal*, 601–619.

McLaclilan C., 'Investment Treaties and General International Law' (2008) 57(2) *International and Comparative Law Quarterly*, 361–401.

Melo A. & Modensi R., 'Capital Controls and Financial Liberalization: Removing the Ideological Bias' (2008) 30(4) *Journal of Post Keynesian Economics*, 561–582.

Mestral A. D., 'Investor-States Arbitration between Developed Democratic States' (2015) 1 *Investor-States Arbitration Series*, 1–33.

Meyer K. & Rottig D., 'International Trade and Investment Agreements: Sovereignty at Bay in the 21st Century?' (2016) 16(1) *AIB Insights*, 3–6.

Miamb O. E., 'How Can Economic and Political Liberalisation Improve Financial Development in African States?' (2010) 2(1) *Journal of Financial Economic Policy*, 35–59.

Mills A., 'Antinomies of Public and Private at the Foundations of International Investment Law and Arbitration' (2011) 14(2) *Journal of International Economic Law*, 469–503.

Mitchell A. D., Hawkins K. J. & Mishra N., 'Dear Prudence: Allowances under International Trade and Investment Law for Prudential Regulations in the Financial Services Sector' (2016) 19 *Journal of International Economic Law*, 787–820

Mitchell A. D. & Munro J., 'Someone Else's Deal: Interpreting International Investment Agreements in the Light of Third-Party Agreements' (2017) 28(3) *The European Journal of International Law*, 669–695.

Mohan S. C., 'The Amicus Curiae: Friends No More' (December 2010) 2 *Singapore Journal of Legal Studies*, 352–374.

Moon W. J., 'Essential Security Interests in International Investment Agreements' (2012) 15(2) *Journal of International Economic Law,* 481–502.

Motola Z., 'Free Trade, the Washington Consensus, and Bilateral Investment Treaties the South African Journey: A Rethink on the Rules on Foreign Investment by Developing States' (2017) 61(1) *American University Business Law Review*, 31–56.

Muchlinski P. T., 'Regulating Multinationals: Foreign Investment, Development, and the Balance of Corporate and home State Rights and Responsibilities in a Globalized World' in Jose E. Alvarez & Karl P. Sauvant (eds), *The Evolving International Investment Regime: Expectations, Realities, Options* (Oxford University Press 2011).

Muir H. W. & Arroyo D. P. F., *Private International Law and Global Governance* (Oxford University Press 2014).

Mysore S. & Vora A., 'Tussle for Policy Space in International Investment Norm Setting: The Search for a Middle Path' (2016) 7(2) *Jindal Global Law Review*, 135–156.

Nam J., 'Model BIT: An Ideal Prototype or a Tool for Efficient Breach' (Summer 2017) 48(4) *Georgetown Journal of International Law*, 1275–1308.

Ndongko W. A., 'Indigenisation Policy and the Development of Private Enterprise in Nigeria' (1980) 15(1) *Africa Spectrum*, 53–71.

Neuymer E., Nunnenkamp P. & Roy M., 'Are Stricter Investment Rules Contagious? Host State Competition for Foreign Direct Investment through International Agreements' (2015) 152(1) *Journal Review of World Economics*, 177–213.

Neumayer E. & Spess L., 'Do Bilateral Investment Treaties Increase Foreign Direct Investment to Developing States?' (2005) 33(10) *World Development*, 1567–1585.

Newcombe A., 'Sustainable Development and Investment Treaty Law' (2007) 8(1) *Journal of World Investment and Trade*, 357–407.

Nnabue S. F. N., 'Principles of International Economic Law and the Right to Economic Development' (2011) 2 *Nnamdi Azikiwe University Journal of International Law*, 1–13

Noy U. & Vu T. B., 'Capital Account Liberalization and Foreign Direct Investment' (2007) 18 *North American Journal of Economic and Finance*, 175–194.

Ocampo J. A. & Palma G. B., 'The Role of Preventative Capital Account Regulation', in Jose Antonio Ocampo & Joseph E. Stiglitz (eds), *Capital Market Liberalization and Development* (Oxford University Press 2008).

Odumosu-Aganu I. T., 'South-South Investment Treaties, Transnational Capital and African People' (2013) 21(2) *African Journal of International and Comparative Law*, 172–201.

Ofodile U. E., 'African-China Bilateral Investment Treaties: A Critique' (2013) 35(1) *Michigan Journal of International Law*, 131–212.

Ogbuagu C. S. A., 'The Nigerian Indigenization Policy: Nationalism or Pragmatism?' (1983) 82(327) *African Affairs*, 241–266.

Oji A. E. & Ozioko M. V. C., 'Effect of Globalisation on Sovereignty of State' (2011) 2 *Nnamdi Azikiwe University Journal of International Law*, 256–270.

Olokoyo F. O., 'Foreign Direct Investment and Economic Growth: A Case of Nigeria' (2012) 4(1) *BVIMSR Journal of Management Research*, 1–30.

Onuoha C. A., 'Relationship between Foreign Direct Investment Inflow, Sub-Saharan Africa and Nigeria Economic Development' (2012) 1(11) *Kuwait Chapter of the Arabian Journal of Business and Management Review*, 29–45.

Oruaze D. M., 'Rebalancing International Investment Agreements in Favour of Host States' (2018) 60(2) *International Journal of Law and Management*, 452–469.

Osiander A., 'Sovereignty, International Relations, and the Westphalian Myth' (2001) 55(2) *International Organization*, 251–287.

Pabian D. H., 'Capital Controls in International Law: Clarity through a Central Regulatory System' (2015) 24(3) *Minnesota Journal of International Law*, 1–32.

Paddock J. V., 'IMF Policy and the Argentine Financial Crisis' (2002) 34(1) *The University of Miami Inter-American Law Review*, 155–187.

Palomi A. P., 'Emergency Economic Intervention and the Rights of Foreign Investors: US-Argentina Practice' (2009) 20(1) *Journal of Interdisciplinary Economics*, 169–191.

Perrone N. M., 'The International Investment Regime and Foreign Investors Right: Another View of Popular Story' (2014) 11(3) *Manchester Journal of International Economic Law*, 397–420.

Perrone N. M., 'The Governance of Foreign Investment at a Crossroad: Is an Overlapping Consensus the Way Forward?' (2015) 15(1) *Global Jurist*, 1–28.

Perrone N. M., 'The International Investment Regime after the Global Crisis of Neoliberalism: Rupture of Continuity' (2016) 23(2) *Indiana Journal of Global Legal Studies*, 603–627.

Perrone N. M., 'The Emerging Global Right to Investment: Understanding the Reason Behind Foreign Investor Rights' (2017) 8 *Journal of International Dispute Settlement*, 673–694.

Picciotto S., 'Linkages in International Investment Regulation: The Antinomies of the Draft Multilateral Agreement on Investment' (1988) 19(3) *University of Pennsylvania Journal of International Economic Law*, 731–768.

Pitlik H., 'A Race to Liberalization? Diffusion of Economic Policy Reform among OECD Economies' (2007) 132 *Public Choice*, 159–178.

Poulsen L. S., 'The Significance of South-South BITs for the International Investment Regime: A Quantitative Analysis' (2010) 30(1) *Northwestern Journal of International Law & Business*, 101–130.

Poulsen S. L. N., *Bounded Nationality and Economic Diplomacy: The Politics of Investment Treaties in Developing States* (Cambridge University Press 2015).

Poulsen S. L. N. & Aisbett E., 'When the Claim Hits: Bilateral Investment Treaties & Bounded Rational Learning' (2013) 65(2) *World Politics*, 273–313.

Powelyn J., 'At the Edge of Chaos? Foreign Investment Law as a Complex Adaptive System, How it Emerged and How it Can be Reformed' (2014) 29(2) *ICSID Review*, 372–418

Price D., 'Indonesia's Bold Strategy on Bilateral Investment Treaties: Seeking an Equitable Climate for Investment?' (2017) 7(1) *Asia Journal of International Law*, 124–151.

Quiggin J., 'Globalization and Economic Sovereignty' (2001) 9(3) *The Journal of Political Philosophy*, 56–80.

Qumba M. F., 'The Exhaustion of Local Judicial Remedies in Investor-States Dispute Settlement: A Proposal for the African Continental Free Trade Agreement on Investment Protocol' (2021) 25 *Law, Democracy and Development,* 156–192.

Qureshi A. H. A., 'Necessity in International Economic Law' in I. F. Dekker & E. Hey (eds), *Netherlands Yearbook of International Law* (Cambridge University Press 2010).

Rajput A., 'Safeguarding India's Regulatory Autonomy: Analysis of the New Model Bilateral Investment Treaty' (2017) 14(3) *Manchester Journal of International Economic Law,* 279–300.

Randelovic M. P., Ksenija D. M. & Milenkovic-Kerkovic T., 'An Analysis of the Location Determinants of Foreign Direct Investment: The Case of Serbia' (2013) 81(1) *Social and Behavioural Science*, 181–187.

Randeria S., 'The States of Globalization: Legal Plurality, Overlapping Sovereignties and Ambiguous Alliances' (2007) 24(1) *Theory Culture and Society*, 1–33.

Ranjan P., 'Definition of Investment in BITs of South Asian States and Regulatory Discretion' (2009) 26(2) *Journal of International Arbitration*, 217–235.

Ranjan P., '"Necessary" in Non-Precluded Measures Provisions in Bilateral Investment Treaties: The Indian Contribution' (2020) 67 *Netherlands International Law Review*, 473–501.

Ranjan P. & Amand P., 'The 2016 Model Indian BIT: A Critical Deconstruction' (2017) 38(1) *Northwestern Journal of International Law and Business*, 1–58.

Rasekhi S. & Seyedi Z., 'An Examination of Economic Liberalisation Impact on Foreign Direct Investment in Selected Developing States' (2010) 14(25) *Iranian Economic Review*, 1–17.

Raustiala K., 'Rethinking the Sovereignty Debate in International Economic Law' (2003) 6(4) *Journal of International Economic Law*, 841–878.

Reinisch A., 'Legality of Expropriations' in August Reinisch (ed), *Standards of Investment Protection* (Oxford University Press 2009).

Reinisch A., *Standards of Investment Protection* (Oxford University of Press 2009).

Richardson M. & Stahler F., 'International Agreements, Economic Sovereignty and Exit' (2019) 120 *European Economic Review*, 1–16.

Ripinsky S., 'Global Economic Crisis and the Danger of Protectionism: Does International Law Help?' (2009) 1(3) *Amsterdam Law Forum*, 3–16.

Roberts A., 'Power and Persuasion in Investment Treaty Interpretations: The Dual Role of States' (2010) 107 *American Journal of International Law*, 179–225.

Roberts A., 'Triangular Treaties: The Extent and Limits of Investment Treaty Rights' (2015) 56(2) *Harvard International Law Journal*, 35–417.

Rosa P. D., 'The Recent Wave of Arbitrations against Argentina under Bilateral Investment Treaties and Principle Legal Issues' (2004) 36(1) *The University of Miami Inter-American Law Review*, 41–74.

Rothgeb Jr J. M., 'Foreign Investment and the Decapitalization of Underdeveloped Host States' (1990) 27(4) *The Social Science Journal*, 457–473.

Sacerdoti G., 'BIT Protections and Economic Crises: Limits to Their Coverage, the Impact of Multilateral Financial Regulation and the Defence of Necessity' (2013) 28(2) *ICSID Review*, 351–383.

Sachdeva A. M., 'International Investment: A Developing Perspective' (2007) 8(1) *Journal of World Investment and Trade*, 532–548.

Salacuse J. W., 'BIT by BIT: The Growth of Bilateral Investment Treaties and Their Impact on Foreign Investment in Developing States' (1990) 24(3) *The International Lawyer*, 655–675.

Salacuse J. W., 'The Emerging Global Regime for Investment' (2010) 51(2) *Harvard International Law Journal*, 427–473.

Salacuse J. W. & Sullivan N. P., 'Do BITs Really Work? An Evaluation of Bilateral Investment Treaties and Their Grand Bargain' (2005) 46(1) *Harvard International Law Journal*, 67–136.

Saputo N. M., 'Paradoxical Pacts: Understanding the BIT Phenomenon and the Rejection of a Multilateral Agreement on Investment' (2014) 41(1) *Ohio Northern University Law Review*, 121–170.

Sattorova M., 'Defining Investment under ICSID Convention and BITs: Of Ordinary Meaning, Telos and Beyond' (2012) 2(2) *Asian Journal of International Law*, 267–290.

Sattorova M., *The Impact of Investment Treaty Law on Host States: Enabling Good Governance?* (Hart Publishing 2018).

Satyanand P. N., 'Once BITten, Forever Shy: Explaining India's Rethink of its Bilateral Investment Treaty Provisions' (2016) 16(1) *AIB Insights*, 17–20.

Sauvant K. P. & Lisa S., *The Effect of Treaties on Foreign Direct Investment: Bilateral Investment Treaties, Double Taxation Treaties, and Investment Flows* (Oxford University Press 2009).

Schill S. W., 'International Investment Law and the Host State's Power to Handle Economic Crises: Comment on the ICSID Decision LG&E v Argentina' (2007) 24(3) *Journal of International Arbitration*, 265–286.

Schill S. W., 'Enhancing International Investment Law's Legitimacy: Conceptual and Methodological Foundations of a New Public Law Approach' (2011) 52(1) *Virginia Journal of International Law*, 57–102.

Schill S. W., 'Deference in Investment Treaty Arbitration: Reconceptualising the Standard Review' (2012) 3(3) *Journal of International Dispute Settlement*, 577–607.

Schill S. W., 'In Defence of International Investment Law' in Marc Bungenberg, Christoph Herrmann, Markus Krajewski & Jorg Philipp Terhechte (eds), *European Yearbook of International Economic Law* (Springer International Publishing 2016).

Schill S. W. & Briese R., 'If the State Considers: Self-Judging Clauses in International Dispute Settlement' (2009) 13 *Max Planck Yearbook of United Nations Law*, 69–140.

Schlemmer E. C., 'An Overview of South Africa's Bilateral Investment Treaties and Investment Policy' (2016) 31(1) *ICSID Review*, 167–193.

Schneidermsn D., 'Investing in Democracy: Political Process and International Investment Law' (2010) 60(1) *University of Toronto Law Journal*, 909–940.

Schrijver N., 'The Changing Nature of State Sovereignty' (2000) 70(1) *The British Year of International Law*, 65–98.

Schwartz P., 'Capitalism, International Investment Law and the Development Conundrum' (2013) 6(2) *Law and Development Review*, 217–253.

Seifu G., 'Regulatory Space in the Treatment of Foreign Investment in Ethiopian Investment Laws' (2008) 9(5) *Journal of World Investment & Trade*, 405–426.

Sepulveda-Amor B. & Lawry-White M., 'State Responsibility and the Enforcement of Arbitral Awards' (2017) 33(1) *Arbitration International*, 35–61.

Seyoum M., Wu R. & Lin J., 'Foreign Direct Investment and Economic Growth: The Case of Developing African Economies' (2015) 122(1) *Peer Reviewed Journal*, 45–64.

Shaikh A., *Globalization and the Myths of Free Trade: History, Theory and Empirical Evidence* (Routledge 2007).

Siddiqui K. & Armstrong P., 'Capital Control Reconsidered: Financialisation and Economic Policy' (2018) 32(6) *International Review of Applied Economics*, 713–731.

Siegel D. E., 'Using Free Trade Agreements to Control Capital Accounts Restrictions: Summary of Remarks on the Relationship to the Mandate of the IMF' (2004) 10 *ILSA Journal of International and Comparative Law*, 297–304.

Simmons B. A., 'The Legalization of International Monetary Affairs' (2000) 54(3) *International Organization*, 573–602.

Simmons B. A., 'Bargaining over BITs, Arbitrating Awards: The Regime for Protection and Promotion of International Investment' (2014) 66(1) *World Politics*, 12–46.

Simmons B. A. & Elkins Z., 'The Globalisation of Liberalisation: Policy Diffusion in the International Political Economy' (2004) 98(1) *American Political Science Review*, 171–189.

Singh K. & Ilge B., *Rethinking Bilateral Investment Treaties: Critical Issues and Policy Choices* (Both Ends, Madhyam, Somo 2016).

Singh M., *A Decade of Decay* (1st edn, Rare Publication 2013).

Singh M., Cremer W. & Kumar N., *Open Markets, Free Trade and Sustainable Development* (Springer 2019).

Sirr G., Garrey J. & Gallagher L., 'Bilateral Investment Treaties and Foreign Direct Investment: Evidence of Asymmetric Effects on Vertical and Horizontal Investment' (2017) 35(1) *Development Policy Review*, 93–113.

Skovgaard L. N. & Aisbett E., 'When the Claim Hits: Bilateral Investment Treaties and Bounded Rationality' (2013) 65(2) *World Politics*, 273–313.

Sloane R. D., 'On the Use and Abuse of Necessity in the Law of States Responsibility' (2012) 106 (3) *American Journal of International Law*, 447–508.

Smit D. B. L., 'Treaty Rights as Tradable Assets: Can Investors Waive Investment Treaty Protection?' (2010) 25(2) *ICSID Review*, 404–420.

Sneij F., 'Are IIAs Old-Fashioned? How Consistency in the Use of Public Policy Fosters the Object and Purpose of Investment Agreements' (2016) 21(2–3) *Uniform Law Review*, 197–215.

Sornarajah M., 'State Responsibility and Bilateral Investment Treaties' (1986) 20(1) *Journal of World Trade Law*, 79–80.

Sornarajah M., 'Protection and Guarantees of Investment' (2000) 26(2) *Commonwealth Bulletin*, 1290–1299.

Sornarajah M., 'A Law for Need or a Law for Greed? Restoring the Lost Law in the International Law of Foreign Investment' (2006) 6 *Int Environ Agreements*, 329–357.

Sornarajah M., 'Portfolio Investments and the Definition of Investment' (2009) 24(2) *ICSID Review*, 516–520.

Sornarajah M., 'Mutations of Neo-Liberalism in International Investment Law' (2011) 3(1) *Trade Law and Development*, 203–232.

Sornarajah M., *The International Law on Foreign Investment* (Cambridge University Press 2021).

Sourmare I. & Gohou G., 'Does Foreign Direct Investment Reduce Poverty in Africa and Are There Regional Differences?' (2012) 40(1) *World Development*, 75–95.

Spears S. A., 'The Quest for Policy Space in a New Generation of International Investment Agreements' (2010) 13(4) *Journal of International Economic Law*, 1037–1075.

Stern B., 'The Future of International Investment Law: A Balance between the Protection of Investors and the States Capacity to Regulate' in Jose E. Alvarez & Karl P. Sauvant (eds), *The Evolving International Investment Regime: Expectations, Realities, Options* (Oxford University Press 2011).

Stevens M., 'ICSID at the Crossroads: Some Thoughts and Recommendations for Improving the Dispute Settlement System' in Pierre Sauve & Roberto Echandi (eds), *Prospects in International Investment Law and Policy: World Trade Forum* (Cambridge University Press 2013).

Stiglitz J. E., 'Proceedings of the Annual Meetings' (2007) 101 *American Society of International Law*, 3–60.

Stiglitz J. E., 'Regulating Multinational Corporations: Towards Principles of Cross-Border Legal Frameworks in a Globalized World: Balancing Rights with Responsibilities' (2007) 23(3) *American University International Law Review*, 451–558.

Subedi S. P., *International Investment Law: Reconciling Policy and Principle* (3rd edn, Hart Publishing 2016).

Subramanian S. R., 'Too Similar or Too Difficult: States of Necessity as a Defence under Customary International Law and the Bilateral Investment Treaty and Their Relationship' (2012) 9(1) *Manchester Journal of International Economic Law*, 68–91.

Sykes A. O., 'The Economic Structure of International Investment Agreement with Implications for Treaty Interpretation and Design' (2019) 113(3) *American Journal of International Law*, 482–534.

Sykes A. O., 'Economic "Necessity" in International Law' (2015) 109(2) *The American Journal of International Law*, 296–323.

Szewczyk B. M. J., 'Sempra Energy International v. Argentine Republic' (2011) 105(3) *The American Journal of International Law*, 547–553.

Thaliath J., 'Bilateral Investment Treaties and Sovereignty: An Analysis with Respect to International Investment Law' (2106) 5(2) *Christ University Law Journal*, 1–8

Thomas C., 'Balance of Payment Crises in the Developing World: Balancing Trade, Finance and Development in the New Economic Order' (2000) 15(6) *American University International Law Review*, 1249–1277.

Thomas W., *Jus Cogens: International Law and Social Contract* (Cambridge University Press 2015).

Thrasher R. D., Sklar S. & Gallagher K. P., 'Policy Space for Capital Flow Management: An Empirical Investigation' (2021) *Journal of International Economic Law*, 779–798

Tienhaara K., 'Once BITten, Twice Shy? The Uncertain Future of "Shared Sovereignty" in Investment Treaty Arbitration' (2011) 30 *Policy and Society*, 185–196.

Tillman R. B., 'Globalization-Driven Innovation: The Investor as a Partial Subject in Public International Law – An Inquiry into the Nature of and Limits of Investors Rights' (2014) 15(1–2) *American University International Law Review*, 73–116.

Tobin J. L. & Rose-Ackerman S., 'When BITs Have Some Bite: The Political-Economic Environment for Bilateral Investment Treaties' (2011) 6(1) *Review of International Organisation*, 1–32.

Trachtman J. P., 'The International Economic Law Revolution' (1996) 17(1) *University of Pennsylvania Journal of International Economic Law*, 33–62.

Trakman L. E., 'Foreign Direct Investment: Hazard or Opportunity?' (2009) 4(1) *The George Washington International Law Review*, 1–66.

Tyurina N., 'Regional Economic Integration and States Sovereignty' (2014) 1(1) *Journal of International and European Law, Economics and Market*, 43–50.

Vadi V. & Gruszczynski L., 'Standards of Review in International Investment Law and Arbitration: Multilevel Governance and the Commonweal' (2013) 16(3) *Journal of International Economic Law*, 613–633.

Van Der Ploeg K. P., 'Protection of Regulatory Autonomy and Investor Obligations: Latest Trends in Investment Treaty Design' (2018) 51(1) *International Lawyer*, 1–7.

Vandevelde K. J., 'Investment Liberalization and Economic Development: The Role of Bilateral Investment Treaties' (1998) 36(3) *Columbia Journal of Transnational Law*, 501–528.

Vandevelde K. J., 'The Political Economy of a Bilateral Investment Treaty' (1988) 92(4) *The American Journal of International Law*, 621–641.

Vandevelde K. J. 'Sustainable Liberalism and the International Investment Regime' (1988) 19(2) *Michigan Journal of International Law*, 373–399.

Vandevelde K. J., 'The Economics of Bilateral Investment Treaties' (2000) 41(2) *Harvard International Law Journal*, 469–502.

Vandevelde K. J., 'A Brief History of International Investment Agreements' (2009) 12 *UC-Davis Journal of International Law and Policy*, 157–194.

Vandevelde K. J., 'Model Bilateral Investment Treaties: The Way Forward' (2011) 18(1) *Southwestern Journal of International Law*, 307–316.

Vandevelde K. J., 'Rebalancing through Exceptions' (2013) 17(2) *Lewis & Clark Law Review*, 449–460.

VanDuzer A. J., 'Canadian Investment Treaties with African States: What Do They Tell Us About Investment Treaty Making in Africa?' (2017) 18(3) *The Journal of World Investment & Trade*, 556–584.

Vernon R., 'Economic Sovereignty at Bay' (1986) 47(1) *Foreign Affairs*, 110–122

Vinuales J. E., 'Amicus Intervention in Investor-States Arbitration' (2007) 61(4) *Dispute Resolution Journal*, 72–81.

Vinuales J. E., 'Sovereignty in Foreign Investment Law' in Zachary Douglas, Joost Pauwelyn & Jorge E. Vinuales (eds), *The Foundations of International Investment Law* (Oxford University Press 2014).

Viterbo A., *International Economic Law and Monetary Measures. Limitations to States' Sovereignty and Dispute Settlement* (Elgar International Economic Law 2012).

Von Mehron G. M., Salmon C. T. & Paroutsas A. A., 'Navigating through Investor-States Arbitrations: An Overview of Bilateral Investment Treaty Claims' (2004) 59(1) *Dispute Resolution Journal*, 69–77.

Voon T., 'Multinational Enterprises and States Sovereignty under International Law' (1999) 21(2) *Adelaide Law Review*, 219–252.

Voon T. & Mitchell A. D., 'Denunciation, Termination and Survival: The Interplay of Treaty Law and International Investment Law' (2016) 31(2) *ICSID Review*, 413–433.

Vu D., 'Reasons Not To Exit? A Survey of the Effectiveness and Spillover Effects of International Investment Arbitration' (2019) 47(2) *European Journal of Law and Economics*, 291–319.

Waibel M., 'BIT by BIT: The Silent Liberalization' in Christina Binder, Ursula Kriebaum, August Reinisch & Stephan Wittich (eds), *International Investment Law for the 21st Century: Essays in Honour of Christopher Schreur* (Oxford University Press 2009).

Waibel M., 'Demystifying the Art of Interpretation' (2011) 22(2) *European Journal of International Law*, 571–588.

Walde T. & Kolo A., 'Investor-States Disputes: The Interface between Treaty-Based International Investment Protection and Fiscal Sovereignty' (2007) 35(8–9) *Intertax*, 424–449.

Waller S. W. & Simon A. M., 'Analyzing Claims of Sovereignty in International Economic Disputes' (1985) 7(1) *Northwestern Journal of International Law and Business*, 1–11.

Wang W., 'The Non-Precluded Measure Type Clause in International Investment Agreements: Significances, Challenges, and Reactions' (2017) 32(2) *ICSID Review*, 447–456.

Wassem M., 'Political Risk Guarantees and Capital Inflow: The Role of Bilateral Investment Treaties' (2015) 9(26) *Peer Review Journal*, 1–38.

Weidenmier M. K. J., 'The Barring Crisis and the Great Latin American Meltdown of the 1980's' (2008) 68(2) *The Journal of Economic History*, 462–500

Welsh N. A., Schneider A. & Rimpfel K., 'Using the Theories of Exit, Voice, Loyalty, and Procedural Justice to Reconceptualize Brazil's Rejection of Bilateral Investment Treaties' (2014) 45 *Washington University Journal of Law and Policy*, 105–143.
Williams C., Luoianova T. & Marinez C., 'The Moderating Effect of Bilateral Investment Treaty Stringency between Political Instability and Subsidiary Ownership Choice' (2017) 26(1) *International Business Review*, 1–11.
Williams D. E., 'Policy Perspectives on the Use of Capital Controls in Emerging Market Nations: Lessons from the Asian Financial Crisis and a Look at the International Legal Regime' (2001) 70(2) *Fordham Law Review*, 561–621.
Witherell W. H., 'Developing International Rules for Foreign Investment: OECD'S Multilateral Agreement on Investment' (1997) 32(1) *Business Economics*, 38–43.
Yackee J. W., 'Are BITs Such a Bright Idea? Exploring the Ideational Basis of Investment Treaty Enthusiasm' (2005) 12(1) *U.C. Davis Journal of International Law & Policy*, 195–225.
Yackee J. W., 'Bilateral Investment Treaties, Credible Commitment, and the Rule of (International) Law: Do BITs Promote Foreign Direct Investment?' (2008) 42(4) *Law & Society Review,* 805–832.
Yackee J. W., 'Pacta Sunt Servanda and States Promises to Foreign Investors before Bilateral Investment Treaties: Myth and Reality' (2009) 32(5) *Fordham International Law Journal*, 1550–1613.
Yarbrough B. V. & Yarbrough R. M., 'Cooperation in the Liberalization of International Trade: After Hegemony What?' (1987) 4(1) *International Organisation*, 1–26.
Yarbrough B. V. & Yarbrough R. M., 'Reciprocity, Bilateralism and Economic "Hostages": Self Enforcing Agreements in International Trade' (1986) 30(1) *International Studies Quarterly*, 7–21.
Yianni A. & Vera C., 'The Return of Capital Controls?' (2010) 73(4) *Law and Contemporary Problems*, 357–372.
Zarra G., 'The Issue of Incoherence in Investment Arbitration: Is There Need for a Systemic Reform?' (2018) 17(1) *The Chinese Journal of International Law*, 137–185.
Zimmermann C. D., 'The Promotion of Transfer-of-Funds Liberalisation across International Economic Law' (2011) 12(5) *Journal of World Investment and Trade*, 725–742.
Zimmermann C. D., 'The Concept of Monetary Sovereignty Revisited' (2013) 24(3) The European Journal of International Law, 797–818.
Zimmermann C. D., *A Contemporary Concept of Monetary Sovereignty* (Oxford University Press 2013).
Zugliani N., 'Human Rights in International Investment Law: The 2016 Morocco-Nigeria BIT' (2019) 68(3) *International and Comparative Law Quarterly*, 761–770.

WEBSITES

Angola-Japan BIT. Available on https://investmentpolicy.unctad.org [Accessed on 5 December 2024].
Article XIV (s 1–2) of the International Monetary Fund Articles of Agreement. Available on https://www.imf.org/external/pubs/ft/aa/pdf/aa.pdf [Accessed on 4 December 2024].
Bilateral Investment Treaties 1995–2006: Trends in Investment Rule Making, p. 56. Available on https://unctad.org/system/files/official-document/iteiia20065_en.pdf [Accessed on 2 December 2024].
Bilateral Investment Treaties and Development Policy-Making, 30. By Luke Eric Peterson. Available on https://www.iisd.org/library/bilateral-investment-treaties-and-development-policy-making [Accessed on 4 December 2024].
Bilateral Investment Treaties Treatment of International Capital Movement: Time for Reform, p. 26. By Amr Abbas Mohammed Adel Abbas Aly Hussein. Available on

https://qmro.qmul.ac.uk/xmlui/bitstream/handle/123456789/2514/HUSSEINBilateralInvestment2012.pdf?sequence=1 [Accessed on 4 November 2024].

Canada-China BIT. Available on https://investmentpolicy.unctad.org/international-investment-agreements [Accessed on 4 December 2024].

Economic Instability, Capital Controls and Bilateral Investment Treaties. By Terra Lawson-Remer. Available on https://www.cfr.org/blog/economic-instability-capital-controls-and-bilateral-investment-treaties [Accessed on 4 November 2024].

Germany-Nigeria BIT. Available on http://investmentpolicyhub.unctad.org/Download/TreatyFile/1382 [Accessed on 4 December 2024].

How May Tribunals Apply the Customary Necessity to Rule to the Argentine Cases?, p. 29. By Javier El-Hage. Available on https://papers.ssrn.com/sol3/papers.cfm?abstract_id=2480059 [Accessed on 6 December 2024].

ICSID Convention. Available on https://icsid.worldbank.org/en/Documents/resources/2006%20CRR_English-final.pdf [Accessed on 5 December 2024].

Investment Policy Framework on Sustainable Development. By UNCTAD. Available on https://unctad.org/en/PublicationsLibrary/diaepcb2015d5_en.pdf [Accessed on 5 December 2024].

Investment Policy Hub. Available on https://investmentpolicy.unctad.org [Accessed on 5 December 2024].

Assessing the Benefits of Allowing Amicus Curiae Briefs in Investor-State Arbitrations: A Developing State's Perspective, 7. By Kinyua Paul Kenneth. Available on https://www.researchgate.net/publication/255967036_Assessing_the_Benefits_of_Accepting_Amici_Curiae_Briefs_in_Investor-StateState_Arbitrations_A_Developing_State%27S_Perspective [Accessed on 7 December].

Bilateral Investment Treaties and Development Policy-Making. By Luke Eric Peterson. Available on https://pravo.hse.ru/data/2012/10/05/1244483607/READER_Bilateral%20Investment%20Treaties%202004.pdf [Accessed on 4 November 2024].

Morocco-Nigeria BIT (2016) Available on https://investmentpolicyhub.unctad.org/IIA/State/153/treaty/3711 [Accessed on 5 December 2024].

Multilateral Liberalization through Bilateral Treaties? A Workshop on Global Investment Governance. Available on https://www.bsg.ox.ac.uk/sites/default/files/documents/Multilateral%20Liberalization%20through%20Bilateral%20Treaties_Final%20Memos%2028%20June.pdf [Accessed on 4 November 2024].

Nigeria-Algeria BIT. Available on https://investmentpolicy.unctad.org [Accessed on 5 December 2024].

Nigeria-Canada BIT. Available on https://investmentpolicy.unctad.org [Accessed on 5 December 2024].

Nigeria-Finland BIT. Available on https://investmentpolicy.unctad.org/international-investment-agreements/treaty-files/1206/download [Accessed on 4 November 2024].

Nigeria-Morocco BIT. Available on https://investmentpolicy.unctad.org [Accessed on 5 December 2024].

Nigeria-Morocco BIT and Nigeria-Singapore BIT. Available on http://investmentpolicyhub.unctad.org/Download/TreatyFile/1382 [Accessed on 4 December 2024].

Nigeria-UAE BIT. Available on https://investmentpolicy.unctad.org [Accessed on 5 December 2024].

Nigerian-Romanian BIT. Available on https://investmentpolicy.unctad.org [Accessed on 5 December 2024].

Restrictions on Foreign Investors/Currency Exchange Controls. Available on (https://ppp.worldbank.org/public-private-partnership/legislation-regulation/framework-assessment/legal-environment/foreign-investor-currency-exchange-restrictions [Accessed on 4 November 2024].

Safeguarding Policy Space in Investment Agreements, 5. By Simon Lester & Bryan Mercurio. Available on https://www.cato.org/sites/cato.org/files/articles/lester-mercurio-iiel-issue-brief-december-2017.pdf [Accessed on 4 December 2024].

The Evolving International Investment Law and Policy Regime, p. 7. By Karl P. Sauvant. Available on http://www3.weforum.org/docs/E15/WEF_Investment_Law_Policy_regime_report_2015_1501.pdf [Accessed on 6 December 2024].

The Morocco-Nigeria BIT. Available on https://investmentpolicy.unctad.org/international-investment-agreements/treaties/otheriia/3711/morocco---nigeria-bit-2016- [Accessed on 5 December 2024].

The Morocco-Nigeria BIT: A New Breed of Investment Treaty? By Thomas Reuters. Available on http://arbitrationblog.practicallaw.com/the-morocco-nigeria-bit-a-new-breed-of-investment-treaty/ [Accessed on 5 December 2024].

The Use, Non-Use and Abuse of Economics in WTO and Investor-State Dispute Settlement, 15. By Joost Pauwelyn. Available on https://papers.ssrn.com/sol3/papers.cfm?abstract_id=2141357 [Accessed on 7 December 2024].

Turkey-China BIT. Available on https://investmentpolicy.unctad.org/international-investment-agreements [Accessed on 4 December 2024].

Using Capital Controls to Deal with a Financial Crisis. By Martin Khor. Available on https://StateState.globalpolicy.org/component/content/article/220/47393.html [Accessed on 5 December 2024].

United Nations, *Vienna Convention on the Law of Treaties*, 23 May 1969, United Nations, Treaty Series, vol. 1155, p. 331. Available on https://www.refworld.org/docid/3ae6b3a10.html [Accessed on 6 December 2024].

Index

FSC
www.fsc.org
MIX
Papier | Fördert gute Waldnutzung
FSC® C083411

Kolibri 360 GmbH
Ferdinand-Jühlke-Straße 7
99095 Erfurt, Deutschland
produktsicherheit@kolibri360.de